Circuit Chautauqua

Circuit Chautauqua

*From Rural Education to
Popular Entertainment in
Early Twentieth Century America*

by JOHN E. TAPIA

with a foreword by ROBERT A. McCOWN

McFarland & Company, Inc., Publishers
Jefferson, North Carolina, and London

To my wife, Denise A. Bartles, and to Mr. Chips

The present work is a reprint of the library bound edition of Circuit Chautauqua: From Rural Education to Popular Entertainment in Early Twentieth Century America, *first published in 1997 by McFarland.*

LIBRARY OF CONGRESS CATALOGUING-IN-PUBLICATION DATA

Tapia, John E., 1950–
    Circuit chautauqua : from rural education to popular entertainment in early twentieth century America / by John E. Tapia ; with a foreword by Robert A. McCown.
      p. cm
    Includes bibliographical references (p.) and index.

    ISBN 978-0-7864-4084-9
    softcover : 50# alkaline paper ∞

    1. Chautauquas — History.   2. Lyceums — United States — History. I. Title.
LC6301.C5T27   2008   374.973 — dc20   96-41623

British Library cataloguing data are available

©1997 John E. Tapia. All rights reserved

No part of this book may be reproduced or transmitted in any form or by any means, electronic or mechanical, including photocopying or recording, or by any information storage and retrieval system, without permission in writing from the publisher.

On the cover: Small town tent chautauqua, a photograph courtesy of the Swarthmore Chautauqua, New York Public Library; vintage decorative frame ©2008 Shutterstock

Manufactured in the United States of America

McFarland & Company, Inc., Publishers
  Box 611, Jefferson, North Carolina 28640
    www.mcfarlandpub.com

Table of Contents

Foreword by Robert A. McCown	1
Preface	3
Introduction	7

I. ADULT EDUCATION IN NINETEENTH-CENTURY AMERICA — 11
   Lyceum — 12
   Permanent Chautauqua — 19
   Introduction of Circuit Chautauqua — 25

II. THE MOVEMENT TOWARD STANDARDIZATION AND COMMERCIALIZATION — 27
   The Standard Chautauqua — 27
   Standardization and Commercialization in America — 29
   Growth of Circuit Chautauqua Into Big Business — 30
   The Selling and Promotion of Circuit Chautauqua — 32
   Other Circuit Chautauqua Jobs — 38
   "Chautauqua Week" and the Program — 45
   Tracing Changes in America, 1904 to 1930 — 47

III. BEGINNINGS IN RURAL AMERICA — 48
   The Country Versus the City — 49
   Pervasiveness of the Chautauqua Lecturer — 53
   Musical Features — 61
   Dramatic Arts — 66
   Children's Activities, Magicians, and Illusionists — 72
   Circuit Chautauqua in Rural America — 76

IV. Coming of Age: The Movement into the National Marketplace Before World War I — 78
- Factors of Expansion — 78
- The Lecture "Message" Begins to Lapse — 82
- Shakespeare, Drama, and Readers — 90
- The Versatility of the Music — 96
- Ethnic Images — 100
- Junior Chautauqua and "Entertainers" — 105
- Beyond the Rural Heartland — 109

V. "Making the World Safe for Democracy": Chautauqua Goes to War — 111
- Silence on the Platform — 111
- Chautauqua Goes to War — 113
- The "War Tax" — 116
- Lectures — 117
- Music and Patriotism — 125
- Dramatic Arts — 134
- The Junior Chautauqua — 140
- The Nineteenth Amendment — 144
- Chautauqua as a Gateway into the 1920s — 145

VI. The Post–World War I Era: From "The Hand at the Nation's Throat" to Comedy — 146
- Henry Cabot Lodge and the League of Nations — 146
- Disarmament and Chautauqua Rhetoric — 147
- Bolshevism in America — 149
- Chautauqua Rhetoric in the Postwar Era — 151
- The Response to Unrest — 155
- Financial Troubles Begin — 157
- "Straight from Broadway" — 160
- Fading from Center Stage: Opera, Readers, Impersonators, and Magicians — 165
- The Musical Variety Continues — 170
- The Diversity of Exhibitions for Community Youth — 173
- The Call of the 1920s: Entertainment and Comedy — 177

VII. THE JUBILEE YEAR AND THE VESTIGES OF HOPE	178
Chautauqua Success	178
Chautauqua and Modern America	184
The Program: From *Applesauce* to "Leisure Time"	187
Music: Sidesplitting "Climaxes and Anti-Climaxes"	190
The Lecturer as Media Figure	191
Chautauqua as a Stepping Stone: From Late Nineteenth- to Twentieth-Century Entertainment	195
The "Spirit" of Chautauqua	201
Life After Death	203
VIII. CIRCUIT CHAUTAUQUA AS AN AGENT OF SOCIAL CHANGE	205
Appendix	209
Selected Bibliography	215
Index	219

Foreword

Circuit or "tent" chautauqua was created by Iowan Keith Vawter, and Iowa towns were included in the first attempt at circuit chautauqua in 1904. While circuit chautauqua was eventually a nationwide movement, Iowa was always its heart. How appropriate, then, that the largest collection of archival records concerning circuit chautauqua is housed at the University of Iowa in Iowa City. In April 1951, 13,500 pounds of records from the Chicago office of the Redpath Bureau arrived in Iowa City. The collection contained business correspondence, letters to and from talent, contracts, photographs, programs, handbills, tickets, posters, newspaper clippings, telegrams, route books, reports, and accounting records (cash books, day books, journals, and ledgers).

The collection is presently divided into four series. The first series deals with talent and is arranged alphabetically. The second series is filed by agents and the third by business records. The fourth series is filed alphabetically by states and then by towns within states. A two-volume, unpublished inventory for the collection has been prepared. In the Redpath records, the researcher interested in state and local history will find material on chautauqua and lyceum in many of the states, as well as material dealing with particular towns.

Besides being very large, the Redpath Chautauqua Collection is also one of the most frequently used holdings. Hardly a week has gone by in the last twenty-five years that a letter or telephone call has not arrived asking about the collection. In 1976, John Edward Tapia, the author of the present study, made his first trip to Iowa City to do research in the collection. Since then, he has visited the Special Collections Department in the main library many times pursuing his interest.

This book is an encyclopedic study of circuit chautauqua in America. The author's analysis of the marketing strategies of chautauqua booking agencies through a close look at advertising brochures is a new contribution. He thoroughly explores changes in the chautauqua program over the years, especially the development of drama on the chautauqua stage. Children's programs or junior chautauqua also receive special consideration. Finally, the switch of chautauqua talent to radio and motion pictures as chautauqua declined in the late 1920s is examined as well. The many illustrations in the volume give the reader a sense of the phenomenon that was circuit chautauqua.

Robert A. McCown
University of Iowa

Preface

My purpose in writing this book is twofold. First, the word *chautauqua* has been recently associated with various nostalgic "rebirths" of the circuit chautauqua idea. Currently, midwestern states such as Kansas, Missouri, and South Dakota sponsor traveling summer chautauquas through their respective humanities councils. A number of very talented individuals portray various historical characters such as William Jennings Bryan, Andrew Carnegie, and Carrie Nation beneath modern chautauqua tents.

As a Missouri Committee for the Humanities lecturer, who speaks anywhere from 12 to 20 times a year about circuit chautauqua, I find that many younger people have a genuine curiosity about the chautauqua their parents, grandparents, or even great-grandparents attended. Many are inquisitive about why it was "such a big deal" and how the movement influenced American life. This book attempts to respond to these curiosities.

The second reason for writing this book is to address my interest in American ideological and historical linkages. Before circuit chautauqua began in 1904, platform arts reigned supreme in terms of providing adult education and, to a lesser extent, entertainment. After circuit chautauqua ended in about 1930, Americans readily accepted radio and sound movies (and later television) as a means of acquiring information and as a thoroughfare of entertainment. The question for me became: What was the missing link between nineteenth-century platform arts and twentieth-century forms of electronic mass media? The answer that I came up with was the circuit chautauqua movement. Thus, my second reason for writing this book is to make the argument that the circuit chautauqua movement literally transformed nineteenth-century platform arts and popular education into a standardized commercial product that eventually fostered the acceptance of the radio, sound movies, and perhaps television.

The major works written about circuit chautauqua were written prior to the mid–1950s. Many of these books present chautauqua from the perspective of the circuit managers, superintendents, or performers. Manager Henry P. Harrison's excellent work *Culture Under Canvas* (1945), as told to Karl Detzer; Victoria and Raymond Case's *We Called It Culture* (1948), based on recollections of superintendent J. Roy Ellison; and performer Gay MacLaren's *Morally We Roll Along* (1938) all relate information concerning the movement through a vast number of interesting personal reflections. All of these books, in conjunction with manager Hugh Orchard's *Fifty Years of Chautauqua* (1923), assisted me in understanding the day-to-day operations of circuit chautauqua. The newest book on the subject of chautauqua, at this writing, is Theodore Morrison's *Chautauqua: A Center for Education, Religion, and the Arts in America* (1974). The circuit movement is mentioned by Morrison, but the bulk of his book is devoted to the operation and cultural significance of the New York Chautauqua Institute.

Circuit Chautauqua discusses the social, historical, and commercial motivations as groundwork for understanding circuit chautauqua as a linkage between the nineteenth and twentieth centuries with regard to mass media. In examining circuit chautauqua, the book relies heavily on primary sources. Based upon the analysis of program brochures, speeches, dramas, readings, and entertainment, my book presents the argument that circuit chautauqua was a sequential and important step in the evolution of electronic mass media in America.

The sources and places from which I acquired the information used in the writing of this book are varied. I owe a great debt to the following libraries and their respective staffs: the Special Collections Library at the State University of Iowa, Iowa City; the River Bluffs Regional Library, Central Branch, St. Joseph, Missouri; the Andrew County Museum, Savannah, Missouri; the Plattsburg Historical Society, Plattsburg, Missouri; the State Historical Society of Iowa, Iowa City; and the Special Collections Library at the University of Arizona, Tucson. I also want to express my special thanks to the library staff, especially Dr. Barbara Palling and Joyce Shutte, of Missouri Western State College in St. Joseph, Missouri, for assisting me in obtaining source material.

The interviews and conversations I had with individuals who were associated with chautauqua in one way or another were of great importance in allowing me to understand the personal and social side of the movement. To this end, I would like to thank Christian Buehler,

Merlin Carstenson, Sue Humphrey, Gilbert Kelly, M.D., former governor Alfred M. Landon, Edwin McDonald, Lorraine Rausch, Simon Rositzky, Isabel Sparks, Leah Spratt, Merlyn J. (Saunders) Tapia, and Ina Wachtel. I would also like to acknowledge the help of the following individuals in assisting me to attain the necessary permissions to use quotations in my book: Nancy Davenport, Laura Sue Hancock, and Senator Nancy Landon Kassebaum.

Those who assisted me in locating pictures and additional sources about chautauqua and in some instances lent me their personal collections include Linda Farber, Steve Edson, Dorothy Elliott, Audry Hart, Gilbert Kelly, Mary Goldberg, "Buster" Johns, Peggy and Herb Iffert, Robert McCown, John Quinton, Anne Redmond, Monya Rositzky, John and Shirley Shober, Lee and Polly Strang, "Cousin" Bob Turner, J. Marshall White, and W. Cole Woodbury.

The pictures included in this text that come from the Special Collections of the State University of Iowa were photographically copied on site by Kate Johnson. The other pictures included in the book were photographically copied at the Instructional Media Center at Missouri Western State College by Anne Adams, assisted by the center's director, Max Schlesinger. The care which Zercher Photographic of St. Joseph, Missouri, took in developing the pictures was deeply appreciated.

The sabbatical granted me by Missouri Western State College made the task of completing this book much easier. The grants and encouragement I received from the Missouri Western State College Foundation, directed by Dr. James McCarthy, and from Dr. Martin Johnson, Dean of Liberal Arts and Sciences at the same college, toward the completion of my book are greatly appreciated. I would also like to acknowledge the careful proofreading and examination given my manuscript by Denise Bartles, Monya Rositzky, and Alice Shue.

It is easy to stray from a project of this magnitude. Sometimes a little encouragement goes a long way. The people who especially encouraged me to "stay with it" are my very patient wife, Denise Bartles, who assisted me in much of the research; Simon and Monya Rositzky; my in-laws, Betty Lou and Bill Bartles; my parents Carl and Merlyn (Saunders) Tapia; C. Irvin Parmenter; Steve Huff; Robert McCown; Lee and Polly Strang; "Cousin" Bob Turner; Ina Wachtel; and Mr. Chips.

John E. Tapia, Ph.D.
Summer 1996

Introduction

Huge brown circuit chautauqua tents were a common summer sight in many early twentieth-century American communities. Circuit chautauqua was first introduced to fifteen Iowa villages in 1904. Within the span of a decade, circuit chautauqua had become a yearly event in many rural and urban towns throughout the United States. The circuit chautauqua programs exposed countless Americans to many new ideas and customs, national and international issues, and popular forms of entertainment that otherwise would have been inaccessible to them. The period of five, six, or seven days set aside for the program also provided opportunities for families, friends, and neighbors to visit one another.

Between 1920 and 1924, the popularity of and demand for circuit chautauqua flourished. More than 10,000 communities sponsored a program each year during this period, and in 1924, or what is known as the Jubilee Anniversary Year, approximately 40 million Americans attended chautauqua. After 1924, the demand for circuit chautauqua dramatically declined. Circuit managers encountered increasing difficulty in getting towns to rebook chautauqua, and the programs more and more frequently failed to draw audiences. By the mid–1920s, advancements in film, radio, and transportation provided new and exciting alternatives for personal enrichment and entertainment. The alarming number of bank failures after 1926 also made it more difficult, and in many instances impossible, for communities to sponsor chautauqua. The Great Crash of 1929, for all practical purposes, ended the circuit chautauqua movement in the United States.

The circuit chautauqua movement initially developed out of the merger of two popular nineteenth-century forms of adult education: the lyceum and the permanent chautauqua. Lyceum and permanent chautauqua activities capitalized on American desires for personal self-enrichment and betterment. From the beginning of the American lyceum in 1826 until the early 1840s, New England lyceum groups sponsored lecture-demonstrations in order to help textile workers cope with the demands of their jobs. Beginning in 1845 and lasting until the outbreak of the Civil War in 1860, literary societies in the East and upper Midwest took over the planning of community lyceum programs. These societies brought professional speakers from Boston and New York into their communities to discuss various literary and social topics. During the Civil War, however, the support for lyceum abated. When lyceum again emerged after the war, it was associated with large commercial bureaus that booked popular lecturers and, after the mid-1870s, other kinds of entertainment.

While the lyceum was taking on a commercial character, the New York Chautauqua Institute, the first permanent chautauqua, was founded and was becoming an important vehicle for adult education in America. The Chautauqua Institute began as a religious assembly in the summer of 1874 on the northeastern shore of Lake Chautauqua in New York State. Although the institute remained dominantly religious in orientation, under the guidance of its founder and president, the Rev. John Heyl Vincent, practical programs of adult instruction and "constructive" entertainment were integrated into the curriculum between 1880 and 1900. Many of the early lecturers, instructors, and performers who were featured at Lake Chautauqua were booked through New York City or Boston lyceum bureaus.

The success of the New York chautauqua prompted literally hundreds of midwestern communities to sponsor their own chautauqua. Community-based chautauqua programs were generally a combination of local talent and noted lyceum features. The popular features were acquired through eastern lyceum agencies. By 1913 many of the community chautauquas had been displaced by circuit chautauqua. Circuit chautauqua basically won out over community chautauqua because it could deliver a better program at a more competitive price.

Characteristic of both nineteenth-century lyceum and chautauqua operations was the ability of local groups to control what would or would not be included as part of a program. Programs were generally aimed at attracting audiences interested in self-improvement, cultural enrichment, and, occasionally, spiritual betterment. As the circuit chautauqua movement evolved into a vast commercial venture, it built upon the intellectual, literary, and religious underpinnings of nineteenth-century lyceum and chautauqua. In doing so, the movement transformed locally governed forms of personal enrichment into a standardized commercial entertainment package.

Circuit chautauqua bureaus "sold" communities on a week-long prepackaged program of education and entertainment that was designed for mass consumption. As the circuit chautauqua movement grew, rural and urban peoples were drawn together through the common denominator of the program. In this way, circuit chautauqua was responsible for fostering a "melting pot" ideology among early twentieth-century Americans. The purpose of this book is to examine how the circuit chautauqua movement transformed locally governed lyceum and chautauqua programs of adult education into a standardized commercial entertainment product, flourished, and then faded into other entertainment fields.

I
Adult Education in Nineteenth-Century America

Adult education throughout the history of nineteenth-century America was generally accomplished through public discourse and discussion. The New England "town hall" tradition, held over from colonial days, was carried westward by settlers. The importance of this custom as a vehicle of local decision making was recognized at the end of the century by historian Frederick Jackson Turner at the 1893 World's Columbian Exposition. There he delivered "The Significance of the Frontier in American History" to the World's Congress of Historians. Turner's "frontier thesis" advocated that as settlers pushed westward into the American frontier, a "perennial rebirth" of American democracy occurred each time popular decision making was established at the local level.

In addition, the nineteenth-century American pulpit also kept communities aware of local social and political issues, as did the innumerable speeches heard on town squares on almost every imaginable occasion. The political debates sponsored by concerned citizen groups were also an important source of information for communities about regional and national issues. The information and issues presented in such public forums were subsequently discussed and argued in countless farmhouse kitchens, dry goods stores, and barber shops. Cultural historian James Trusdale Adams characterized nineteenth-century adult education through "talk" in the following way:

> If there were "giants in those days" in the Senate and in public life, so were there also ... simple but sincere folk wrestling with problems that were not beyond their capacity to deal with in detail and which, at the same time, were fairly clearly defined in their broader outlines and principles. Life itself was still comprehensible and there was plenty of Adult Education, though technique was wholly unorganized and practically undreamed of.

Lyceum

BEFORE THE CIVIL WAR

One of the earliest attempts at providing some structure to early nineteenth-century American adult education occurred through the lyceum. The first lyceum course in this country was started in 1826. Borrowing the name *lyceum* from the ancient Greek reference to the garden of the Temple of Apollo Lyceus at which Aristotle had taught, Josiah Holbrook established that year a lecture-demonstration lyceum course for textile workers in Milbury, Massachusetts. The main method of instruction was carried out through a series of lecture-demonstrations and dealt with topics about science and mechanics as they pertained to the jobs carried out by the textile workers.

The official opening of the Erie Canal in 1825 was in part responsible for the growth of the lyceum movement in New England. As the canal became a major commercial artery for textile goods, the villages and trading posts along the waterway grew into towns and, in some instances, into powerful economic centers. The increase in population along the canal, coupled with an active economy, resulted in more community-sponsored lyceums. By 1840, there were more than 1,000 active lyceum groups operating in New England. As the canal region became civilized, there was an increasing demand for cultural enrichment and general adult education. As a result, the programs provided through lyceum focused decreasingly on science and mechanics and increasingly on literary and cultural subjects.

After 1840, professional lecturers were frequently requested to lead New England lyceum activities. Many well-known authors, biographers, explorers, and religious philosophers from New York City or Boston conducted these courses in New England. The courses covered such subjects as literary works and authors, history, travel, and religion. The broadening of lyceum subject matter in turn attracted a more diversified audience for the programs. In addition to the men who attended, women and, on certain days, children were also included in lyceum discussions. By the time of the Civil War, lyceum had become equated with popular adult education.

As the lyceum movement grew along the eastern seaboard, it also moved inland and westward. A series of public land disposal acts passed by the United States Congress beginning in 1836 opened up vast lands for settlement to the West. Encouraged in part by the twelve thousand miles of railroad track laid throughout the Ohio Valley during the 1840s, many Easterners migrated west of the Alleghenies—first south of the Great Lakes, then down the Ohio River, and finally toward the Pacific Ocean. Settlers tried to preserve the elements of the civilized world they had left behind, which included town hall democracy and lyceum. Notable lecturers such as Henry Ward Beecher, Ralph Waldo Emerson, Horace Greeley, Oliver Wendell Holmes, James Russell Lowell, Theodore Parker, Wendell Phillips, and Henry David Thoreau were brought into western states to conduct lyceums programs. In the southern region of the country, lyceum activities never flourished, before or after the Civil War. Southern financial leaders were antagonistic to anything that might upset the slave-based economy, and that included educating blacks and poor whites through lyceum.

Despite the development and popularity of the lyceum movement prior to the Civil War, it lacked centralized organization and commercial coordination. The several attempts that were made at creating a nationally coordinated lyceum organization during the 1840s and 1850s, including Holbrook's proposal for a National Lyceum League, all failed. The basic obstacle to centralized coordination was that individual communities refused to relinquish the control of their lyceum to an outside authority. Consequently, professional lecturers dealt directly with community lyceum organizers in negotiating the date, fee, and topic for the program.

The lyceum movement was interrupted by a depression that began in 1857. By the time the depression was receding and prospects for lyceum once again appeared good, the country was on the verge of a great conflict. President Lincoln declared war on April 15, 1861, against the Confederate states. Once the war got underway, the few remaining lyceum speakers bluntly defended either the South or the North. Carl Bode noted that the direct result of the Civil War on the lyceum movement "or rather such small parts of it as could maintain themselves was of course that lecturing became propaganda instead of education or even amusement."

AFTER THE CIVIL WAR

When lyceum reappeared after the Civil War, it was coordinated through centralized and commercial booking agencies. The commercialization of lyceum was in part initiated through the efforts of what

The Redpath Lyceum Bureau in Chicago, ca. 1900. The Redpath name became almost synonymous with circuit chautauqua. Redpath Collection, University of Iowa.

remained of postwar community lyceum organizations. Approximately one hundred of these surviving associations, which were located primarily in the Midwest, banded together in 1865 to create the Associated Western Literary Society. Through this alliance, the members cooperatively booked speakers for their respective lyceum programs and, by doing so, were better able to negotiate lecture fees through the coordination of travel schedules. In the spring of 1868, the Associated Western Literary Society merged with the American Literary Bureau of New York to create the first large commercial lyceum booking agency.

The most prominent and commercially successful lyceum bureau ever to operate in America was the Boston Lyceum Bureau, also known as the Redpath Lyceum Bureau. James Redpath (1833 to 1891) founded the Redpath Lyceum Bureau in Boston during the fall of 1868. Even before the establishment of the bureau, the Redpath name had been associated with education, history, and social commentary. Redpath had served as a war correspondent for the *New York Tribune*, was the coeditor of Jefferson Davis' *History of the Southern Confederacy*, wrote several social histories, served as the general superintendent of education in Charleston, South Carolina, and had been a lyceum lecturer before the war.

There was so much demand in the Midwest for lyceum that Redpath established a regional office in Chicago in 1871. Upon assuming the position of managing editor of the *North American Review* in 1875, Redpath sold his bureau to George Hathaway and Major J. B. Pond. Hathaway bought out Pond's interest in the agency in 1880 and remained sole owner of the Redpath Lyceum Bureau until 1903. In 1903 the bureau was set up as an investment corporation that operated both lyceum and, within several years, circuit chautauqua. Two other notable lyceum bureaus started operation within a year or two of the founding of the Redpath Bureau — the Williams Lecture and Musical Bureau and the Midland Lyceum Bureau. By the turn of the century, there were a total of twelve lyceum bureaus in operation and each was booking programs for at least 3,000 events a year. The Midland Lyceum Bureau, following the lead of the Redpath agency, also began its own chautauqua circuit in the early 1900s.

At the end of the 1870s, the Redpath Lyceum Bureau had in place what were called "star lecture courses." Star courses were designed to promote the popular and expensive lecturers. Late nineteenth-century Redpath star courses were built around lecturers such as Susan B. Anthony, Henry Ward Beecher, William Jennings Bryan, Edward Everett Hale, Wendell Phillips, Charles Sumner, Henry M. Stanley, and Mark Twain. Even Phineas T. Barnum was placed under contract by the Redpath bureau in 1869 as a "star lecturer." Barnum was, however, only booked once by the Redpath bureau. He had been placed under contract to present "The Art of Making Money" at a lyceum function in Troy, New York. At the close of the lecture, Barnum persuaded the sponsors to pay him an additional five dollars beyond the contracted amount to cover his hotel bill. When James Redpath learned of this, he became enraged. The idea that his talent would independently squabble over a fee after it had already been agreed upon seemed inexcusable to him. Redpath never booked Barnum again.

The general nature of lyceum programs after the Civil War was directed toward providing popular entertainment to smaller towns. John Noffsinger noted that lyceum was almost always a "village function," with the vast majority of the programs (even into the 1920s) being sponsored by communities of less than 1500 population. Talent features were gradually extended to include animal acts, singers,

James Redpath founded the Redpath Lyceum Bureau in 1868. Occasionally, Redpath performed in some of the lyceum plays booked through his agency. Redpath Collection, University of Iowa.

dancers, readers, humorists, impersonators, magicians, and some play productions. In *Eccentricities of Genius*, Major J. B. Pond provided an explanation of why lyceum began to focus so much on popular entertainment after the war: "When over a million men had returned from military strife to civil pursuits ... there came an unprecedented demand for entertainments and amusements."

Nineteenth-century lyceum bureaus supplied programs to three general types of gatherings: social clubs, lyceum theatres (or opera houses) and community chautauquas. Single lecture features were usually booked by literary or reading circles, as had been the case before the Civil War, to promote discussions about some literary work or author. The typical program usually lasted an entire day and occasionally two. The 1869 completion of the first transcontinental rail line and the vast expansion of the railroad in the 1870s not only encouraged lyceum lecturers westward but also prompted eastern dramatic companies to travel into the hinterland.

To encourage the westward expansion of culture, many affluent midwestern communities built spacious lyceum theatres or opera houses in the last quarter of the nineteenth century. The majority of these towns booked the production companies and other attractions for their lyceum theatres through eastern lyceum agencies. By 1890, more than 1,300 midwestern towns were regularly sponsoring national touring companies to appear at their lyceum theatres. In areas which wanted to sponsor a production but were not reachable by railroad, the lyceum bureaus arranged to have performers, costumes, instruments, lighting, scenery, and a "theatre" tent transported by wagon.

The availability of large production companies for booking in the West was generally limited by the lyceum bureaus to the months between June and September. This was roughly the same span of the year in which circuit chautauqua would operate. To transport large production companies when snow was likely increased the risk of delays, missed bookings, frustrated talent, and additional expenditures. Yet the lyceum bureaus wanted to keep their talent working as much as possible throughout the year. It was also important from the standpoint of promotion to keep a bureau's name as visible as possible in a community no matter what the time of year. To accomplish both of these goals, most bureaus booked single lecturers or small companies in the West during the winter months. Although a performer or small group of performers could be delayed because of the weather, the additional expense was much less in comparison to the detainment of a large production company. As railroad travel become more dependable in the last decade of the nineteenth century, the months for booking larger production companies in the West gradually expanded.

Unlike the carefully structured circuit chautauqua contract, rarely was there a written contract or agreement between lyceum bureaus of the late nineteenth century and the groups sponsoring their programs. The major reason for this was that the lyceum bureaus wanted as much flexibility as possible in booking agreements. The uncertainty of

Uncle Tom's Cabin was a very popular post–Civil War lyceum production. Redpath Collection, University of Iowa.

transportation, as well as talent, frequently translated into delays, postponements, and cancellations. A written contract specifying exact times, dates, and performers would have brought about many legal problems for the lyceum bureaus. The lyceum bureaus, however, made every attempt to deliver the program as promised because future bookings hinged on their ability to present what was pledged.

Circuit entertainment was not just limited to lyceum after the Civil War. Large traveling circuses such as the Barnum and Bailey Circus, the Ringling Brothers Circus, and Hunt's Three Ring Circus traveled to countless communities. The circus was, in fact, so popular between the years of 1871 and 1920 that circus historian Earl Chapin May called the period the "golden age of the circus." In the meanwhile, out of the hodgepodge of entertainment found in honky-tonks, free-and-easies, beer halls, local theaters, and special attraction museums of the 1880s and 1890s, vaudeville was emerging. Popular talent and other entertainers traveled from engagement to engagement and usually acted as their own agents.

By the early 1900s, vaudeville, as had been the case with lyceum and the circus, had been organized into a system of commercial circuits. The Keith-Orpheum circuit, the Keith-Albee circuit, and the Kohl-Castle circuit coordinated and supplied different kinds of attractions to theatres, museums, showboats and music halls, all typically found in urban areas. Vaudeville tended to be promoted as what Able Green and

Joe Laurie, Jr., called, "glittering showmanship and gaudy showplaces." The entertainment was frequently rough and lusty and accompanied by drink. It was not particularly suited to women or children. Whereas lyceum served a "village" function, vaudeville and the circus were generally sponsored in larger communities of 3,000 or more population.

Although they served different types of audiences, the line between vaudeville and lyceum (and later chautauqua) was not always well defined. Sometimes vaudeville and lyceum talent were one and the same. Entertainers such as Edwin Brush, John Bunny, Ruth Gordon, Bill Nye, among a host of others, worked back and forth between vaudeville and lyceum (and later chautauqua). Some of these vaudevillians also found work in the "legitimate" Broadway theatre and appeared in early silent movie features. When the circuit chautauqua movement began to flourish in the pre–World War I era, many vaudeville and lyceum entertainers also found themselves performing in a Redpath tent.

Permanent Chautauqua

REVEREND VINCENT'S NEW YORK INSTITUTE

While the lyceum movement was moving westward, Reverend John Heyl Vincent, with financial backing from Lewis Miller, began a Methodist Sunday school retreat on the northern shore of Lake Chautauqua. The retreat, which was officially opened in 1874, eventually evolved into the "Chautauqua Institute" after a number of vast changes and additions. The first "chautauqua" assembly was held August 12–28, and was attended by forty men and women. According to "Pansy," the author of *The Chautauqua Girls at Home*, written in the 1870s, the assembly was a rather euphoric experience: "The last Sabbath of August was a lovely day; it was the first Sabbath that our girls had spent at home since the revelation of Chautauqua. It seemed lovely to them."

There are many different meanings for the word "*chautauqua*." In the early 1700s, the Seneca Indians of the Iroquois Federation used phonetic variations of *chautauqua* when referring to a body of water located in the southwest corner of what is now New York State. The Senecas had several different connotations for the term *chautauqua* when associated with this body of water: "water of plentiful fish," "place of sudden death," or "bag tied in middle." As the French and English explorers and trappers moved into the region, the spelling and pronunciation of chautauqua went through any number of changes. Different spellings of chautauqua persisted until 1859, at which point a proclamation approving the current spelling was passed by the county supervisors of the New York county containing the chautauqua area.

Through the efforts of Methodist minister John Heyl Vincent, the word *chautauqua* had taken on a new and popular meaning by 1900. It was dominantly associated with education, culture, and inspiration. In 1885, Vincent summed up the mission of chautauqua as follows: "It exalts education, — the mental, social, moral, and religious culture of all who have mental, social, moral, and religious faculties." The early programs offered through chautauqua dealt with such topics as leading singing and prayer, the importance of Bible reading and biblical geography, public oration, and effective Sunday school management. "Alf" Landon, former Kansas governor and 1936 Republican presidential hopeful, recalled in a 1980 interview that his grandfather (Reverend W. H. Mossman) was "an old Methodist preacher at chautauqua" and would train students in oratory and biblical reading by having them "stand on the stumps after trees were cleared and deliver sermons."

Beginning in the late 1870s under Vincent's direction, programs of general education and entertainment activities were integrated into Chautauqua's summer curriculum. Vincent believed that the men and women attending Chautauqua needed something "constructive" to do between lessons in religion and Sunday school instruction. He turned in part to the commercial lyceum agencies as a source of suitable educational workshops and entertainment. Among the "star" lyceum names that appeared at the Chautauqua Institute prior to 1900, were Jane Addams, Elsie Baker, Admiral Richard E. Byrd, William Jennings Bryan, Thomas A. Edison, Ulysses S. Grant, Rutherford B. Hayes, Upton Sinclair, Billy Sunday, Ida M. Tarbell, Count Ilya Tolstoy, Booker T. Washington, and George Westinghouse.

The popularity of the summer programs increasingly attracted more people to Chautauqua each year throughout the late nineteenth and early twentieth centuries. Nearly five hundred persons attended the Chautauqua Institute in 1878, and by the early 1900s, literally thousands of people from all over the United States were in attendance. In 1878, Reverend Vincent began a home study course called the Chautauqua Literary and Scientific Circle. The course was frequently referred to as either the C.L.S.C. or the "Circle." The purpose of the Circle was to provide men and women deprived of schooling at home an avenue through which they could obtain an education.

During the 1880s, the Circle developed into a four-year course of directed home reading. When the program was completed, a diploma was awarded. The ninth assembly of the Chautauqua Institute, held in 1882, graduated the first C.L.S.C. class. Eight hundred diplomas were awarded to those attending the ceremony, and at least that many were distributed through the mail to those who could not be present. The *Chautauquan* was a monthly magazine begun in 1881 under auspices of the Circle. It contained most of the articles required for the home reading course and advice about how to run local circles. In 1898, the Chautauqua Press was founded and acted as the publishing agency for the Circle-sponsored book-a-month club.

More than 8,400 people, primarily in rural areas of the Midwest, joined the Circle during 1878. Circle enrollment climbed to 100,000 in 1888, and by 1900 more than 2,500,000 belonged. The Circle was especially important to those living in small towns, where chances for adult learning were limited. In isolated areas, local circles provided an opportunity for adults to gather and discuss guided readings with one another. Vincent encouraged people not just to join a circle but to create their own circles. In a February 1883 issue of the *Chautauquan*, he wrote:

> First of all, good friends, don't let the idea prevail anywhere that the local circle is indispensable to the work of the C.L.S.C. [Chautauqua Literary and Scientific Circle]....
>
> Where people come together voluntarily for mutual improvement, the local circle is of very great advantage, and the more circles we can have the better, and the more you attend the local circle the better for you. Any effort put forth to establish a local circle is worthy of praise.
>
> Again, small local circles are better than large ones. Where there are six persons who "take to" each other, who work easily together, they will do better work than a large circle.

Between 1878 and 1898, 10,000 local circles came into existence, most of them in towns of less than 3,000 in population. The significance of the Circle in American adult education was summed up in Joseph Gould's *The Chautauqua Movement*:

> In an incredibly short period of time, nearly every community of any size ... had at least one person following the Chautauqua reading program as a member of C.L.S.C.... Travelers reported finding crews on western railroads who had constituted themselves a Circle, and there were crossroad store keepers who dragooned their cracker barrel philosophers into joining.

The widespread interest in the Circle as an educational vehicle for adults motivated Vincent to create additional instructional programs to be offered through the summer Chautauqua Assembly. The Normal School of Languages and the Teacher's Retreat were established in 1879. In the same year, the Chautauqua College of Liberal Arts began providing summer programs of academic study. The work of all of these schools was carried on the rest of the year through correspondence and extension lecture courses. In addition to these schools, the Chautauqua School of Theology was chartered in 1881. It provided courses in religious studies, and all courses were conducted only at the Assembly. The significance of the Chautauqua Assembly's work in adult education was recognized on March 30, 1883, when the New York Legislature empowered it to grant college degrees as Chautauqua University. The original Chautauqua Assembly in essence pioneered three of the most popular forms of late nineteenth-century adult education — summer schools, guided home reading, and correspondence/extension courses.

COMMUNITY-BASED CHAUTAUQUAS

The desire for adult education in the last quarter of the nineteenth century was not met by only the Chautauqua Institute or lyceum bureaus, however. After 1880, many local circles began their own community-based chautauqua. Community chautauquas tried, whenever possible, to model their program after the Chautauqua Institute in New York. Many eastern and southeastern community chautauquas were initiated and run by the Baptists or Methodists, while in the West, it was more common to have a broader-based, usually nondenominational, community effort in the planning and operation of the chautauqua. Frequently, civic and business leaders provided economic support for the chautauqua in their community.

The *Biographical History of Atchison County, Missouri*, printed in 1905, explained how the Lecture Congress and Chautauqua evolved in Rock Port, Missouri:

> The first session was held in the late summer of 1900, under Mr. Dopf's personal management. He was so delighted with the appreciation of the people that he held another session, in July of 1901; but, notwithstanding the success of the undertaking from the public's point of view, the promoter lost several hundred dollars each year, and in 1902 Mr. Dopf turned the management of the

Adult Education in Nineteenth-Century America 23

The Lake Contrary Chautauqua Grounds, St. Joseph, Missouri, by 1900 had a horse racing track, boating, fishery, dance hall, hotel, theatre, and street car access. Courtesy of St. Joseph Public Library, St. Joseph, Missouri.

chautauqua over to thirty-seven public spirited citizens of Rock Port, who pledged themselves to be responsible for the expenses of the coming session....

Since 1902 the chautauqua had been conducted in the same manner, the citizens meeting annually to hear the report of the treasurer and elect a board of managers for the ensuing year. There has been a steady and widening interest in the institution, throughout the country.... Among the noted men who have been heard at the annual sessions are W. J. Bryan, Senator La Follette, J. Adam Bede, R. P. Hobson, Opie Read, DeWitt Miller, Thos. McClary, Dr. A. A. Willitts, Rev. L. B. Wickersham, Frank Dixon, Col. G. W. Bain, James Hedley, Hon. G. A. Gearhart, Edward Amherst Ott, and others of national fame and ability.

As noted in the Rock Port example, the managers of community-based chautauquas, in consultation with sponsors (as well as local educators and clergy), booked speakers and other performers on their ability to lead study classes and provide educational workshops. The majority of the Rock Port programs were booked through the Redpath Lyceum Bureau. The typical program lasted anywhere from five to seven days and was created by the intermingling of lyceum professionals and local talent. It was, of course, desirable to have enough big names to draw a crowd.

The actual features and workshops offered through community chautauquas covered a variety of topics such as Bible reading, literature and interpretive reading, health and science, history and social

The Chautauqua Auditorium, Clarinda, Iowa. Postcard, ca. 1904. Clarinda hosted a Chautauqua every year from 1900 to 1930.

studies, and public speaking. Because of the cost, and sometimes the distance, involved in attending chautauqua, frequently only one member of a family came to the program. Subsequently, that family member shared what he or she had learned at the program with other family members and friends. Bette Davis' mother, for example, spent several summers during the early 1900s learning the Delsarte art of expression at the Free Baptist Chautauqua Assembly in Ocean Park, Maine. She in turn "tutored" Bette Davis in these performance methods.

The better community chautauqua programs were usually sponsored in towns that had a population of at least 3,500 within a five-mile radius. The larger population base usually meant that a community had enough financial backing to bring "star" attractions to its chautauqua. Sometimes a local "star" emerged and commanded the attention of regional chautauquas and lyceums. One well-known Kansas lecturer, who spoke almost exclusively in the Midwest, was Carrie Nation. Another locally popular performer was the Reverend Sam Jones of Kansas. The *Illustrated Doniphan County* (circa 1900) noted of Reverend Jones: "The people never seemed to tire of him, with his scathing denunciations of sin and his vivid descriptions of the wrath of God. Not only were his hearers amused, but shocked, sometimes, for he often called names and told ... the sins of men before him in no uncertain tones."

Some attempts were made on the part of smaller community chautauquas to negotiate lyceum bookings cooperatively. They hoped that by pooling resources and booking lecturers as a group they could bring better feature attractions to all of their chautauquas. The Western Federation of Chautauquas was created in 1889, then the International Chautauqua Alliance in 1889, and, finally, the Chautauqua Union in 1913. None of these attempts succeeded, largely for the same reasons that collaborative efforts among lyceum groups had failed. Regional chautauqua or lyceum groups did not want anyone from the outside interfering with or having control over their programs. Squabble after squabble erupted over talent selection, programs dates, and cost.

Introduction of Circuit Chautauqua

As the chautauqua movement grew, first in the East and then in the West, it drew heavily from lyceum bureaus to recruit talent for programs. But by the beginning of the twentieth century, many lyceum agencies owned and operated their own circuit of chautauquas. The largest and most prestigious circuit chautauqua bureau was that managed by the Redpath Lyceum and Chautauqua Bureau. What the Redpath Bureau did, starting in 1903, was to sell a circuit program on the basis of its overall quality and cost in comparison to what the community chautauqua could offer. What the community lost under the Redpath scheme was the ability to control the makeup of the program and the program dates.

In exchange for these losses, the Redpath, and later circuit bureaus, provided programs of predictably good quality at an affordable price. By necessity the circuit chautauqua bureaus always had to control the programming and dates. Bureau managers realized that if they began negotiating with each town over features and program dates, they would encounter the same problems that had brought about the failure of earlier cooperative chautauqua efforts.

As the circuit chautauqua movement gained momentum, it gradually pushed aside the community-based chautauqua. In 1910, approximately 1,800 American communities hosted their own chautauqua, but within four years, the majority of these community chautauquas had ceased operation. The "onslaught of the little Chautauqua," reported the *New York Times* in 1914, was due to the rise of the commercial circuit chautauqua bureau. By the close of World War I in 1919, only a handful of communities continued to sustain their own chautauqua operation and most existed in name only.

After 1919, the vast majority of the community-based chautauqua programs were in fact actually booked through the circuit chautauqua bureaus. The name of the local chautauqua manager and committee appeared in the program booklet, without mentioning the name of the circuit chautauqua that was really providing the program. The community-based chautauqua that was offered in King City, Missouri, in 1919, for example, was made up of exactly the same features presented roughly in the same order as the Redpath Circuit Chautauqua program that appeared in that same year in Savannah, Missouri. In this way, the illusion, but not the substance, of community control over chautauqua persisted.

II

The Movement Toward Standardization and Commercialization

In 1900, Keith Vawter, an agent for the Redpath Lyceum Bureau, began studying the problems associated with the inability of community chautauquas to work together. During the next three years, Vawter created a proposal that he believed would allow the Redpath bureau to provide programs to communities without the many problems associated with cooperative efforts. Under his plan, Vawter suggested that a standardized Redpath chautauqua program be created and sold to a group of towns close to one another that had established community chautauquas. The overall advantage of his proposal was that once the talent that made up a program was sent to an area, they stayed there. The biggest benefit to the bureau was that money could be saved by transporting talent and equipment less frequently back and forth between the East and West. And the communities booking a Redpath Chautauqua program would receive a standardized program of good quality at an affordable cost.

The Standard Chautauqua

Keith Vawter and a newly acquired partner by the name of Roy J. Ellison established the Standard Redpath Chautauqua in 1903 under certain agreements with the Redpath Lyceum Bureau. That year Vawter and Ellison tried to persuade the managers of 30 independent chautauquas in Iowa to let the Standard Redpath Chautauqua provide their community's 1904 chautauqua program. Most of the chautauqua managers (and sponsors) they visited with were hostile to the idea of having an outsider come into their town to operate "their" chautauqua. Of the thirty contacts Vawter and Ellison made, only nine consented to have the Standard Redpath Chautauqua provide their 1904 program.

Both men realized that more bookings were absolutely necessary if the Standard Redpath Chautauqua venture was to be financially feasible. The distances between engagements and idle weeks of time between programs needed somehow to be filled in with other towns. They made the decision to offer small towns without established chautauquas that were located near those already booked a chance to book a Standard Chautauqua. In those towns without an established chautauqua organization, Ellison and Vawter looked to community leaders and business people to pledge enough money for the program. Six additional Iowa towns were booked, making a total of fifteen towns the Standard Redpath Chautauqua journeyed to in 1904.

In all of the communities that sponsored the Standard program through their established chautauqua organization, there was either a chautauqua pavilion or a large building set aside for holding the program. There was, however, no specific building in the six towns added to the list of 1904 Standard Chautauqua towns. Vawter came up with the idea of using a circus tent in these towns. By 1910, the Redpath Chautauqua, as did other chautauqua bureaus, used what was called a "chautauqua tent." This tent was of a different design and color from the typical circus tent in use at that time.

As the circuit chautauqua movement grew, the chautauqua tent was used more frequently, even in towns with pavilions, for several practical reasons. First, if a town did have a chautauqua pavilion, it was frequently too small for the crowds that attended chautauqua. Second, circuit chautauqua managers could never predict what kind of shape they would find community pavilions in. And, third, upon seeing the huge chautauqua tent, local people became inquisitive and attended the program. The tent in essence was an effective public relations device for chautauqua.

Although the Standard Redpath Chautauqua was not financially successful in 1904, the efforts of Vawter and Ellison paved the way for the future operation of circuit chautauqua. What they did establish, wrote former circuit manager Hugh Orchard in *Fifty Years of Chautauqua*, was the practice of "booking uniform programs of Chautauqua talent through consecutive dates, to a considerable number of communities, and supplying from a central headquarters the equipment, as well as the management of all transactions entering into the building and delivery of such Circuits." After modifying the contractual guarantee and broadening the area in which the chautauqua traveled, Vawter and Ellison delivered the Redpath Chautauqua program (the name Standard having been dropped by the bureau) to 33 Iowa, Nebraska, and Wisconsin towns in 1907.

The goal of the Redpath Chautauqua, which was to provide better programs than the traditional community chautauqua could provide and provide them at a more affordable price, was accomplished in 1907. In a 1907 edition of the *Audubon Republican*, an Iowa newspaper, the following statement was made:

> The independent Chautauqua cannot easily compete with those run by a Bureau because they go into the market and buy talent at retail, while the Bureau buys it up wholesale. And we are assured by one of the managers that the difference in the expenses of the Audubon Chautauqua would have amounted to five or six hundred dollars. It seems to us that the Redpath Lyceum Bureau has solved the problem of putting these entertainments before the people in smaller towns in a practical and successful way.

Standardization and Commercialization in America

Circuit chautauqua emerged at a point in history where the accumulative effects of post–Civil War mechanization, railroad expansion, and centralized economic markets had come together to create a new industrial order for the country. Well into the 1870s, small-town life was the norm in America. Social historian Robert Wiebe wrote that "depending upon the line of transportation, groups of these towns fell into satellite patterns about larger centers, to which they looked to for market places and supplies, credit and news.... With farms, generally fanning around them, these communities moved by the rhythms of agriculture." The almost 200,000 miles of railroad track laid between Lee's surrender at Appomattox in 1865 and the outbreak of World War I in 1914 drew countless small towns into national markets, however, and made them increasingly dependent upon decisions and products made elsewhere.

The development of the railroad after the Civil War was paralleled by the evolution of mass marketing mail services. During the 1870s and

1880s, there came into being numerous popular magazines—the *Atlantic, Century, Harpers, North American Review,* and *Ladies Home Journal*—that were designed to sell mail-order products. Mail-order catalog businesses were also a result of the new markets made possible by railroad. The Montgomery Ward mail-order business was started in 1872. Operating out of Chicago, Ward's primary market was in the Midwest, where it worked with various farm organizations, especially the Grange, to capture the farm and seed market. In 1889, H. W. Sears and Alvah C. Roebuck began a mail-order house that also operated out of Chicago. By 1900, the *Sears, Roebuck Catalogue* was essentially the Bible of rural midwestern consumption, offering farm and seed supplies, as well as dishes, clothes, furniture, and just about anything else.

Mail-order supply houses like Montgomery Wards and Sears Roebuck offered rural residents standardized and affordable products of predictable quality. In the post–Civil War era, lyceum bureaus used a mail-order approach in selling their features to various community groups. A multitude of one-page promotional fliers describing the type of entertainment and cost were commonly sent to those who might be interested in sponsoring a lyceum feature or program. From the information provided on the fliers, potential sponsors determined what feature or features they wanted to book for their literary program, opera house, or community chautauqua. The local group was solely responsible for the promotion and advertising of the particular feature.

The bureaus' approach to booking circuit chautauqua, on the other hand, did not allow the sponsors to choose what specific features were included on a program. The features that made up the five, six, or seven day circuit chautauqua program were exclusively determined by the bureaus and were sold to a community as a complete package. In addition, the promotion and advertising of the circuit program was coordinated by the bureaus, not the local participants. The promotion of circuit chautauqua programs largely involved the direct mass mailings of promotional materials to citizens and business leaders, as well as special display materials for the sponsoring committee.

Growth of Circuit Chautauqua Into Big Business

Circuit chautauqua grew into a sophisticated commercial enterprise prior to 1917, the year America became directly involved in World War I. Attracted by the growing success of the Redpath Chautauqua, other lyceum bureaus entered the field of circuit chautauqua. Six lyceum bureaus operated circuit chautauquas in 1910 and together delivered programs to about a hundred towns that same year. Circuit chautauqua was not very profitable, however, for most of the lyceum bureaus that had entered the field until after 1912. The reluctance of many communities to relinquish the control of their chautauqua to a circuit bureau persisted until early 1913. In addition, prior to this year, the marketplace for circuit chautauqua programs was generally limited to small midwestern towns.

The summer of 1913 was the turning point when circuit chautauqua became a successful business. The Western Redpath Chautauqua branch alone journeyed to 250 communities that year, and by the following year, the 15 large lyceum and chautauqua companies engaged in circuit operations collectively provided programs to 2,400 towns throughout the country. Each of these 15 circuit chautauqua bureaus operated one or more circuits, with each circuit including anywhere from 40 to 90 towns.

The competition over "chautauqua territory" was at times fierce. For example, in 1912, the Ellison-White Chautauqua Bureau (Roy Ellison had left Vawter and the Redpath Bureau by this time) provided a free program in the same town and at the same time that a Redpath program was being held. The Ellison-White bureau wanted to "get even with" the Redpath bureau for encroaching upon what it considered to be its territory. Squabbles like this were not uncommon among the early circuit companies. To resolve territorial issues and other matters, the owners and operators of the larger bureaus joined in 1914 and created the International Lyceum and Chautauqua Manager's Association.

Through the Manager's Association, circuit chautauqua managers negotiated with one another about territory, selection and sharing of talent, and sharing of transportation and equipment costs. The subtle impact of the International Lyceum and Chautauqua Manager's Association was that it operated as an informal monopoly that benefited its members. By overseeing chautauqua territories, talent availability, and the general coordination of the movement, the Manager's Association discouraged the development of new circuit chautauqua companies.

By the time that the United States had joined Allied forces against Germany in 1917, all of the large circuit bureaus operated under a rather complex corporate structure. Donald Graham explained the intricacy of the circuit chautauqua corporate structure, using the Redpath system as an example, in the following manner:

The Redpath system consisted of a number of Chautauqua circuits allied together under a single name, but owned separately. The parent organization, The Redpath Lyceum Bureau, continued to function throughout the period of Chautauqua history as a single corporation. The managers of several Redpath Lyceum offices established chautauquas as separate corporations and were thus actually operating two businesses simultaneously, lyceum and chautauqua. For the privilege of using the corporation name for their own undertakings, the Redpath Chautauqua managers paid a royalty to the Redpath Lyceum Bureau.

The popularity of circuit chautauqua continued to grow so much throughout the years of World War I that approximately 8,000 communities sponsored programs in 1918, the year in which the armistice was signed. The biggest year of the circuit chautauqua movement occurred in 1924, when it was sponsored in 10,000 American communities and an estimated 40,000,000 Americans were in attendance. The demand for circuit chautauqua diminished abruptly after 1924, however, for reasons discussed later. Although the focus of this work is on the American circuit chautauqua, it is also important to note that after 1914, several of the larger circuit bureaus took programs abroad. Beginning in 1915, the Redpath Bureau and the Ellison-White Bureau provided chautauqua to English-speaking towns in Canada and Mexico. In addition, the Ellison-White Bureau experimented with programs in Australia starting in 1917, and in New Zealand and Tahiti during 1918. The overseas circuits, however, were not financially successful and were abandoned after 1918. But in the rural areas of Canada and Mexico, chautauqua programs continued to be sponsored as late as 1940, although not through American-based bureaus.

The Selling and Promotion of Circuit Chautauqua

THE BOOKING AGENT

The booking agents of almost all the circuit chautauquas reported directly to the bureau managers. The primary job of the booking agent was selling the circuit program to the leaders of a community. If the agent was successful, local business and civic leaders became sponsors of the program and signed the bureau's contract. The standard chautauqua contract basically stipulated that the sponsors would

(1) guarantee a certain figure in ticket sales (usually $2,500), (2) agree to the bureau manager receiving all of the gate receipts (before 1910, managers received a percentage above the amount guaranteed), and (3) not request any changes in the program or program dates. In return, the bureau was obligated to provide a chautauqua program lasting five, six, or seven days, promotion and advertising for the program, and the necessary equipment, such as the tent, seating, and lighting.

In situations in which a community was currently backing a successful circuit program, the agent usually tried to get a contract for the following year signed before the program closed. Although any standard chautauqua contract placed the immediate financial risk on the shoulders of the sponsors, a large program deficit could result in future financial loss for the bureau. In towns where large deficits occurred, the agent had difficulty in finding sponsors for future programs. Moreover, the loss of one town on an established circuit, unless it could be replaced by another, meant less overall return for a bureau.

Booking agents used various appeals and strategies to sell local business and civic leaders on sponsoring a circuit chautauqua program. Potential contract guarantors were frequently challenged by the booking agent with a question about whether they wanted their community to be "just as good" as those neighboring communities that had already signed for the program. The agent also asked community business leaders to reflect on how many people chautauqua had brought into their town last year and how the activity had translated into commercial activity. Community leaders were also reminded that it was their civic responsibility to bring "education, culture and uplift" to their town and that chautauqua was, of course, the most effective means of doing so. Decorative promotional fliers describing each of the main attractions on the forthcoming chautauqua program were handed to potential sponsors. "Imagine," the agent might have said, "Broadway plays, travelogues, and Mr. Bryan. Right here on Main Street."

Once a desirable number of contract guarantees had been secured, the agent, in conjunction with the bureau manager, reviewed the number of days, dates, and places for the next year's program and developed a geographic and time schedule. The individual features that made up the circuit program followed one another successively from town to town with no days lost en route. The features that constituted the first day of the program in one town also comprised the first day's features in the next town on the circuit. Because the order of appearance of the features on a program was basically unchanged from town to town, advertising materials and promotional techniques were also standardized. Blanket program brochures, for example, were printed for all of the stops on a particular circuit, with the town name and program dates being filled in at a later time. Press releases about the program, poster cards, and banners were also all standardized for a given group of circuit towns sharing a particular program.

Print media were basically used to promote circuit chautauqua programs. So important was print to the promotion of the Horner-Redpath Bureau that manager Charles Horner bought the controlling interest in the *Olathe Register* to assure that he had sufficient equipment for his advertising needs. The sheer vastness of the advertising materials used to promote circuit programs is described by Hugh Orchard:

> Calendars, street car cards, program folders, herald programs, window cards, window card spreads, large muslin banners, small muslin banners, thirty-six inch pennants, muslin daters, street streamers, automobile banners, windshield stickers, arrow tack cards, for sale cards, lecture window cards, one sheet posters, circular letter to underwriters, newspaper chautauqua stories, display advertisements, direct mail advertisements, special display for special attractions.

MARKETING THE PROGRAM IN THE COMMUNITY

About a month before the opening of the chautauqua, the bureau sent large packages of promotional materials along with advance men and women into the community. Strategically designed and executed advertising materials for a given program were essential in assuring its success. Hugh Orchard explains how circuit marketing was planned and accomplished: "Trained publicity agents begin the study of the quantity, quality, variety and distribution of advertising materials six months in advance of the opening date, and where well handled, every detail is considered and recorded so that the whole scheme of publicity unfolds in a natural and effective way at the appointed time and place for which it is attended [*sic*]."

Advertising cards were tacked up on fences and barns by the publicity agents and children who had been recruited into service. Buttons were distributed that proclaimed, "I Bought Mine" or "I'm Going." One-page fliers featuring the star attractions appeared in the windows of local merchants. And a huge banner hung over Main Street boldly proclaimed the dates of the program.

The Movement Toward Standardization and Commercialization   35

The local newspaper was used to promote the forthcoming chautauqua in a variety of ways. There were standard promotional pieces about star talent and the overall program, in addition to some contests that drew attention to the program. *The Committeeman's Manual: How to Run a Lyceum Course* explained how the advertising of "missing word contests, misspelled word contests, word-forming contests" could benefit chautauqua. The following example of how these contests worked was included in the *Manual*:

> Hobart, Oklahoma, is a young town of about 1,500 population. While the chautauqua was in progress, the *Hobart Republican* announced that on a certain day five advertisements in its issue of that day would contain misspelled words.
>
> The first person discovering the five errors and reporting to the newspaper office would receive three free tickets to the chautauqua. The second reporting would receive two, and the third reporting would receive one.
>
> The *Republican*, the next day, announced the winners, and reported that the next hour after the papers were off the press about 125 telephone calls came to the office reporting errors. This simple scheme set the entire town to searching, and was good for the paper, the advertisers and the chautauqua.

The program booklet or brochure was by far the most effective and versatile form of chautauqua print advertising. The brochure described each of the individual attractions that made up the program, included a schedule of when features were to appear on the program, provided pictorial glimpses of what one might see at the actual program, and detailed the importance of chautauqua for any given community. Unfolded, the brochure was a large poster, and while folded it could be used as a mailing flier. The circuit bureaus made every effort to deliver the program as outlined in the brochure because substituting talent, especially the feature attractions, usually meant a decline in ticket sales. The decision about what talent to use on a circuit program was based upon the superintendent's "grading" of the performers, questionnaires filled out by circuit sponsors, the availability of the performers, and, of course, cost.

TICKET SELLERS AND THE CHAUTAUQUA BOOSTERS

A single season pass for the entire week-long chautauqua program was available and cost anywhere from $7 to $10. Single tickets to specific performances ranged in price from a quarter to fifty cents. Season

A Redpath tent boy, William S. Ealy, who later became an osteopathic physician. Courtesy of Ann Ealy Redmond, St. Joseph, Missouri.

tickets cost considerably less when compared to purchasing individual tickets for six or seven events per each day of the program. The family season pass made it possible to reduce the cost of attending a program even further. The family pass ranged from $15 to $25 and allowed the purchaser and immediate family members entrance into any circuit feature. The bureaus always liked selling as many season tickets, whether individual or family, as possible because it usually meant that there would be good audiences present for all the program features. Moreover, a large sale of season tickets generated more overall interest in the program and made it easier for the agent to get the sponsoring committee to rebook a program for the following year.

The Movement Toward Standardization and Commercialization   37

By World War I, the Redpath Bureau had purchased several trains for the sole purpose of moving its circuit chautauqua programs from town to town. Redpath Collection, University of Iowa.

The importance of the personal touch, especially when selling tickets, was indicated in the following Redpath release to its ticket agents:

> The foundation of a successful ticket campaign is advertising, propaganda and publicity. But none or all of these three will sell tickets without personal solicitation.... The people who are selling tickets must be thoroughly and everlastingly "sold" on the program for which they are selling the tickets. They must feel that they are selling not simply pieces of cardboard, but means of admission to a wonderful program.

The "Chautauqua Boosters" were an important local component of the personal touch when it came to the selling of chautauqua tickets. Chautauqua boosters were usually local business people, civic leaders, and educators who worked together to encourage townspeople to attend the forthcoming circuit program. Sometimes a sole club took on the entire job of "boostering" the circuit program. Advance workers from the bureau organized the activities of the boosters and provided them with pendants, banners, posters, and, most importantly, rolls of tickets.

Boosters stirred up interest in the forthcoming chautauqua by talking with friends and neighbors about it, assisting with the placement of promotional literature about town and in the planning of various activities during which tickets were sold. In return for their assistance, some boosters received free chautauqua tickets and a few were pictured

North End Club Chautauqua Boosters welcoming a seven-day Redpath Chautauqua program, ca. 1914. Redpath Collection, University of Iowa.

in publicity releases. This tactic also weakened the animosity toward circuit chautauqua felt by some who had once been directly involved in the planning and operation of their permanent chautauqua. The booster idea allowed local citizens to feel that they were participating in the development of their community's chautauqua, but the circuit bureaus did not give up any of their decision-making power over the program or dates.

Other Circuit Chautauqua Jobs

THE SUPERINTENDENT

The day before the actual opening of the program a chautauqua superintendent appeared in town. Sometimes the superintendent was the agent who initially booked the program. The superintendent's job was basically to make sure that the program was delivered as promised and to stir up any last minute excitement that would draw attention to the program. Si Rositzky recalled how the superintendent created enthusiasm for a 1914 circuit program he attended at Craig, Missouri: "On the day prior to the opening, the chautauqua managers announced that there would be a treasure hunt in the big tent for kids the next morning. I was right on time. At the proper moment all the kids were turned loose to find the treasure. Lucky Me! I found tickets to all the presentations for the entire weekend."

As the chautauqua program started to get underway, the superintendent assumed a vast assortment of roles. He or she picked up the performers at the railroad or coach station and delivered them to local boardinghouses or other accommodations. The superintendent also made sure that talent appeared on the program when scheduled. If a tent crew lacked manpower to erect the tent, the superintendent hired local men to assist. In the event that a crew member used language that was offensive to someone in the community, the responsibility of the position included reprimanding that crew member. If ticket sales were slow, the superintendent was responsible for hiring additional people to go door-to-door to sell tickets. At the conclusion of the program, it was often the job of the superintendent, in the capacity of an agent, to secure a contract from the sponsoring committee for the following year. Not all of the superintendents, at least on the Redpath circuit, were men. Redpath management, in fact, found that in "difficult" chautauqua towns, it was frequently their female superintendents who could get the contract signed.

The superintendent had to be ready to handle almost any kind of situation. Hallie Kinney wrote of one such situation that he encountered as a Redpath superintendent during 1918:

> During the war, I had an assignment as Superintendent on the Seven Day program and my route included a town in the Missouri Ozarks that insisted the chautauqua tent should be pitched outside the city limits, so that County authorities would be obliged to furnish aid in keeping the peace if the hillbilly neighbors raised a disturbance. Everything ran smoothly until Sunday evening — Ada Ward was the feature — Miss Ward was from England and was easily annoyed. The seats were all taken and people standing at the edge of the tent were inclined to talk. I was trying to "Hush! Hush!" them as diplomatically as possible when I glanced back toward the entrance gate and saw our Property Man, white as a sheet, surrounded by a mob of young fellows from the hills. I pushed through the crowd to help John — for he was one, against forty or fifty. Luckily for me the gang disbanded after my announcement that there was to be no disturbance. Several of the chautauqua committee told me that the guys who did not have guns carried knives! Later, I learned the invaders had staged a riot; and had called chautauqua — a Methodist Circus.

The talent and features that would appear on future chautauqua programs were also influenced by the superintendent. At the conclusion of each circuit program, the superintendent filled out a report book. In one section of the book, there was a place set aside for the grading of the program talent. A grade was awarded for each of the following categories: platform presence, audience response, and adherence to time limitations. Completed report books were sent directly to the bureau's manager and board of directors. The impressions of talent provided by the superintendent assisted the manager and board in choosing what talent and features to include in future programs.

TENT CREWS

The morning of the day that the local chautauqua was to be officially opened, a tent crew arrived. By the afternoon, they had the huge brown canvas tent set up in a local park or in a field on the edge of town. The raising of the tent was usually watched by the youngsters of the community and on occasion could create great excitement. As a youngster, Merlyn J. Saunders-Tapia saw chautauqua "on the prairie": "My two sisters and I, three small girls with Buster Brown hair cuts, went to watch the boys put up the biggest tent that we had ever seen. As we looked on all of a sudden a tent pole fell down and broke the leg of one of the chautauqua workmen. We had not dreamed of such excitement."

A standard chautauqua tent was 80 feet by 120 feet and had the capacity to seat about 1,000 people. The sides of the tent could be rolled up to encourage cross-ventilation, which was essential, especially to the performers, during hot and humid weather. The temperatures inside a crowded tent could easily rise to above 100 degrees, and on the elevated stage, especially if lighting was in use, a performer might experience temperatures in excess of 110 degrees. Planks or chairs or both were used for seating within the tent. Often the planks were borrowed from a nearby lumberyard and the chairs obtained from local churches and schools. An elevated platform at the far end of the tent served as the "chautauqua platform" or stage. Right behind the platform, often inside the big tent, a smaller tent was set up. The smaller tent served as a dressing room for talent and also doubled as a sleeping room for the tent crew and dark-skinned ethnic performers.

The young men who worked the tent crews were usually college men and used their summer earnings from chautauqua to finance their college education. Reflecting about the "very important role chautauqua

Chautauqua boosters in Mound City, Missouri, getting ready to escort Redpath talent down Main Street to the community's Chautauqua Park, ca. 1915. Redpath Collection, University of Iowa.

played in my life," former Redpath tent boy Ezra Christian Buehler wrote in 1981: "Chautauqua opened the window to help me find the road to my professional life. I became a college Speech Teacher serving 7 different universities for 46 years. It helped me get the first M.A. degree in Speech ever offered by North Western University — 1923."

The tent crew usually consisted of three men. The crew was responsible for the tent and the equipment used on the particular circuit they traveled. As with the other chautauqua personnel, a crew moved successively from town to town. The men who made up the tent crews were held to exacting standards of moral and personal conduct by the bureau. They were to be well-groomed, smiling, and polite, and they were to attend to the job at hand; they were not to smoke, drink, or converse with the young women in town. The bureaus frequently issued bulletins to crew members, reminding them how to behave: "Don't be a grouch! THERE IS TO BE ABSOLUTELY NO ENGAGEMENT WITH THE LADIES. No gossip."

The most important and arduous job of the tent boys was to secure the tent. During the violent summer rain and electric storms common to the Midwest, the tent boys frequently had to reinforce the lead ropes of the tent. In the Northwest, occasionally a very late or early snowstorm required them to brush snow from the top of the tent. Despite precautions concerning the security of the tent, sometimes the decision had to be made by the superintendent to evacuate it during a storm. C. L. Hotchkiss, a former Redpath superintendent, remembered one such occasion:

> In Elk City, Oklahoma, a storm cloud was approaching behind the platform section of the tent. It was during the night program of "The Melting Pot."... I advised the large crowd to leave the tent as quickly as possible.... We had just enough time to tie down the side walls and anchor the lowered peaks before the storm hit. Stakes were jerked from the ground and we could hear the canvas snapping and ripping in the dark. It lasted only a few minutes, but was severe enough to riddle several sections of the tent. Nevertheless, we stretched it again and the final act of "The Melting Pot" was shown the next morning.

The tent crew also had the responsibility of setting up the stage lighting and hanging scenery backdrops as required for drama. At first, lighting effects were accomplished by placing a series of candles or carbide fixtures shielded by hoods along the front edge of the stage. From 1913 until 1917, gasoline lanterns were hung from tent braces and directed at the stage for illumination. After 1917, the lighting of the stage was usually achieved through a series of portable electric spotlights that were controlled from a central panel. Whatever the type of lighting used, anytime the stage was lighted, chautauqua personnel took extra safety precautions. Usually crew members stood on each side of the stage with buckets of sand ready to douse sparks or flames.

THE TALENT

The day that marked the beginning of a town's chautauqua was filled with anticipation for the arrival of the first of the chautauqua talent. When talent did arrive and emerge from a wagon or train or bus, the chautauqua boosters, children, and other citizens welcomed them to their town. The chautauqua boosters then escorted the talent down Main Street in highly decorated parade wagons or automobiles with children trailing behind. While in the town, some entertainers were invited to stay the night with local families. Most performers, however, found lodging in hotels or boardinghouses. Others spent the night camped out beneath the stars or in railroad boxcars or in the small tent that served as a changing room, especially if they had dark-pigmented skin.

Being a chautauqua performer was a demanding job. There were long hauls between engagements, vigorous schedules to maintain and performances to keep polished. Moreover, the continuous circuit schedule did not allow performers any holidays or days off between engagements. Popular entertainers faced anywhere from 6 to 20 weeks of solid booking or up to 140 consecutive daily appearances. Between July 1 and August 31 of 1915, William Jennings Bryan made 33 speeches at different chautauquas while serving as secretary of state under President Woodrow Wilson. Many performers lasted less than a season on the chautauqua circuit because of travel hardships.

Edwin McDonald, interviewed in 1990, recalled how hectic the life of a chautauqua was for him as a performer:

> Right out of the University of Missouri, I joined a musical group in 1928 called the Fads and Fancy which was under contract with the Horner-Redpath Bureau of Kansas City. I served as both a musician and the driver of a Dodge truck that had been converted into kind of a bus. In that year [1928], I visited more than fourteen states and performed in many, many programs. Sometimes we would travel 300 to 400 miles between engagements on highways that were dirt and gravel. The marimba player and I traded off on the driving. When not driving and needing sleep, I would stretch out on the top of the bus among the baggage and instruments. Once the marimba player drove the bus into a railroad car, throwing the leader of the group, a Mrs. Handley, from the bus. She was knocked unconscious. We left her with a local doctor and traveled to the next engagement. If we did not show up for an engagement, it meant a loss of pay.

The sources for circuit chautauqua entertainers were varied. The Redpath Chautauqua Bureau, of course, drew talent from its lyceum listings. The Kaffair African Boys and Tyrolean Alpine Singers were foreign attractions held under contract by the Redpath Lyceum Bureau; they eventually ended up on the Redpath circuit. Both groups had originally been brought to the United States by Mrs. Potter Palmer, exclusively for the 1893 Columbian Exposition held in Chicago. The Redpath Bureau placed them under contract at the close of the Exposition.

In Chicago, a trade journal called *The Lyceumite* was published; it advertised the entertainers and features available for chautauqua or lyceum tours. Carl Sandburg was the advertising manager and assistant editor of the *Lyceumite* during the early 1900s. Sandburg described how the office operated:

> Into this office came scores of travelers, fresh from their platform tours. If they were already advertising I pointed them to space for larger ads. If they were not advertising I told them that among our subscribers were all the bureaus who booked talent and all the local committeemen and Chautauqua managers who picked up for next season's course the lecturers, elocutionists, quartets, solo star singers, violinists, pianists, chalk talkers.

Among the many performers who advertised through this trade publication and ended up on circuit chautauqua, sometimes only briefly, were Albert Beveridge, William Jennings Bryan, Edmund Vance Cooke, Eugene Debs, Robert La Follette, Alton Packard, Katherine Ridgeway, Carl Sandburg, and Lincoln Steffens.

Early twentieth-century film actor–writer John Bunny juggled his work schedule between vaudeville, Broadway theatre, the silent screen, and circuit chautauqua. Bunny's professional work arrangement was typical of that of many "star" performers who appeared on circuit chautauqua. Performers such as Edgar Bergen, Ruth Gordon, Dean Jagger, Everett Kemp, Conrad Nagel, Alice Nielsen, the Ben Greet Players, Opie Read, Carl Sandburg, Martha Scott, and Rhys Williams worked back and forth between chautauqua work in the summer and vaudeville or Broadway or film in the other months of the year.

The Redpath Bureau hired the Ralph Dunbar Maryland Singers, a black jubilee group, through its vaudeville manager, Ralph Dunbar, to perform before circuit audiences. The circuit chautauqua bureaus also sent agents overseas to book foreign performers and features for programs. In election years, politicians were in abundance to speak from the chautauqua platform. Six presidents spoke from the chautauqua platform — Calvin Coolidge, Warren G. Harding, Herbert Hoover, Theodore Roosevelt, William Howard Taft, and Woodrow Wilson, and at least as many vice presidents. Reformers with a cause were welcomed to join circuit chautauqua because controversy attracted audiences to the tent. The more fervent the cause, the better. Although Carrie Nation's antics resulted in her being escorted away from more than one chautauqua tent, she was always sought after for bookings.

Talent was even "discovered" in the various towns the chautauqua visited. In "A Chautauqua Lady in 1921," Roena Gates Clements explains how she was hired by a circuit bureau: "One day as I was walking home from school in May 1921, a friend, Mrs. Allen, came out of her house and met me with the words 'how would you like to tell stories to children on Chautauqua this summer?' Without any questions I said, 'Of course, I would.'" Local clergy were sometimes engaged by the bureaus to deliver a sermon, especially on Sunday programs. Circuit performers, in short, came from a wide variety of backgrounds, professions, and cultures.

"Chautauqua Week" and the Program

"LADIES AND GENTLEMEN, LET ME INTRODUCE..."

Whatever the length of circuit chautauqua programs, five, six, or even up to nine days, the period during which the program was presented was always referred to as Chautauqua Week. During the opening evening of Chautauqua Week, the superintendent welcomed the community to the "best chautauqua program ever," asked a local clergyman to bless the event, and then introduced the main attraction of the evening. The introduction of the feature would begin with a statement like "Ladies and gentlemen, it is with great pleasure that I present to you the Honorable William Jennings Bryan, the next president of the United States." Chautauqua Week for many American communities was the most important week in the year. Recalling her chautauqua experiences, Sue Humphrey wrote: "The town [Havensville, Kansas] never was the same after chautauqua started coming [in about 1910]. The chautauqua brought a new touch of culture which we immediately applied to our lives: new ways of speech, dress, ways of entertainment.... It broadened our lives in many ways."

The yearly interval during which the bureaus toured their programs lasted from the beginning of June until the end of September. These four months generally enabled the crews to transport circuit programs without too many complications arising from adverse weather. The actual length of the program fluctuated, depending on the chautauqua bureau and the territory in which it operated. Before 1917, the Redpath Bureau provided seven- or nine-day programs in the Midwest and frequently a six-day program in the East. The Ellison-White chautauqua generally offered a six-day midwestern program and a four- or five-day western program. Between 1917 and 1919, while America was actively involved in the war in Europe and its aftermath, most of the bureaus shortened the length of their programs to a maximum of five days. During the last half of the 1920s, when circuit chautauqua faced economic hardship, the programs were shortened to as little as a day, but they were more typically two to three days in length.

THE SUNDAY PROGRAM

Late nineteenth- and early twentieth-century Americans generally devoted the Sabbath to worship and fellowship. In fact, the decision to keep the 1893 Chicago Exposition and the 1904 World's Fair open on Sunday was ardently protested by midwestern senators and congressmen. In order to accommodate rural sentiments about the Sabbath, the early circuit chautauquas did not hold programs on Sunday. In *Instructions to Superintendents*, printed about 1910, Keith Vawter related the following advice to circuit managers: "Sunday should be a day of quiet about the grounds. Any necessary work should be done early in the morning and without noise or boisterousness. I should be glad, indeed, if the superintendent and crew should attend services at some church, Sunday morning." Holding up a circuit program for a day in observance of Sunday resulted in extra expenses for the bureaus. Sunday layovers not only meant additional lodging and food costs, but fewer overall bookings for the bureaus.

As the demand for circuit chautauqua expanded after 1912, the pressure for using Sunday as a program day grew. Subsequently, the bureaus gave the sponsoring committees an option of either paying an additional amount to delay the program or having the program that was scheduled on Sunday canceled. Neither of these choices was acceptable to most sponsoring committees. Striving not to alienate the sponsors or lose money from ticket sales, the bureaus modified the Sunday program in such a way as to make it palatable to rural audiences. The program held on Sunday did not begin until early afternoon, allowing people time to attend church and dine with their families. The features that constituted the afternoon Sunday program were chosen by the superintendent on the basis of their moral, inspirational, and spiritual value. A local clergyman was also asked to deliver a sermon at some point during the program. In return, the chautauqua bureau would often make a cash donation to local churches. Once Americans became involved in World War I, however, the practice of providing special Sunday programs was abandoned.

VARIETY

The variety of features, talent, and performances viewed on the circuit chautauqua platform was astounding, even by today's standards. Circuit performer Gay MacLaren noted that the chautauqua programs were made up of

> the greatest aggregation of public performers the world has ever known. There were teachers, preachers, scientists, explorers, travelers, statesmen, and politicians; singers, pianists, violinists, banjoists, xylophonists, harpists, accordionists, and bell ringers; orchestras, bands, glee clubs, concert companies, quartets, sextets, and quintets; elocutionists, readers, monologuists, jugglers, magicians, yodelers, and whistlers.

From the beginning of the movement until 1925, however, the circuit chautauqua program was always built around five types of general features—lectures, music, dramatic arts, funny entertainment, and children's activities.

The individual features and talent that were included on any given program were carefully selected by the bureau's manager and board of directors. The decision about whether to keep or replace a performer on a program was based upon five factors: the superintendent's evaluation in the report book, questionnaires filled out by sponsors, critiques by publicity agents, ticket receipts, and the cost and availability of a performer or feature. As a business, circuit bureaus wanted to attract as many people as possible to the big tent. To do this, programs had to be modified as the marketplace demands changed.

Tracing Changes in America, 1904 to 1930

The following five chapters describe how circuit chautauqua programs were altered to accommodate the changes in the American marketplace between 1904 and 1930. The chapters trace the process by which circuit chautauqua transformed nineteenth-century private, independent, and secular attempts at adult education into a vast commercial system of prepackaged entertainment. Circuit chautauqua was, in a sense, the first twentieth-century mass media organization that dealt with popular culture, eduation and entertainment as a collective package. Because the program was standardized, rural towns and large cities on the same circuit saw the same program. In this manner, circuit chautauqua gradually broke down the barrier between agrarian and urban attitudes, beliefs, and values, thereby fostering a melting pot ideology for the country.

III

Beginnings in Rural America

Under the auspices of the Redpath Lyceum Bureau, the Standard Redpath Chautauqua circuit began in 1904. After a brief interlude, the circuit reappeared in 1907 and was known as the Redpath Chautauqua. By early 1913, at least six other circuit chautauqua bureaus had been started, the majority being managed by established lyceum bureaus. Up until that year, circuit chautauqua was largely a rural midwestern phenomenon. The typical town that sponsored a circuit chautauqua ranged in size from 500 to 1,500 in population. And even though the movement eventually spread into other areas of the country, circuit chautauqua always found its most loyal and supportive audiences in the Midwest. Circuit manager and owner Harry P. Harrison noted that it was in the "lush Middle West where Chautauquas grew greenest."

The states in which circuit chautauqua most frequently operated were Arkansas, Colorado, Illinois, Indiana, Iowa, Kansas, Kentucky, Missouri, Nebraska, New Mexico, North Dakota, Ohio, Oklahoma, Pennsylvania, South Dakota, West Virginia, and Wyoming. The vast majority of chautauqua bureaus in operation by 1913 were headquartered in midwestern cities that were major railroad centers. Centrally located railroad lines were necessary for transporting chautauqua programs in a number of different directions. The Redpath Bureau located its major offices in Cedar Rapids, Iowa; Chicago, Illinois; Columbus, Ohio; Des Moines, Iowa; Lincoln, Nebraska; and Kansas City, Missouri; it also had many smaller offices. The Midland Bureau operated out of Des Moines, Iowa; the Cadmean Chautauqua was managed from Topeka, Kansas; the Lincoln Chautauqua was headquartered in Lincoln, Nebraska; and the Swarthmore Chautauqua Association was located in Swarthmore, Pennsylvania.

Initially, the attraction circuit chautauqua had for those in rural areas was similar to the appeal that the Circle, permanent chautauqua, and lyceum had possessed. Circuit programs fulfilled their desire for popular education, enlightenment, and socializing. Harrison noted that midwesterners were "weary of mud-road isolation, they thirsted for knowledge, for exposition of new ideas not accessible to them in the ordinary course of their reading.... And above all, they were hungry for escape from their own flat horizons into the fascinating world that lay beyond." To illustrate this point, circuit manager C. L. Hotchkiss related the following incident:

> Marge was on her way to the tent in a western Kansas town, one hot, disagreeable windy dusty day. She was joined by a local lady who said she was also going to the Chautauqua. Marge remarked "If it were not my job, I certainly would not be going on a day like this." This reply came back, "If you lived in this part of the country where the Chautauqua is your only chance from one year to the next to see and hear programs like these, you would not miss it for anything."

The Country Versus the City

While operating almost exclusively in the rural Midwest, the circuit bureaus used a promotional theme that dated back to Thomas Jefferson. The theme extolled agrarian values over industrial pursuits and tied the well-being of the country exclusively to agriculture. This vision of America had been readily adaptable to the rhetoric of many of the late nineteenth-century farm movements such as the 1870s Grange Revolt, the Farmers' Alliance in the 1880s, and the Populist Movement of the 1890s. Salutations for agriculture could be respected and even taken seriously in a nineteenth-century America where the "island" community was dependent on local agriculture, markets, and politics. Post–Civil War expansion of the railroad and inventions such as the telegraph, however, drew countless communities into the complexities of an industrial world. By the beginning of the twentieth century, the way of life Jefferson had envisioned for America was antiquated. National hubs of power with corresponding centralized economic and political structures ended any hope of returning to an agrarian way of life.

Circuit chautauqua began at a point in history where the industrial model was beginning to benefit rural areas through the distribution of

Circuit chautauqua began during the horse and buggy days of the early 1900s. Redpath Collection, University of Iowa.

standardized and less expensive products and by creating new markets for farm production. On the surface, it appears ironic that circuit promotion would rely so much on an agrarian view of America that was essentially outdated. The nature of this paradox was explained in Robert Wiebe's *Search for Order*. Accustomed to the ways of small town life and autonomy, many Americans could not readily "master an impersonal world through the customs of a personal society." Being frustrated by not understanding exactly how or why their lives were changing, Americans, especially those in rural areas, struck out at politicians, big business, urbanization, and, in general, anything that was identified as undermining society as they knew it. In a sense, the nineteenth-century accolades honoring agrarianism as a way of life were supplanted early in the twentieth century by eulogies that romanticized agriculture and small-town life.

RURAL CHARACTER

In hundreds of early 1900s circuit chautauqua brochures, rural midwesterners were portrayed as the most intelligent, moral, and virtuous beings on the face of the earth. The "lure" of the big city with its "false ideals" was held out as being the culprit for all major economic, political, and social problems. In "A Personal Note to Our Thousands of Patrons," which appeared in Redpath programs before 1913, Keith Vawter wrote:

> Find a good, live, up-to-date, clean, wholesome and educated city with a correspondingly intelligent farmer patronage, and you have an ideal Chautauqua town.
>
> The greatest industrial problem of this country today comes from the congestion of population in the great cities, and the correspondingly [sic] scarcity of labor on the farm.
>
> Every year thousands of young men and women leave the quiet natural life of the farm and the country town and flock to the great cities, and there generally speaking, land in the lowest stratum of the city's working class, and far too often of the city's criminal class....
>
> Here is the greatest of the many missions of the modern Chautauqua. If it makes life in the country cities more enjoyable, if it furnishes a glimpse of the great outside world, if it not only raises the standard of living, but furnishes a period of relaxation and of vacation, if it makes life in the country brighter and happier, and tends to keep a fraction of those young men and women at home, ... then the Chautauqua is worth all of the support and assistance you can possibly render it.
>
> Every year the great middle west is becoming more important to the life of the nation. In no other like area in the world does so high an average of intelligence prevail. Here reforms find a beginning, and from the agricultural community comes first the demand for improvement in national affairs. The Chautauqua has had its part in bringing about this condition of affairs and in perpetuating them, it has become a necessity. It is an independent promoter of education and morality, and thank God, it is subservient to no political party, and to no force, but law, Christianity and the people.

Chautauqua advertising assured rural audiences that agriculture and their community still controlled their destiny. But the circuit program itself, in conjunction with the reality of what most midwesterners faced, reflected the paradox of the situation. Farmers listened to the circuit speakers condemn the unsoundness of the banking industry, knowing full well that next year's planting money was dependent upon the decisions made by bankers elsewhere. Farm youth were told that their ambitions were better fulfilled at home at a time when literally thousands of young men and women were leaving the farm each year to pursue jobs in the city. Local social conventions might have deemed it improper for a community member to watch a performance of *Lorna Doone* in a Chicago or New York theatre, but it was perfectly acceptable to see it from beneath a chautauqua tent.

But no matter what the reality was for the early twentieth-century midwesterner, circuit chautauqua brochures constantly glorified the virtues of being rural and damned the ways of larger cities. Redpath manager Charles Horner's open letter published in a 1910 Redpath-Vawter brochure echoed this contrast between rural America and the big city:

> The rigors of pioneer life in these states of the middle west have developed a sturdy citizenship and a degree of intelligence that are compelling the attention of the nation.... We are producing some of the greatest men of the greatest minds and grandest purposes....
>
> The Chautauqua claims its part and demands due credit for its share in crystallizing the new thought of the virile west. From a hundred platforms in Nebraska, Kansas, Colorado, Oklahoma and Wyoming this summer eloquent and authoritative speakers will expose the skeletons of civic and social unrighteousness as they exist and thrive in the seats of the wicked.... In no more fertile soil can this seed be planted and nowhere can more intelligent and sympathetic audiences be addressed.
>
> The largest percentage of the independent thinkers of the world today populate the great prairie states of this nation.... They have hewed out a civilization that is rugged, intelligent and honest....
>
> It is the boy of today, the man of tomorrow, in whose hands rests the destiny of the future. It is in his interest that I make a special appeal. The lure of the city with its false ideals of rapid wealth and easy honor should be exploded before he has had time to establish fictitious ideals of life. He must be taught that "The groves were God's first Temples" and that "The country was made for man but man made for the city."...
>
> The Chautauqua undertakes to bring to a community the refinement, the culture, and the entertainment of the city with none of its attendant temptations and vices. It seeks to carry a broad and liberal education....
>
> One of the profoundest social problems of today is the congestion of population in the big cities. The consumers out number the producers and the necessities of life are forced to prices almost

prohibitive. Want ensues, then vice. God encourages ambition but he never intended that the boys and girls from wholesome country homes should go to the cities to seek fame and fortune until they have first lived up to the full capacity of their home opportunities.

And so, good friends of education, I particularly appeal to you to join hands with us in the Chautauqua crusade of 1910.

Pervasiveness of the Chautauqua Lecturer

POLITICAL AND SOCIAL REFORM

Circuit chautauqua programs prior to 1917 were dominated by the platform lecture feature. Until 1913, the two most popular types of lecture on the circuit were the reform speech and the inspirational talk. The primary function of the reform lecture was to attack those institutions, people, issues, and habits that rural America denounced. In terms of political and social issues, there was a group of nationally recognized speakers who regularly "exposed" the corruption going on in "big city" politics and "big business" from the chautauqua platform. The complexity of the issues brought about by American industrialization was condensed in the reform lecture to several simple themes: rural against urban, agriculture against big business and politics, and, in more general terms, "the people" against centralized federal government and the trusts.

The reform lecturers received a great deal of attention and fanfare in the circuit chautauqua promotional materials. "Fighting Bob" La Follette, then governor of Wisconsin, was portrayed in Redpath circuit advertising between 1909 and 1912 as "a record breaker, a giant among men, a power in the Senate of the United States. He has risen to eminence by faithful work, integrity of character and hard fighting against the political machinery and corporate industrial combinations." In La Follette's lecture titled "Representative Government," he told circuit audiences that the main way to combat corruption in government was to push for the establishment of primary elections. During his presentation of "Special Privilege," La Follette outlined how corrupt politicians and "the trusts" take unfair advantage of the farmer and urban poor "who are often from the farm."

Missouri Senator Champ Clark was extolled in early chautauqua brochures in the following manner:

> He is magnificent physically, standing as he does, tall, erect and athletic. He is magnificent mentally, and with his wonderful knowledge of history, of law, and of men, he holds a record for oratory and debate that few have equaled and none surpassed. He is magnificent morally, with a courage of his convictions that is clean-cut and unshaded.... His speech against Tammany has achieved a fame that surpasses that of Daniel Webster.

In many of Clark's chautauqua speeches, he pressed for reform in government and business through the formation of farm blocs and using the "wise vote."

Clark's political counterpart to the west was Governor Edward W. Hoch of Kansas. Hoch was well known throughout the region for his attempts at trying to control the price fixing practices of the Standard Oil Company and the railroads that ran through his state. He was promoted in chautauqua brochures as being largely responsible for putting "the machine out of business" in Kansas. In "A Message from Kansas," Hoch explained to circuit patrons how he accomplished this feat almost "single-handedly."

The "reformers" who appeared on circuit chautauqua programs were usually well-known midwestern politicos. Blind Senator Gore of Oklahoma spoke on the theme of "good government versus the grafter and his graft" before many midwestern circuit audiences. Judge Ben Lindsey of Colorado described how he sentenced "crooked politicians and crooked businessmen." Congressman J. Adam Bede of Minnesota spoke in 1904 at all of the fourteen towns that constituted the first Standard Chautauqua circuit about "political issues of the day." The governor of Missouri, Herbert S. Hadley, already an established voice for the farmer through his attacks on the lumber and harvester trusts operating in the state, joined the Redpath system after retiring from government in 1908.

Governor Joseph Folk, Hadley's predecessor in office, pushed a progressive agenda while he was in office. Among other reforms, Folk managed to put a St. Louis–based racetrack syndicate out of business, established child labor laws, introduced compulsory education, and initiated statewide primary, initiative, and referendum. When Folk's governorship ended, he joined the Redpath Chautauqua to speak about the reforms he had led while governor. He delivered "A Fight for a State" over 100 times before 1913 Redpath audiences. Folk always closed this lecture by stating, "If the government anywhere neglects the people, it's because the people neglect the government."

Senator Joseph L. Bristow of Kansas, who had already appointed Dwight D. Eisenhower to West Point, joined the Redpath Chautauqua in 1912. The title of his lecture was "Necessary Political Reform." Senator and former governor Albert B. Cummins of Iowa was well known throughout his state, as well as in Nebraska and Missouri, for trying to halt barbed wire and railroad price fixing. His presentation of the "Iowa Idea" detailed his "battles against corruption." Cummin's friend and colleague Jonathan P. Dolliver, reelected five times to the Senate by Iowans, also frequently spoke to midwestern circuit audiences about politics and graft.

In addition to these and many other midwestern chautauqua orators who discussed reform, there were several well-publicized "muckrakers" who appeared on circuit chautauqua programs. Ida Tarbell (*History of the Standard Oil Company*, 1904), Lincoln Steffens (*Shame of the Cities*, 1910), and William Allen White (*The Old Order Changeth*, 1910) all spoke many times before circuit audiences. These individuals not only advanced their causes by chautauqua appearances but also promoted books they had written. In reaction to the dominance of the reform rhetoric so characteristic of the early circuit programs, William Allen White once remarked that "the Progressive Party was born from a dozen Chautauqua speeches."

Women's suffrage was also a popular reform topic that was addressed from the chautauqua platform. Jane Addams of Chicago's Hull House had spoken about the suffrage issue on numerous occasions at Lake Chautauqua in New York. Late in 1908, Vawter convinced Addams that there were rural audiences interested in what she had to say about suffrage. Beginning in the following year as a feature on the Redpath program, she became the first woman to advocate women's suffrage before circuit chautauqua audiences. She appealed to the mothers in her audience by explaining what resulted in a male-dominated society: inadequate child labor laws and "sweat shops" that used children in a "disgusting, ill-advised and unhealthy manner." Jeannette Rankin, who in 1914 became the first woman to be elected to the United States Congress, discussed the need for women's suffrage and child labor laws on the circuit. Even the militant Emmeline Pankhurst was brought from England to tour with the Redpath Chautauqua in 1910 and 1911. She explained to rural audiences why Great Britain's Liberal Party should enfranchise women.

PERSONAL HABITS AND REFORM

The need to reform personal "bad habits," especially alcohol consumption, was fiercely addressed from the chautauqua platform. By the time circuit chautauqua had started in 1904, Carrie Nation was well known for her extreme theatrics in speaking out about the "evils" associated with the drinking of alcohol. To counteract Nation's extreme and at times bizarre behavior, chautauqua bureaus had to occasionally soft-pedal the image presented of the outspoken Nation. A chautauqua audience in King City, Missouri, for example, was promised in a 1907 brochure that Nation's "days of freakishness are over, she buried the hatchet and now wields the sword of argument." But before her presentation in King City was over, Nation had to be escorted from the chautauqua grounds for throwing miniature hatchets and temperance literature at members of the audience.

Stories about Nation's behavior at public gatherings were frequently put into print. The reporting of her "freakish" episodes sensationalized the image of the hatchet-wielding Carrie Nation. Large audiences were always expected to turn out to hear and see Carrie Nation. When she appeared at the 1910 Wathena Chautauqua in Kansas, "armed with sixteen hundred little hatchets," the audience flocked about her. Even the ticket of admittance for a Carrie Nation lecture was frequently a card with a hatchet design on the front.

Billy Sunday, the former baseball player and reformed alcoholic who had turned evangelist, began speaking out against alcohol during the early 1900s at the Winona Lake Chautauqua Assembly in northern Indiana. Upon hearing Sunday speak at a Winona Assembly, Keith Vawter persuaded him that he could reach more people if he were to travel with the Redpath Chautauqua. Sunday began touring with the Redpath circuit in 1910 and continued to appear on Redpath program into the 1920s. Several other notable speakers who also probed the "evils" associated with alcohol on the chautauqua circuit were William Jennings Bryan, Governor J. Frank Hanly of Indiana, and John L. Sullivan, the former heavy-weight boxing champion. Sullivan did not condemn alcohol so much from a religious or social perspective as on the grounds that its usage ruined one's health. Hanly received so much publicity for his condemnation of alcohol that in 1920 he was nominated on the Prohibition ticket for president of the United States.

Although Leonora Lake advocated temperance from the circuit platform, she was best known for her presentation of "The Case Against

Beginnings in Rural America 57

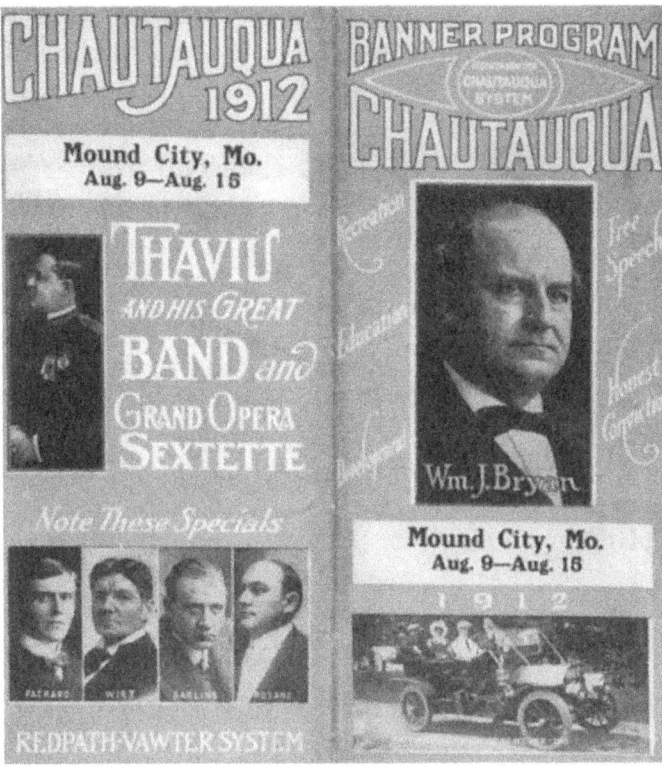

The front cover of a 1912 Redpath-Vawter program brochure featuring William Jennings Bryan and the Band and Orchestra Leader Thaviu. Bryan was always a chautauqua crowd pleaser and frequently drew record crowds to the tent. Author's collection.

Cigarette Smoking." When she reached the climax of the speech, she pounded the podium and proclaimed that "God never intended man to smoke. If he had, he would have put a smokestack on his head!" Maud Ballington Booth, known as the "Mother of the Prison," tried to motivate the women in the chautauqua audiences to become involved in prison reform. "Every man," she promised, "can be redeemed by Divine Power provided he will second that power" with the help of a woman.

INSPIRATION

Second only to the popularity of reform and controversy on the early circuit chautauqua was the inspirational lecture. The basic message of the majority of the inspirational lectures was that agrarians lead an honorable and almost celestial life-style. Midwesterners were told time and time again that they needed to have faith in themselves, in their God, and in the agrarian way of doing things. The inspirational lecture in essence reiterated many of the same promises as found in early chautauqua advertising and social and political platform lectures. By keeping "the faith" in traditional values, the audience was promised a central place in the American destiny.

One of the greatest inspirational speakers of the late nineteenth and early twentieth centuries was Russell Conwell. His most famous speech, "Acres of Diamonds," was given before thousands of lyceum and chautauqua audiences. The speech, built on a series of parables, led to the conclusion that people were better off seeking their fame and fortune where they were rather than seeking these things elsewhere. Conwell could simply change the stories to adapt to the audience to whom he was talking.

The first part of "Acres," at least as presented from the rural chautauqua platform, dealt with the failures encountered by those seeking success in distance places. The second part consisted of success stories of those who had "stayed at home" and applied hard work to their ambitions. "Distant pastures are not fairer," Conwell would tell audiences, "your wealth is next to you. You are looking right over it." "Acres" was the answer to what adults in rural farming areas wanted of their children, many of whom had or were thinking about abandoning the farm or small-town life to find fame and fortune in the city.

Conwell described his most supportive followers in terms of what might be called the "grain belt" of circuit chautauqua. In *Russell H. Conwell and His Work*, he was quoted as saying: "There is a belt of civilization running across the country from a point at Philadelphia on the South and extending North to the international boundary. In that belt I find most responsive audiences." What was amazing about Conwell's "Acres," in terms of circuit chautauqua audiences, was that the same people would come back to hear it year after year. Conwell delivered the speech over five thousand times on chautauqua and lyceum circuits. He used the money he earned from delivering "Acres" to finance the construction of Temple University in Philadelphia, Pennsylvania. Conwell served as the university's first president until his death in 1925.

Without a doubt, the best-known and most popular orator on the chautauqua circuit was William Jennings Bryan. Originally from a small town in rural Illinois, Bryan later moved to Nebraska and represented that state in Congress. He achieved political, religious, and social notoriety. He was a populist leader in the 1890s, secretary of state under

Jubilee singers were always a popular chautauqua attraction. The Booker Washington's Tuskegee Singers were promoted as performing a "program of old fashioned melodies, folk songs and dialect readings." Author's collection.

Woodrow Wilson from 1913 to 1915, a Presbyterian preacher, a Democratic candidate for president of the United States in 1896, 1900, and 1908, and advocate of the cause of fundamentalism in the 1925 Scopes Trial. Politically, Bryan was best known for his "Cross of Gold" speech, first delivered before the 1896 Democratic National Convention in Chicago.

Bryan delivered the "Cross of Gold" to countless chautauqua audiences in the rural Midwest, voicing what was in the hearts of all agrarians: "The great cities rest upon our broad and fertile prairies. Burn down your cities and leave our farms, and your cities will spring up again as if by magic; but destroy our farms and the grass will grow in the streets of every city in the country." So popular was Bryan's "Cross of Gold" speech that in a 1992 interview, Ina Wachtel recalled that when Bryan finished this speech at a chautauqua in Savannah, Missouri, "everyone stood to look at him, even Republicans."

Bryan's single most popular circuit chautauqua lecture was "The Prince of Peace." He promised his listeners that if they accepted and had faith in the teachings of Christ as the "Prince of Peace," their lives would be filled "with purpose, earnestness and happiness." Bryan was always quick to point out to chautauqua audiences that the acceptance of the "Prince of Peace" was easier for them because of their ties with the natural goodness of the land. Rufus Limpp, who drove Bryan to another town to catch a train after his appearance at the King City, Missouri Chautauqua, recalled him saying that "the southeast corner of Nebraska, the northeast corner of Kansas, the southwest corner of Iowa and the northwest corner of Missouri would have made the greatest state in the Union."

Bryan, more than any other single performer, drew the largest audiences to the chautauqua tent prior to World War I. People who today recall seeing and listening to him when they attended chautauqua still characterize him as "truly remarkable" and "full of vitality." In order to combat the heat so characteristic of midwestern summers, Bryan usually fanned himself with a large palm leaf while speaking. When the heat was very extreme, he used the palm fan in conjunction with holding chunks of ice to his head. A chautauqua sponsor remembered that "everyone believed Bryan had to be earnest because of all of that sweat which rolled from his brow." Until 1916, Bryan was among the highest-paid lecturers on the chautauqua circuit. He usually received five hundred dollars per lecture. Between 1908 and 1916, it was not uncommon for Bryan to make anywhere from thirty-five to forty-five appearances at different chautauquas each year.

Another tremendously popular inspirational lecturer was a former Methodist preacher, Dr. A. A. Willetts. His advanced age in conjunction with his active chautauqua schedule was said to be "inspirational in itself." Known as the "Apostle of Sunshine," Willetts appeared on more than a thousand chautauqua programs between 1908 and 1913. In 1913, after filling 127 chautauqua engagements that year, he passed away at the age of eighty-eight. That same year Clara Hinton recorded in her diary the impressions she had of Willetts after hearing him speak at a chautauqua outside of Iowa City, Iowa:

> Dr. A. A. Willetts, the Apostle of Sunshine, was greeted by the chautauqua salute (the waving of white handkerchiefs). He is 88 years old, has been married 65 years, has been on the lecture platform 28 years, and a public speaker 60 years. He said everybody sought

happiness and couldn't find it often. The secret was in making others happy; count your blessings never complain at any time.... He gave some advice to unmarried girls.... Tell me, he said, whether a person is pleasant to live with and I'll tell you whether he's a good man or not. The kind of home was the greatest part of life. He said before people are married the girl is all dressed so nicely ... when he calls; then after they are married she often comes downstairs with her hair down, her stockings down, and her mouth down. The man was apt to lose his care for her when this happened.

Many of the inspirational speakers on the circuit were either educators or clergymen. Edward Amherst Ott, a speech professor at Drake University, toured with the Crawford Peffer, Ellison-White, and Redpath circuits through the years. The theme of his most popular lecture, "Sour Grapes," was that heredity controlled a person's moral character and it was, therefore, critical to know whether two people were compatible prior to marriage, especially if they were planning a family. "People," he frequently concluded, "have to be aware of their past to assure the future." Dr. Frank Wakely Gunsaulus lectured for many years on the Redpath circuit. Gunsaulus was best known for his work in establishing the Armour Institute of Technology in Chicago in 1898. He was the Institute's first president and held the office for several decades.

The central message of Gunsaulus' chautauqua speech, "Gates of the Soul," was that the difficulties one experienced in life taught integrity. Or, as Gunsaulus said, "the harder you're thrown, the higher you bounce." He usually ended his presentation with some lines from poet Edmund Vance Cooke, who at that time was also appearing on chautauqua: "It isn't the fact that you're licked that counts, / But how did you fight, and why?" Other inspirational speakers on the early circuit included Samuel Parkes Cadman of the Central Congregational Church in Brooklyn; Newell Dwight Hillis of the Plymouth Church; Methodist bishop William A. Quayle; George Bradford, the chancellor of Oklahoma Methodist University (who was popular largely because he looked like Bryan); "Take the Sunny Side" Lou Beauchamp; and "Sunshine Dietrick."

Musical Features

MARCHING AND CLASSICAL BAND MUSIC

The circuit chautauqua program always featured a variety of musical styles and performances, but classical numbers and Sousa-type marches tended to dominate the musical numbers offered during circuit chautauqua's first decade. According to a 1909 Redpath brochure, the selections of the popular Royal English Hand Bell Orchestra, which intermittently wandered back and forth between the Redpath chautauqua circuit and New York vaudeville and lyceum, included "Handle [sic], Hayden [sic], Mozart, Mendelssohn, Wagner, Weber, Meyerbee [sic], Wallace."

Bohumir Kryl's Orchestra and Band performed both marches and classical music before hundreds of circuit audiences. A 1912 brochure described the Kryl company in the following way:

HEAVY TO SWEET AND GENTLE

The silvery cornets, the resonant trombone, the blasting horns, the thundering kettle drums, the penetrating chimes and the resounding anvil, on down through the instrumentation to the melodious harp, contribute of their marvels to a range of beauty, from tone blasts that wake the echoes, to the coo of the turtle dove. A Kryl program searches all through the human heart.

Kryl had been recruited by John Philip Sousa to play in the John Philip Sousa Marching Band. Sousa's band appeared on several early Redpath circuit chautauqua programs, including a day-long program in 1910 at Mound City, Missouri. The bureau, however, could never get Sousa to commit his band for an entire season. Kryl, who had learned Sousa's marching band techniques, left Sousa in 1911, joined the Redpath Chautauqua, and stayed with it until 1926. One of Kryl's most popular ending numbers was the "Anvil Chorus." As the band played the piece, four timpanists each banged on an anvil that had an electric device attached to it that caused sparks to fly out. In a 1992 interview, Ina Wachtel recalled the theatrics of Kryl's performance of the "Anvil Chorus": "Kryl's Band would wear bright red shirts and have on leather aprons. Kryl's band would always end with the Anvil Chorus in evening performances. The lights would be turned down in the tent so that we could see the sparks fly from the hammering on the anvils."

Another chautauqua band leader who was associated with Sousa was Arthur Pryor of St. Joseph, Missouri. Pryor worked as Sousa's band assistant before forming the Arthur Pryor Chautauqua Band in the early 1900s. Pryor's band performed before permanent chautauqua assemblies and also toured with various chautauqua circuit companies. Pryor was always so proud of his hometown that no matter where he might

Bohumir Kryl and His Great Band provided chautauqua patrons music that went from "heavy to sweet and gentle." His band also cut records for Victor Records. Author's collection.

be while on tour he always signed the hotel register "Arthur B. Pryor, St. Joseph, Missouri." Pryor was one of the first band leaders on the chautauqua circuit to introduce audiences to ragtime music, including his own "Razzazza Mazzazza" and "The March of the White Rats."

Ina Wachtel also recalled seeing Thaviu's Great Orchestra and Grand Band composed of thirty artists perform at various chautauquas sponsored in Savannah, Missouri. "The Thaviu Band," she said, "was not as exciting as Kryl's, but it did play wonderful rousing marches." She also recalled hearing the music of Sam Schildkret's Hungarian Orchestra. Schildkret's company was well known for having played at Alice Roosevelt's wedding. A 1910 Redpath brochure characterized Schildkret's Orchestra as performing music that would appeal to a variety of tastes: "classics for the 'way ups' in music, and the popular jingles for the masses."

Some orchestras and bands comprised entirely of women musicians appeared on the program. The Kirksmith Orchestra, made up of six sisters, presented "masterful music rendered without the aid of a man." Clara Hinton recalled that one time when she saw the Kirksmith

Orchestra: "Their baggage had not arrived ... and they had on the worst they had. They seemed so ashamed of their attire that two of the best lookin [sic], with their hair fixed puff-iest laughed so they could hardly play." Other all female companies included the Fox Sisters Orchestra, promoted as the "Winsome girls with a wish to please," and the Pilgrim Girls Orchestra, described as a "bright, snappy and interesting" sextet. When the country later entered World War I, the Pilgrim Girls changed the name of their group to the Liberty Maids.

JUBILEE SINGERS

Jubilee singers and "plantation singers" or "jubes," as they were commonly referred to on the circuit, were always, from the very beginning of circuit chautauqua until the end, a popular attraction. Black jubilee singers had been a favorite feature on late nineteenth-century vaudeville and lyceum circuits, as well as on community-based chautauqua programs. In 1904, the Standard (Redpath) Chautauqua promoted the Sterling Jubilee Singers as a "star attraction" on its program. This jubilee company was described as performing "traditional southern plantation songs." In addition to singing, these entertainers also doubled as actors in the 1904 Redpath production of *Uncle Tom's Cabin*.

After World War I ended in 1919, it became very acceptable to have Caucasian actors and actresses made up in grease paint perform in the role of slaves in the then still fashionable circuit feature of *Uncle Tom's Cabin*. In fact, the practice of using talent in multiple types of programming became commonly practiced by the circuit bureaus as the movement progressed. By allowing talent to crossover into other sorts of features, the circuit bureaus saved money. Fewer entertainers had to be transported, fed, or lodged.

Another jubilee group that toured with the Redpath and several other chautauquas into the 1920s, was the Fisk Jubilee Singers. The members of the Fisk company had been educated and trained at Fisk University in Nashville, Tennessee. The group first became associated with chautauqua in 1880, the year Reverend John Heyl Vincent brought them to the New York Chautauqua Institute to partake in a political rally in support of the election of James A. Garfield to the presidency. By 1912, the Fisk company had become an established "star" attraction on the Redpath circuit. The noted black actor Richard B. Harrison, who played "de Lawd" in Marc Connelly's 1929 and 1930 Pulitzer

Prize-winning production of *Green Pastures*, began as a Fisk Jubilee singer on the Redpath Chautauqua. He was also featured in several Redpath programs as being a "Shakespearian reader of the serious kind."

"BIBBITY BOB"

Prior to 1913, there were but a few musical soloists featured on circuit chautauqua programs. Nonetheless, one of the earliest, and always one of the most popular vocalists on the circuit, was Canadian baritone Ruthven McDonald. He worked for the Redpath Chautauqua Bureau every chautauqua season from 1908 until 1926. McDonald's wife played the piano as an accompaniment to his "warm baritone voice of splendid quality." McDonald frequently slipped into the role of a storyteller while performing before chautauqua audiences. One request that audiences always seemed to make of McDonald was for him to "sing and tell Bibbity Bob."

Clara Hinton recorded how, in 1913, McDonald was asked by an Iowa audience to repeat his performance of "Bibbity Bob," in the same manner as he had done it "when he was here two years ago." His story of "Bibbity Bob," as chronicled by Hinton, went as follows:

> Two young people wanted to marry. But the girl's father would not consent. They said they must elope, and hired a certain man to keep the father employed while they were being married. Finally he had an idea. Seeing the old Dutch clock on the wall he said [to the father] "I'll bet you can't swing your arm back and forth without missing a beat as often as the pendulum does, for fifteen minutes. Brown [the father] was overjoyed at the thought of a bet and said that was a good one. So he began swinging his arm back and forth and singing "Bibbity Bob, Bibbity Bob, here she goes, there she goes, this is the way to do it." Mrs. Brown came in before long, hearing the noise and tha't [*sic*] he had gone crazy. She sent for the doctor next door and soon arriving he told what was the matter with Brown. "Why, he thinks he is the clock and that he has to swing his arm as often as the clock does." He kept on, however, growing entirely exhausted by the end of the fifteen minutes. But he won the bet and all right. In the meanwhile the couple had been married and came home for forgiveness. The father saw the joke was on him then. So he forgave them freely. But he says now that every

time he looks at that clock it makes him think of the time when he wore himself out, letting them get married while he went "Bibbity Bob, Bibbity Bob etc."

Dramatic Arts

The dramatic artists who were associated with circuit chautauqua before 1914 habitually complained of being hindered by not being able to perform a complete play before rural audiences. Gay McLaren, in reference to the early period of circuit history, wrote that "the only way the Chautauqua patrons could hear the plays of Shakespeare or other dramatic literature was in a 'reading.'" Basically, drama was edited to the point where it could be read during 40 or 50 minutes on the circuit program.

SERIOUS READERS

The readers who performed serious literature from the early chautauqua platform were frequently educators or professional Thespians who had been associated with lyceum. As lyceum professionals, many of these individuals had taught or received instruction in literature, reading aloud, and movement. Leland T. Powers, who founded the Leland Powers School of Expression in Boston in 1904, began his career as a reader in the 1890s working for the Redpath Lyceum Bureau. Once the bureau had entered into the circuit chautauqua business, Powers was hired not only as a reader but as a coach to assist fellow readers. In addition, Powers also assisted in shortening scripts and editing out anything that might be offensive to rural audiences.

Carl Sandburg's main chautauqua performance was called "An American Vagabond," which he thought "sounded more attractive than either 'The Good Gray Poet' or just plain 'Walt Whitman and What I know of Him.'" He had first given this presentation at the 1907 International Lyceum and Chautauqua Association convention held in Joliet, Illinois. Although he was hoping to be noticed by the bureau managers attending this meeting, Sandburg recalled what happened in the aftermath of his "Vagabond" lecture: "Not one of [the managers] came afterward to say, 'We must have you on our list.' There was a lone booking agent who handed me his card and said he might start of [sic] bureau of his own and I should look him up in November." Once on the chautauqua circuit, Sandburg found that "the best part of my lecture — I could see it reaching the audience — was not my reciting what I had written but the well-memorized line Whitman wrote in 'Song of Myself' and 'Song of the Open Road.'" Sandburg gradually faded from the chautauqua platform by 1916, only to reappear on it during the 1920s.

Katherine Ridgeway was a contemporary of both Powers and Sandburg; by World War I, she had achieved the status of chautauqua's "Queen of the Platform." Ridgeway began her association with the Redpath Bureau before 1900, first as a reader at lyceum meetings and as a concert company director, and later, after 1909, strictly as a reader on the chautauqua and lyceum circuits. Other notable readers who appeared before circuit chautauqua audiences during the formative years include Wallace Amsbary, Montaville Flowers, Philadelphia Rice, Charles Rose Taggart, Frederick Wade, and Maude Willis. The selections from which they read ranged from *David Garrick*, the *Christmas Carol*, *Ben Hur*, and the *Bible* to *Waitin' fer the Cork to Bob* and *Cornstalk Fiddle*.

Also featured on the circuit as dramatic artists were authors and poets who read from their own works. Fred Emerson Brooks, Edmund Vance Cooke, and Lew Sarett read from their poetry before early circuit audiences. All three poets had also appeared on various late nineteenth-century lyceum programs. Forecasting the change that was yet to come at the close of World War I, rural audiences listened to Cooke read his *Mother's Gone A-Marching*:

She never dreamed of politics, nor cared how they were made,
But ... now well, Mother's marching in the Suffragette parade...
But now she lugs a yellow sign which shrieks "I want a Vote!"
Implying that she'll get it, or else get someone's goat.

Writer-humorist Opie Read appeared before many chautauqua audiences as "Old Lim Jucklin," the main character of his best-selling 1895 novel *The Jucklins*. When standing in front of his public, "Old Lim" described his thoughts about politics and society and spoke of his visits to the big city. Read was a sort of rural Plato who set up the dialogue so that Lim always got the best of anyone to whom he spoke. When discussing the relationship between truth and political success, Lim observed:

Success may after a while enable the candidate to tell the truth, but it seems that when a man breaks into politics he breaks in as a

A banner, featuring the face of James Redpath, was hung over a street in Chicago to welcome the Redpath Chautauqua, ca. 1915. Redpath Collection, University of Iowa.

liar.... If your son-in-law is hesitating between politics and the penitentiary, remember that if he goes to the penitentiary you won't have to take care of him.... A politician's smile may be bright, and so is a sunbeam when it falls on a puddle where the hogs have been wallerin'.

At the close of his performance, Read frequently reminded his audiences that attending chautauqua was important to their "moral sense of well-being," especially if they had "been around politicians, flashy businessmen" or in the "fancy city lights." Read also took material from his other 1902 novel *Starbucks* in creating his monologues for chautauqua. In 1921, a Hollywood movie was made out of *Starbucks*, with Read playing the lead character of Jasper.

A friend and colleague of Read's, author-reader-humorist Strickland W. Gillilan, also appeared on circuit chautauqua programs into the late 1920s. Read and Gillilan had known each other from vaudeville and both began careers with the Redpath Chautauqua bureau around 1910. Year after year Gillilan was promoted by the bureau as "guaranteed to evoke laughter." His two most popular circuit presentations were "Tickles and Trickles" and "Off ag'in, on ag'in, gone ag'in, Finnigan."

Another author-reader-humorist who regularly appeared on early circuit chautauqua programs was Bill (Edgar Wilson) Nye. By the early 1880s, Nye had stopped practicing law and was devoting his time to writing and lecturing. His popular books contained a series of short stories and included, among others, *Bill Nye and the Boomerang, Forty Liars and Other Lies, Goose-Neck Smith, How Came Your Eye Out, Your Nose Not Skin,* and *Baled Hay* (prefaced with: "a drier book than Walt Whitman's 'Leaves o'Grass'"). Prior to 1900, Nye was a well-known humorist on vaudeville and lyceum circuits, occasionally appearing with the popular midwestern poet James Whitcomb Riley.

Before chautauqua audiences, Nye told stories mainly based on his own literary imagination and experience. When asked one time why he avoided writing novels, he replied, using the words from the introduction to "A Novel Novelette" contained in *Baled Hay*: "I never wrote a novel, because I always thought it required more of a mashed raspberry imagination than I could muster, but I was the business manager, once, for a year and a half, of a little two-bit novelette that has never been published."

John Bunny was already well known to eastern vaudeville, Broadway, and silent film audiences before joining the circuit chautauqua. During the early 1900s, Bunny appeared on several vaudeville and lyceum productions as a member of an act called the "Love Waltz." In 1905, he appeared in the Broadway production of *Easy Dawson* with Flora Zabelle and Raymond Hitchcock. During 1908, Bunny starred with Hattie Williams in the Broadway play *Fluffy Ruffles* and with Flora Finch in a silent film called *Fibber McGee and Molly*. Also in 1908, Bunny was placed under contract with the Affiliated Circuit Chautauqua to appear on its circuit as humorist-reader. The materials Bunny performed were usually taken from a vaudeville or film sketch he had written or in which he had recently worked.

Bunny wrote and appeared in a 1913 Vitagraph silent movie entitled *The John Bunny Comedy* and subsequently was referred to as a film star in New York and Chicago theaters. In the same year that Bunny achieved his fame in film, the Redpath Chautauqua wooed him away from the Affiliated Bureau. By 1913, the Redpath Chautauqua was trying to expand its operations into eastern and midwestern urban centers. Redpath management believed that Bunny's name on the Redpath program would entice urban audiences to attend their chautauqua. Bunny continued working for the Redpath Bureau that following year, but in 1915, the vaudeville performer, Broadway actor, film star, and circuit chautauqua humorist died.

There were numerous other dramatic-humorists, many of whom read from their own materials, who appeared on the early circuit programs. Several of the monologues that Ralph Bingham presented before circuit audiences—*Brother Jones' Sermon, Bill Johnson and His One Tune, Mrs. Rastus Johnson's Joy Ride*—were recorded by the Victor Company. Jessie Pugh appeared as Elmer Warts, the "Indiana hawg caller," based on his monologue titled "Homecoming of Elmer Warts, Champion Indiana Hog Caller." Estelle Clark, well known to lyceum and permanent chautauqua audiences, appeared on the first 1904 circuit program and many thereafter. She took her cuttings from a variety of sources, including James Whitcomb Riley's *Out to Old Aunt Mary's*, Edward Eggleston's *The Hoosier Schoolmaster*, and her most popular piece, *Mrs. Wiggs of the Cabbage Patch* by Alice Hegan Rice. In fact, *Mrs. Wiggs* was performed by Estelle Clark before lyceum, permanent, and circuit chautauqua audiences before it opened as a play on Broadway in the fall of 1904.

FROM READINGS TO DRAMATIC PLAYS

The evolution from "readings" and "impersonations" to full-length Broadway play productions on the chautauqua circuit was a slow and difficult progress. Theatre to early circuit audiences, stated Keith Vawter, "meant painted women and dissolute men.... It meant cheap vaudeville and the cancan and chlorine hussies who not only displayed ankles but brazen knees to the public. It meant Flesh and the Devil." If a "play" was presented from the circuit chautauqua stage before 1913, it was strategically promoted in the guise of being a "reading of literary and social merit." One play that met the literary and social criteria of the circuits was Harriet Beecher Stowe's *Uncle Tom's Cabin*. In fact, the play had been included as a "reading feature" on the 1904 Standard Chautauqua program.

Prior to the appearance of *Uncle Tom's Cabin* on the Standard Chautauqua Circuit, the book had won fame not only as a literary piece but also as popular entertainment. By 1900 the work was already a fashionable nickelodeon arcade feature and vaudeville act and had appeared time and time again on lyceum and permanent chautauqua programs as a "reading." In 1903, *Uncle Tom's Cabin* was made into a silent film under the guidance of Thomas Edison. The popular urban appeal of the play was never mentioned in early circuit advertising. The "reading" of *Uncle Tom's Cabin* was promoted by the circuit bureaus as providing "moral lessons to be learned" about cruelty in times of social strife.

R. D. Blackmore's classical play *Lorna Doone* was presented as a "reading" by Albert Armstrong to 1904, 1907, 1908, and 1909 Redpath audiences. The play, described as an "illustrated literary classic" in Redpath advertising, was accompanied by glass slides illuminated by a magic lantern projector. The plot of *Lorna Doone* centered on seventeenth-century England, when, as a 1909 brochure observed: "the division of family estates and the injustice of the courts drove men to desperation, even until they became outlaws, and lived according to the motto: 'The world hath preyed upon me like a wolf. God help me now to prey on the world.'"

The play dealt with many of the same sources of frustration being felt by late nineteenth- and early twentieth-century rural Americans: power centralized in the hands of the few, corruption in government, unworkable economic policies, and markets outside of the control of "the people." *Lorna Doone* had a plot with which rural Americans could identify and, not surprisingly, was one of the readings most frequently requested in the early days of the circuits. Armstrong also presented *The Sky Pilot* and *The Little Minister*, two other "magic lantern slide readings," before chautauqua audiences.

TRAVELOGUES

Another circuit chautauqua feature that incorporated the art of dramatic reading and magic glass slides (or occasionally "real moving" pictures) was the travelogue lecture. Many travelogue lecturers read excerpts from the literature native to the country or place of which they spoke. The reading was used in such a way as to create a mood or to make a point about the scene depicted on the screen. The visual images of foreign places projected through a magic lantern or vitascope device were exciting and unusual to rural America. When circuit chautauqua began in 1904, arcade nickelodeons, film shorts, and tinted glass slides were still a novelty outside of the major metropolitan centers. It would be more than a decade before there was a movie theater in almost every town.

Although vastly crude by today's standards, the visual technology upon which the travelogue lecture hinged provided those living in the rural Midwest an opportunity to see that there was a world beyond Main Street, the corn and wheat fields, and the grain elevators. The quality and diversity of the visuals used by the travelogue lecture was so important that much of the promotion focused on it. Early Redpath advertising promoted Charles Payne's presentation of the "historic city of Rome" on the basis of his use of "meticulously hand colored slides." Dr. Yeuell gave a series of lectures on European sites and art works on the chautauqua circuit between 1908 and 1914. He was advertised as having a "new travelogue and a new slide" for each new season. One of the earliest uses of moving pictures on the chautauqua circuit was in Howard W. DuBois' presentation of the "American Wonder Series," a story of his travels in the "Wild West."

Because circuit audiences liked controversy, the Redpath bureau did not overlook the possibility of using the travelogue to "debate the issues." One of the most controversial travelogues presented on the chautauqua circuit began in 1910, when the Redpath bureau featured "Dr. Frederick Cook's Discovery of the North Pole." Cook's lecture traced his route to the North Pole and his discovery of it on April 21, 1908, which was almost a year before Commodore Robert E. Peary had claimed discovery. Peary countered Cook's version by periodically threatening to sue him. He also wrote a series of articles that appeared in popular and scientific publications and told his side of the story. Peary even went as far as to present a lecture called "The Real Discovery of the North Pole" on the 1911 and 1912 Redpath circuit that refuted Cook's claim.

Children's Activities, Magicians, and Illusionists

As had been the case with late nineteenth-century lyceum and permanent chautauqua, the focus of the early circuit chautauqua program was on adult education and inspiration with a little wit and entertainment thrown in for good measure. To encourage as many adults as possible to attend circuit chautauqua, the program included various children's activities that occupied them while adults attended programs. Without the worry of having to find someone to watch youngsters, all

The Chautauqua Girl telling boys and girls about the fun to be had at chautauqua. Redpath Collection, University of Iowa.

of the adults in the community were afforded the opportunity to attend the chautauqua.

THE CHAUTAUQUA GIRL

The job of coordinating the children's activities was the basic responsibility of the "Chautauqua Girl." Children's activities, as listed in a 1910 program brochure, included: "circle games, races, tag games, ball games, active games, rainy day games, tournaments, games for little tots." Storytelling was also an important part of the chautauqua girl's assignment. A former chautauqua girl, Roena Clements, described this part of her job as follows: "Daily I told stories in the quietest spot in the tent. So many children came.... But they were so good and listened intently as I told them about a Mexican boy and his dog and 'Black Beauty,' etc.... And how I worked with those children. And against terrible odds. No one wanted to be in the choir, every child wanted to be an Indian!"

Although genuine Native American performers were basically absent from all phases of the early circuit programs, "playing Indian"

In the morning, the children's program was presented to eargerly awaiting boys and girls, some with shoes and others without. Redpath Collection, University of Iowa.

was an important part of entertainment for children during Chautauqua Week. The way this activity was conducted is detailed in a 1910 Redpath-Vawter brochure:

> Some boy will have a drum to use as a tom-tom in the war dances. It would be nice if some would have bows and arrows. You can whittle out tomahawks. The girls may bring dolls for papooses.... Oh, yes, about your clothes. Well, mamma can easily fix that matter by sewing some bright red or yellow fringe along the boy's trousers and the girl's skirts. A few feathers in the hair will help to make you look savage.

The chautauqua bureaus never lost an opportunity of making money on any venture pertaining to their circuit. The same 1910 Redpath-Vawter brochure also pointed out to the parents whose children planned to participate in "playing Indian" that "before the Chautauqua opens you may buy at the stores regular Indian play suits, good strong ones, for $1 each. This is the lowest cost price and in the big cities they sell for $2.00." The bureau acted as the supplier of the play suits to the local merchants and in return received a percentage of the sales.

MAGICIANS AND ILLUSIONISTS

Some purely entertainment features such as magic and illusion acts were included in the early children's program. Although strictly entertainment features were generally well received, the circuit bureaus, at least at first, downplayed their appearance on a program. Before 1913, for example, it was not unusual for the Redpath Bureau to feature only one appearance by a magician or cartoonist on a program. Several bureaus did not, in fact, feature anything that might be considered purely entertainment until after 1912. As had been the case with small-town lyceum and permanent chautauqua, the early circuit bureaus wanted to keep the focus of their programs on education, inspiration, and culture. Rural people might enjoy feats of magic and illusion, but they would not sponsor a program built upon these or any other entertainment feature.

One of the few "entertainers" enlisted for the 1904 Vawter-Ellison Standard Chautauqua was the magician Edwin Brush. In fact, Brush canceled a vaudeville engagement in Chicago to join the Standard Chautauqua circuit. He was featured on the 1904 program as "Brush: The Great Magician." When the Vawter-Ellison chautauqua traveled for a second time, in 1907, under the Redpath name, Brush was again included on the program and advertised as posing a challenge to audiences: "Come match your wits against his. See if his hand is quicker than your eye. Fun for young and old." By 1912, when rural audiences were more accepting of entertainment, Brush was so much in demand on the chautauqua circuit that he wrote the following letter, dated October 21, 1912, to Redpath booking agent Harry P. Harrison: "I am sorry but I am sold out for next summer's Chautauquas, the time not sold starts with next Sept."

Alton Packard was another "entertainer" who became part of the first 1904 Vawter-Ellison Standard Chautauqua program. Packard began his professional career as a "cartoon-humorist" in 1895, when he was first placed under contract by the Redpath Lyceum Bureau. Packard continued with the Redpath Bureau for many years, booking chautauqua in the summer and lyceum in the winter. The slogan that was used to promote Packard year after year was "Rare Fun Well Done." In order to live up to this slogan, Packard while drawing caricatures, promised audiences "a new face for every minute and two good laughs to the face."

Packard sketched various characters before circuit audiences, using an 8-foot square easel. Each of the sketches he provided was also accompanied by a story. Clara Hinton recalled seeing Packard perform:

> It was "rare fun well done" all right.... Whenever he came upon a funny picture in human life he would sketch it. One day he saw a funny Old Dutchman in a depot & proceeded to draw his picture. Just then a lady from over his shoulder remarked that the picture was fine. He must be an artist. "Well; that is my business & whenever I see an unusually interesting scene I take it down to use in my next entertainment. I thought that was quite a funny old man" I said. "O. I hadn't exactly thought of that. I suppose I get accustomed to it" she said. "O. so you know him, I beg a thousand pardons, I did not know I was talking that way about a friend of yours" I hastily answered. "O he's no friend of mine. He's my husband" she returned.

As the circuit chautauqua movement developed, the great popular appeal of both Packard and Brush was indicated by the fact that they were always booked far in advance and were requested back in the same town season after season.

Circuit Chautauqua in Rural America

Before 1913, circuit chautauqua was predominantly a rural midwestern phenomenon. It started during a period of American history when the essential principles of the traditional nineteenth-century American community—local autonomy and an agricultural economy—were being eroded away by an industrial age characterized by centralized national politics and economics, as well as urbanization. The earliest circuit chautauqua advertising followed the lead of post-1870s farm movements such as the Grange, the Farmers' Alliance, Populist party, and independent chautauqua in denouncing big business, big politics, and big cities. The word *big* associated with industrialism was synonymous with "corrupt" and "false." Early chautauqua programs and lecturers called upon agrarians to provide the leadership necessary to reform centers of "evil." At the same time, however, the reality was that small towns were becoming increasingly dependent upon the economic and political power centers that they cursed.

The early programs provide a perspective as to what was considered adult education in rural America. The lecturer dominated the early circuit programs, especially those of a social, political, and inspirational

The attraction of the early circuit programs quickly filled the tents to capacity. Redpath Collection, University of Iowa.

nature. The speeches, taken as a whole, covered a wide variety of issues: politics, economics, women's suffrage, temperance, smoking, self-improvement, religion, and faith. The bands and orchestras on chautauqua generally favored classical numbers and marches. "Readings" rather than drama were presented from the circuit platform because drama was associated with painted women, cheap vaudeville, and immorality.

The travelogue lecture was accompanied by readings, stories, and the glass slides of the magic lantern. The activities planned for children were advertised to be constructive and educational. The features that constituted the program were rarely promoted as providing entertainment, with the exception of the masters of magic and illusion. Despite the emphasis placed on traditional views of agrarianism, adult education, and inspiration, the circuit chautauqua movement did introduce rural America to ideas, concepts, and some types of entertainment common to large urban centers. The early circuit programs, almost from the beginning, were breaking down the demarcations between rural and urban America.

IV

Coming of Age: The Movement Into the National Marketplace Before World War I

By the end of 1912, the momentum of the circuit chautauqua movement was becoming self-evident. At the close of that chautauqua season, the number of rural midwestern towns requesting programs for the following year had almost doubled. But more consequential to the financial success of the movement were the demands being made for chautauqua in new marketplaces outside of the rural Midwest. Requests for circuit programs came from the rapidly growing midwestern cities of Chicago and Kansas City, established urban areas like New York City and Washington, D.C., and newly created western towns in states as far away as Nevada, Oregon, and California. The population of a typical chautauqua town jumped from a range of 500 to 1,500 in 1912 to a range of 1,500 to 35,000 by 1915. Circuit chautauqua after 1912 was no longer just a rural midwestern phenomenon. The increase in the overall demand for circuit chautauqua, the expansion of its operating territory, and the movement's ability to attract both a rural and urban following were attributable to several factors.

Factors of Expansion

First, circuit chautauqua had proven by 1913 its ability to deliver at an affordable price a standardized package of education and entertainment that was of predictably good quality. Second, the traditional late nineteenth-century practice of having each individual community book the features for its local chautauqua was not and could not be cost-effective when compared to what circuit chautauqua had to offer.

Once the circuit movement began to catch hold, more and more communities turned to a circuit chautauqua bureau to provide their programs and coordinate promotion and advertising. Even in those towns in which the operation of chautauqua was kept in the hands of a local group, the practice was often illusory. What frequently occurred was that the local chautauqua committee turned to one of the circuit bureaus to supply the program and promoted it as its own.

Another factor that encouraged the phenomenal growth of the circuit chautauqua movement after 1912 was its commercial value. Once the pioneers in the field of circuit chautauqua, especially the Redpath and Midland bureaus, began to make substantial profits, additional circuit chautauqua bureaus began operation. The increase in the number of circuits resulted in greater competition in contracting program engagements. As the competition increased among the circuit companies, new territories and marketplaces were sought out in which to sell their programs.

Expansion of circuit routes was accomplished through a variety of business arrangements, liaisons, and moves. Roy J. Ellison left the Vawter-Redpath bureau in 1912 and joined Clarence H. White in establishing the Ellison-White Chautauqua Bureau, headquartered in Portland, Oregon. The number of western communities the Ellison-White bureau booked each year increased until 1920, at which time its all-time high of more than one thousand engagements was reached. In 1916, the Ellison-White Chautauqua had opened an office in Calgary to facilitate bookings in western Canada. On the other side of the country, Vawter, acting on a recommendation from Crawford A. Peffer, manager of the New York Redpath Lyceum Bureau, established the Redpath Chautauquas of New York and New England in 1912. Its agents booked several hundred towns for the 1913 New York and New England Redpath circuits in the states of Maine, New Hampshire, New York, and Vermont. By 1915, this eastern branch of the Redpath Bureau was traveling to towns along the Atlantic coast as far down as South Carolina.

In 1914, W. L. Radcliffe organized the Radcliffe Chautauqua System of Washington, D.C., which had engagements in seventy-seven towns that same year. Also in 1914, the Central Community Chautauqua System in Indiana, the Redpath Chautauqua of Columbus, Ohio, and the Coit-Alber Chautauqua of Cleveland, Ohio, were all organized. The Cadmean System of Topeka, Kansas, was founded in 1913 and was unique in that it provided chautauqua programs in the winter. The southern part of the country was covered by the Lincoln Chautauqua

Bureau that operated out of Lincoln, Nebraska, and Chicago. These are but a few examples of the chautauqua bureaus that started operation during the 1910s. At least another 30 circuits emerged or originated as spin-offs from other bureaus during this period. It is safe to say that circuit chautauqua had caught hold of the national marketplace before World War I.

RAILROAD SPUR LINES

The phenomenal development of circuit chautauqua would not have been possible without the railroad. Although the country did not experience the same type of transcontinental rail expansion after 1900 as it had in the late 1800s, what did evolve were more and more railroad spur lines. These spurs linked many rural communities to the "main line." The smaller spur lines in conjunction with the major railroad lines made it much easier to transport chautauqua features and equipment from one town to another and, in some instances, from one part of the country to another. By 1916, most of the circuit bureaus had negotiated reduced railroad fares for transporting personnel and equipment.

In some instances, the larger bureaus had their own railroad cars that could be attached to a train going in the direction of the next program. Several of the largest bureaus even owned a railroad train, complete with an engine, cars, and a caboose, and made arrangements to use the lines and spurs necessary to route the program. The Redpath-Chicago circuit, for example, had its own Redpath Special train beginning in 1913. As the train traveled to its various destinations, it was frequently decorated with Redpath Chautauqua banners and posters in order to draw attention to the Redpath name and programs.

The railroad influenced the acceptance and development of circuit chautauqua in another way beyond the transportation of talent and equipment. It brought to the West new customs, ideas, and forms of entertainment that were all essential in laying the groundwork for the acceptance of circuit chautauqua as a standardized and commercial entertainment product. News and feature magazines, mail order catalogs, home and farm products, silent movies and vaudeville were brought into countless rural areas by rail. The exposure to these early forms of standardized popular communication gradually broke down taboos concerning the "evil" city with its wanton ways and wayward citizenry.

COMPETITION

Many of the larger communities that circuit bureaus recruited into their circuits also actively supported theatrical and symphony guilds, lyric opera and vaudeville, nickelodeon arcades and movie houses. In order for the circuit bureaus to compete with such local chapters of entertainment and enrichment, they had to abandon the narrow agrarian image that was associated with earlier programs and provide something that appealed to all of their audiences — those in the far West, the Midwest, the East and, later, the South. In dealing with this marketing dilemma, the circuit bureaus began promoting their programs and activities in a manner that could not be construed as offensive to any American anywhere. A 1914 Britt Chautauqua program brochure, for example, proclaimed that "the modern chautauqua is thoroughly undenominational and non-political. It has big aims and standards. It appeals to thinking people." Moreover, after 1912, the advertisements for chautauqua were cast in such sweeping terms that all Americans could find something beneficial in the program.

A 1913 Redpath promotional brochure explained the benefits of attending a Redpath chautauqua program in the following manner:

GET READY IN EARNEST. You owe yourself this week of pleasure. Discharge that debt fully.

GET READY FOR OTHERS. Help your family and friends to the delights Chautauqua affords.

GET READY FOR THE JOY OF IT. The bacilli of trouble perishes in the sweet atmosphere of Chautauqua enthusiasm.

GET READY FOR THE ENTERTAINMENT. You have serious problems in plenty every day. Let the Chautauqua entertainer help you forget them.

GET READY FOR THE ENTHUSIASM. It is a tonic and brain quickner. It turns the blood redder. It puts "pep" into your system.

GET READY FOR THE SOCIABILITY. Your old friends and neighbors will be there. Clasp hands with them and get acquainted over again. Meet new people.

GET READY FOR THE REST. It is such a change from the daily grind of care. It is good for the tired muscles and the lame back. Your work will be easier after the rest.

GET READY FOR THE RECREATION. You can't afford to work all the time. Even a horse needs an occasional vacation. Recreation makes you over and gives you more power.

GET READY FOR THE UPLIFT. The Chautauqua programs invite all to higher ground. They coax the spirit upward and outward. They cure the hide-bound, brain-bound and heart-bound.

GET READY FOR THE INSPIRATION. The rise of thousands of great characters dates from the thrill of some great Chautauqua attraction. Get ready for yours.

In short, the circuit bureaus began using marketing strategies and appeals after 1912 that no longer identified the Midwest as its exclusive target audience. The circuit chautauqua bureaus changed their approach to the promotion and the delivery of programs in such a way that they could be mass marketed throughout the United States. Because many of the new markets that chautauqua bureaus desired to attract into their circuits were metropolitan (or becoming so) in nature, the programs became more oriented toward entertainment to compete with the avenues of entertainment such areas afforded. There were some complaints made to the Redpath Bureau about the new direction its programs were taking. In an attempt to counter these concerns, Keith Vawter included an open letter in all 1914 Redpath brochures that stated: "Some people may scold a little because there seems to be a good big share of entertainment features. They should not do so, however. Each entertainment feature has a lot of good in it. There is plenty of solid material in this program and a bountiful supply of fun for good measure."

The Lecture "Message" Begins to Lapse

After 1912, as circuit chautauqua moved into the other regions of the country and booked engagements in both urban and rural areas, the rallying calls for agrarian political, economic, and social reform subsided. Even the popular "Fighting Bob LaFollette," an early Redpath-Vawter "headliner" (the term, headliner, usually denoted an expensive attraction), had been dropped by 1914 from the Redpath program and had signed on with the smaller and less prestigious Alkahest Chautauqua Company. The earlier serious reform rhetoric gradually gave way to witty, humorous, and novel speeches about broad social issues, community betterment, and self-improvement, and were promoted on the basis of showmanship.

SOCIAL INTERESTS

Mississippi congressman James K. Vardaman delivered a speech entitled "The Impending Crisis" on various Redpath circuits between 1913 and 1916. In his speech, Vardaman argued that blacks should not be educated because "the educated Negro will threaten the political dominance of the White Man." Despite the debatable social consequences of this message, Vardaman was promoted by the Redpath bureau on the basis of his "wit of the keen and scintillant kind [and] humor which brings the ready smile." When appearing before circuit audiences, Vardaman dressed and acted the part of a Southern gentleman. Harry P. Harrison stated: "I remember him as a tall and impressive-looking gentleman with a voice trained in cotton field political oratory. His long black hair cascaded over the shoulders of an immaculate white suit and ... he had the flashing eyes of a zealot." Vardaman was elected to the Senate of the United States in 1916 and the following year was one of seven senators who voted against President Wilson's declaration of war on Germany.

Harry L. Fogelman, a businessman from New York, joined the Redpath bureau in 1912 and within several years had achieved headliner status. Fogelman could deliver a speech in a staccato manner at three hundred words per minute; this ability won him the nickname of "Gattling Gun Fogelman." Fogelman was also known for his energetic use of gestures and movement, and in some promotional materials he was referred to as the "Billy Sunday of Business," after the well-known baseball player turned evangelist. Fogelman's most successful speech on the circuits was "An Analysis of Success and Failure," in which he defended the right of the leaders of industry to make money. Congressman J. H. (Cyclone) Davis spoke about various social, political, and industrial issues and was promoted in circuit brochures as the "Opie Read of Politics," in reference to the popular humorist.

The former governor of North Carolina, Robert B. Glenn, was featured as an orator on the 1915 and 1916 Redpath-Horner program. He was introduced to circuit audiences as having "vigor and American manhood [which] characterizes every sentence." The first United States senator elected from the state of Utah, Frank J. Cannon, entered the chautauqua field in 1912 upon retiring from office. According to Redpath advertising the ex-senator, who was also an ex-Mormon, deliverd his speech "Modern Mormon Kingdom" with "fire in his eyes." Cannon's speech attacked various tenets and assumptions upon which the Mormon religion was based. Frequently, Mormon missionaries followed Cannon from engagement to engagement and attempted to refute what he had said about their religion. The local press usually was "informed" in advance of the potential confrontation that might occur between Cannon and the missionaries. If a local newspaper story appeared about the possible controversy between the "fire-eyed" Cannon and the Mormons, ticket sales for the program usually increased.

Another popular orator on the circuit chautauqua was Warren Gamaliel Harding. While serving as lieutenant governor of Ohio, Harding had been hired by Vawter in 1908 to lecture on the midwestern Redpath circuit. Initially, Harding spoke about the politics of Alexander Hamilton, but later, after becoming an Ohio senator, he traveled the chautauqua circuits explaining President Teddy Roosevelt's "big stick" policies. Even after being elected to the office of the president in 1920, Harding occasionally spoke at chautauquas about "Effective Government in the Post War."

Circuit managers always encouraged well-known political and social leaders, no matter what their party affiliation or how extreme their views might be, to address chautauqua crowds. Having President Theodore Roosevelt or President William Howard Taft or President Wilson or socialist leader Eugene Debs or "Pitchfork Ben" Tillman of South Carolina or "Uncle" Joe Cannon of Illinois appear on the chautauqua platform, even momentarily, usually meant good attendance and newspaper coverage of the program. Chautauqua provided important exposure for politicians, especially in election years. Theodore Roosevelt once remarked that "chautauqua is the most American thing in America."

BETTERMENT AND SUCCESS

Two popular themes that also ran through much of the chautauqua oratory after 1912 were how a community could collectively better itself and how individuals could achieve their own "personal success." Nels Darling, characterized as the "community expert and town doctor" in 1914, 1915, and 1916 Redpath advertising, delivered two speeches that were always in demand on the circuit, "The Home Town" and "The Village Storekeeper." In both of these speeches, Darling dealt with what he believed to be the strong relationship between community betterment and local business success.

Lecturer Allen Albert, a lawyer by profession, delivered "The Forces that Make Cities" to numerous circuit audiences. Albert would usually arrive in the community in which he was to give this speech a day ahead of time. This allowed him time to scout around until he found an obvious situation in the community that needed improvement. In his presentation the following day, he would identify the problem and suggest ways the community could address it. Because the problem he pointed to was associated particularly with that community, audience members paid a great deal of attention to what he had to say. Similarly, another Redpath flier noted that upon arriving in a community, the "Famous Community Expert" John E. Aubrey finds the "community's weakest spot, dresses it, binds it up, cures it" and discusses it in his lecture "The One-Mile Town."

Probably the best-known personal success or inspirational lecturer on the circuit chautauqua next to Conwell or Bryan was Ralph Parlette. His most famous circuit lecture was entitled the "University of Hard Knocks." The theme and approach he used in this speech had evolved out of a talk Parlette had given at a lyceum meeting to a group of school children sometime in the late 1890s. Using a glass jar full of navy beans and walnuts, Parlette demonstrated what he told the children. He said, shaking his "jar of life," that children must grow to get to the top, for those who are small would always end up on the bottom. Of course, when he shook the jar, the navy beans collected at the bottom and the walnuts remained on top.

Gay MacLaren described Parlette's "jar of life" or the "University of Hard Knocks" presentation in the following way:

> "See this poor little bean down there at the bottom," Parlette would say, holding the jar up where all the children could see; "he whines, I ain't never had no chance — you just help me up where them big fellows are and I'll show 'em.'"
>
> Then, with humorous gestures and grimaces, Parlette would rescue the little bean, place it on the top, and begin to shake the jar, explaining that life never stands still. Of course, the little bean rattled right down to the bottom. In the same way a walnut (one of the "big fellers") placed at the bottom shook back to the top.
>
> In answer to the questions put to the children, "How can you get to the top?" they would all shout in unison: "Change our size and grow greater."

When Parlette first started with chautauqua, he was featured on the children's program. Because so many adults were clamoring to hear about "the jar of life," the Redpath bureau placed him on the adult program in 1913. Trying to adapt his presentation to an adult audience, Parlette planned to do away with the jar containing the beans and walnuts. During his first presentation of the "University of Hard Knocks" before adults, however, the audience demanded to see the "jar of life." After excusing himself for a couple of minutes, Parlette reappeared with the "jar of life."

Parlette delivered the "University of Hard Knocks" approximately 4,000 times in front of circuit chautauqua audiences. After 1925, Parlette was lured away from chautauqua by a national manufacturing firm that wanted him to train their sales executives. Until his death in 1930, Parlette traveled back and forth between Chicago and New York conducting seminars. The advice he gave at these sessions was the same advice he had given to chautauqua audiences for years: "It's all up to the man. He comes to the top or lands at the bottom, depending only on himself."

There was also a wide variety of stories about "how to" accomplish personal success floating around the chautauqua circuit before World War I. George Yarrow's "The Culture of Your Personality" was promoted as assisting chautauqua audiences in discovering ways they could "take the raw material of [their] personality and go out into the world to compete for its honors with the prospect of success." Dr. Charles Baker, who had appeared in the 1910 vaudeville production of William Morris' *Chanticleer* and had served as President Taft's personal physician, delivered a speech called "How to Live One Hundred Years" on the circuit between 1913 and 1916.

Thomas McClary was another self-improvement chautauqua lecturer. Clara Hinton, recalling the message of McClary's "Mission of Mirth," wrote in her diary that

> Mirth produced *health*; *beauty*; *helped over rough places*; and helped *produce success*; "Laugh and grow fat," as he was doing. One who laughs trains the features into suitable lines — arches the eyebrows, brightens the eyes, curves the lips. One who smiles and takes interest in all, is always beautiful, though not pretty.... Always boost, never kick. You may need boosting yourself someday....
>
> > Someone did a golden deed,
> > planted some good seed,
> > said I love to live,
> > [said] it's good to give
> > does ever dare be true,
> > Is this somebody you?

For those interested in home agronomy, Henry Augustus Adrian, popularly known as the "Burbank Man," spoke before numerous 1915 and 1916 chautauqua audiences about the work of agriculturalist Luther Burbank. In his presentation, he would specifically tell audiences how Burbank "succeeded in wonderfully increasing the productivity of soil [and] in conquering plant enemies." Although "inspirationalists" like Conwell, Bryan, Gunsaulus continued to "uplift souls" on the circuit, the majority of improvement messages after 1912 were aimed at assisting listeners in improving their material or community status or bettering health or physical appearance.

ARTS AND CRAFTS

Variations of the "how to" lecture on the circuit included demonstrations of arts and crafts. Artists and craftsmen not only spoke about their particular skills, but frequently conducted workshops during the morning segment of the program. Charles Edgar Rosecrans was a very popular turn-of-the-century vaudeville "chalk artist." In 1910 the Redpath Bureau placed him under contract to perform chalk artistry on one of its circuits. Because some audiences might recognize his name and not like his prior association with vaudeville, Rosecrans was referred to in chautauqua publicity as "Ross Crane." In fact, circuit publicity before the war often changed the names of popular vaudeville or Broadway personalities who had joined chautauqua or simply did not refer to their past. Big city attractions, vaudeville, and Broadway were viewed through the eyes of skepticism in many small towns.

Rosecrans fascinated circuit audiences by drawing designs upside down which became landscapes when he turned his easel right side up. He was also known for his ability to write the name of someone in the audience on his easel and then transform it into a caricature of the person. As additional chalk artists entered into the chautauqua field, he began to distinguish himself from them by adding a clay modeling component to his act. His abilities as a "mud modeler" were described in a 1915 Redpath advertisement as follows: "He throws a handful of mud at a board and then, with a few deft pinches makes it into a likeness of Mckinley [sic]; then a few strokes and it is W. J. B. [Bryan] or President Wilson."

As even more chalk and then also clay artists appeared on the various circuit chautauqua programs, Rosecrans again tried to distinguish himself from them. In 1916, he began lecturing on how to use colors in conjunction with interior design and was from then on referred to as "Rosey Crane." MacLaren recalled that for his lecture on interior decorating he "carried a trunkful of bright draperies and chair coverings with him — chintzes, linens, cretonnes, and so on, and, with furniture borrowed from the local dealer, he would furnish and decorate a room right on the platform."

The Chicago Art Institute sculptor Lorado Taft toured with the Redpath Chautauqua lecturing about art. He also offered workshops in art appreciation and clay modeling on the morning program. Taft first used a magic lantern and glass slides and then later used colloid slides and an electric projector to demonstrate his topic. He was the creator of the Columbus Memorial Fountain in Washington, D.C. Another "how to" circuit artist was Evelyn Bargelt, who combined drawing with music and dramatic reading to instruct audiences in the "fine arts, music, and literature."

The Caveny Company, which was associated with the Alkahest Chautauqua Bureau, consisted of a husband and wife team and a violinist by the name of Edna Crumm. While Mr. Caveny entertained circuit audiences with cartoon sketches or mud modeling, Mrs. Caveny played the piano and was accompanied by Crumm on the violin. Their performance was aimed at not only educating people in the arts but also making their lives a little happier. A 1915 Alkahest brochure stated that the company believed "in mirth and laughter and song as a means for making life brighter and happier and better."

TRAVELOGUES

Many basic attitudes surrounding nineteenth-century American foreign policy were carried into the twentieth century. First, an isolationist attitude prevailed and dictated that the United States should stay out of European entanglements. The one notable exception to this was America's participation in the 1899 World Disarmament Conference at The Hague, in the Netherlands. The second attitude had been established through the Monroe Doctrine and decreed that European powers should be forced to stay out of the Western Hemisphere. And the third, was the concept of manifest destiny or the right of the United States to further its interests throughout the Western Hemisphere and, to a lesser extent, the Orient.

Despite the isolationist philosophy engulfing American foreign policy carried over from the nineteenth century and the platitudes paid to it, the country throughout the 1900s became increasingly involved in world politics. In 1899, Secretary of State John Hay's Open Door Letter was issued, which requested major powers to restrain their leaseholds and influence over China. During the following year, the Boxer Rebellion broke out in China, and the United States became involved in the turmoil. In 1903, during the presidency of Theodore Roosevelt, America started building the Panama Canal and became embroiled in the name of "missionary diplomacy" in the internal affairs of many South American and Caribbean countries. By the time William Howard Taft had become president in 1909, the country had already been engulfed in settling the Russo-Japanese War over Manchuria and continued to be involved in the domestic affairs of many western countries and China. Moreover, at this time, the United States government was also meddling in the affairs of North Africa and Europe.

As the press coverage of foreign episodes increased, the result, according to historian Arthur S. Link, was that Americans became fascinated by foreign countries and customs. By 1912, the chautauqua travel lecture capitalized on this interest by featuring travelogue lecturers who had visited foreign countries and could vividly discuss their customs. To "play it safe," the chautauqua bureaus promoted and presented these lectures in such a manner that they could not be offensive to any American-born chautauqua audience member.

All of the travelogues, whether or not they were delivered by a foreign lecturer, were presented in English, and many of the speakers were said to have been "American" educated. Promoted by the Redpath bureau as a "Japanese orator" educated in America, Yutaka Minakuchi identified in his speech "The East and West and the Borderland" the cultural contributions each hemisphere had made and explained ways that "cultural differences between the two might be bridged." The Britt circuit featured the "American-educated" Kiyo SueInui, the "Japanese Silver Tongue," who lectured about Japanese customs and culture.

The Horner-Redpath Bureau sponsored Dr. Sumner Vinton's "Pagoda Land" which, according to 1915 and 1916 advertisements, allowed audiences to experience through pictures "all the romance of southern climes; all the witchery of the Far East; all the mystery of an ancient civilization." Through his presentation of slides and motion pictures in his lecture "The Land of the Dragon," explorer Dr. Frederick Poole attempted to illustrate how China was changing. As a 1913

Redpath brochure explained, Poole's travelogue "shows the real 'yellow peril'—a boy working in a manufacturing plant at a few cents per day."

Dr. E. A. Brinton presented a travelogue lecture entitled the "Land of War and Women" on the Redpath circuit. Having visited Paraguay in 1910, Brinton offered impressions of the "land of war and women" that were summarized in a Redpath promotional statement: "[He] tells of her vicious element, that make our rough necks look tame. He discusses her women who occupy a position there, unique in the world. He treats exhaustively the social evil, polygamy, institutions, laws." With the attention that had been given to the digging of the Panama Canal and "missionary diplomacy," the Redpath bureau sought out William Rader. Rader had covered the completion of the Panama Canal in 1914 as a journalist. In telling audiences about the most "gigantic enterprize ever performed," he used both stereoptican colored slides and moving pictures to illustrate the presentation.

Some of the circuit travelogues were more global in scope. Julius Caesar Nayphe, promoted as "the son of a Grecian Nobleman" and graduate of Harvard, was featured on the 1916 Redpath circuit as being able to share his knowledge about various parts of the world. The 1916 Jones Chautauqua bureau promoted James T. Nichols on the basis of his ability to take the audience on a "trip around the world" through slides and movies. Whatever part of the world the travelogue lecturer discussed before circuit audiences, the use of magic lantern slides and short silent movies was by this time essential to the presentation.

Shakespeare, Drama, and Readers

Drama, especially Shakespearean drama, became a burgeoning success on the circuit chautauqua after 1912. Prior to this date, the presentation of a "play" was considered immoral and taboo by chautauqua audiences. So during that time, the cautiously guarded plays were presented as "readings" and promoted on the basis of having "moral" or "social" merit. The spreading popularity and availability of the silent film and nickelodeon features, the plots of which were often taken directly from Broadway and vaudeville plays, were a factor in the breakdown of the stigma attached to drama by those living in rural America. But for chautauqua, the most significant single factor that paved the way for the acceptance of drama on Main Street was Ben Greet and his Shakespearian Players.

THE GREET PLAYERS AND SHAKESPEARE

Producer Charles Frohman brought Greet and his company from England to Broadway in 1904 to perform in *Twelfth Night*. The Greet Players were so well received by Broadway audiences that Frohman arranged to have them tour the country in the fall of 1904, including a stopover at the White House. The Greet Players ended up staying in the United States and continued to tour and perform on Broadway.

Crawford Peffer, manager of the New England Redpath Bureau, approached Ben Greet in 1912 about the possibility of having his company tour with his chautauqua the following year. An agreement was subsequently negotiated which stipulated that the company would tour with *A Comedy of Errors* and *She Stoops to Conquer* and that Broadway director William Keighley was to be engaged to produce the plays. In order to sway Keighley to join this venture, the bureau had to promise him that it would support his casting choices. Percival Vivian, who starred in the 1912 Broadway production of *Oliver Twist*, and veteran Broadway star Grace Halsey Mills were chosen as the lead players in the 1913 Redpath production of *A Comedy of Errors*. Irene Bevans, Vivian's wife and a noted Broadway player in her own right, was engaged as the leading lady in the Redpath production of *She Stoops to Conquer*. Thus in the year 1913, the Redpath bureau managed to bring not simply professional theatre to chautauqua audiences but some of the best talent Broadway had to offer.

In an attempt to make Shakespeare "safe" for chautauqua, so that it would offer what one program brochure called "refined art and high moral and cultural standards," Peffer, Greet, and Keighley spent hundreds of hours rewriting and deleting lines from both plays. The initial monetary investment necessary to make the Greet Players tour possible also required the financial backing of several other Redpath bureaus. Each of the bureaus that invested money in the tour in turn wanted "part of the action." As a result, when the Greet Players toured in 1913, they did so on several Redpath circuits, not just the one operated by Peffer. The production of *A Comedy of Errors* appeared on a total of 110 Redpath programs in 1913, primarily in New England and in the Midwest. *She Stoops to Conquer* toured in the eastern branches of the Redpath circuits and appeared on approximately 100 programs.

The following year, the 1914 Redpath circuit toured the Keighley-directed productions of *Twelfth Night* and *Merchant of Venice* in more than 100 eastern communities. Vivian and Mills played the leads in both plays. In addition, *Much Ado About Nothing*, also produced by Keighley, was featured on several midwestern Redpath chautauqua circuits that same year. Ben Greet himself performed in this production and was described in one promotional statement as appearing "in a delightfully funny mood which bubbles over in rich profusion, from first to last."

OTHER FEATURED DRAMAS

The overwhelmingly positive receptions given to the Keighley productions of Shakespeare on the chautauqua circuit prompted the Redpath bureau to underwrite the tour of the then fashionable Broadway production of Charles Rann Kennedy's *The Servant in the House*. The play had opened on Broadway in 1908 and continued its run until the early 1920s. The play had the three essential ingredients that chautauqua audiences were beginning to look for in drama: it was a comedy, had a Shakespearian ambience, and featured an all-star cast.

In 1915, the *Servant in the House* was first presented on chautauqua from beneath a Redpath tent in Jacksonville, Florida. The Broadway cast included such stage legends as William Lindquist (who earlier had been a Redpath circuit jubilee singer), J. W. McConnell, William Owen, Robert Stevens, Margaret Ulrich, and Sarah Willey. The opening night of the play was financially very successful for the bureau. With this cast intact, the play toured that same year in an additional 75 Redpath towns in the South and the Midwest.

Following the lead of the Redpath bureau, other chautauqua companies began featuring "drama" or "plays" on their programs. The Lincoln Chautauqua Bureau induced the Arden Drama Company, which was also at that time a major Broadway company, to tour on its 1916 midwestern circuit with the production of *The Taming of the Shrew*. Examples of other play productions featured on various chautauqua circuits before World War I included the 1915 and 1916 presentation of the *Battlefield*, a comedy that used the Spanish-American War as its backdrop, and the Frank Lea Short Players production of the *Romancers*. In 1916, the year before President Wilson formally declared war on Germany, the Redpath-Horner Bureau of Kansas City engaged a New York production company to present Israel Zangwill's *The Melting Pot*. Broadway actress Dore Davidson, in conjunction with William Keighley as an actor-producer, presented this play to literally hundreds of midwestern chautauqua towns that year. Within five years, Davidson would appear in the Warner Brothers silent film, *Your Best Friend*, which dealt with Jewish family life.

The Melting Pot had been written in 1908 and concerned Jewish immigrants who upon coming to this country had cast off their traditions to become "one-hundred percent" American. In a 1916 Horner-Redpath program brochure, *The Melting Pot* was advertised as follows:

> This is the year that we Americans should renew our patriotism and be proud of our country, but in the face of the world's troubles it should be patriotism well-tempered with the doctrine of brotherly love.
>
> Such is the message of the Melting Pot....
>
> If you were to see this drama in New York City with such a cast, you would expect to pay $2.00. Having a season ticket, you will pay so little for so big an event ...
>
> The play has not been changed, but it has been made to conform to Chautauqua standards.

The Melting Pot was published while Theodore Roosevelt was still in office and was one of his favorite plays. The "melting pot" became a popular rhetorical and literary metaphor that was used on numerous occasions by the president when discussing domestic policies. *The Melting Pot*, moreover, was also a fashionable penny arcade and lyceum attraction in ethnic neighborhoods of large urban areas like Chicago and New York. The play became a "headline" favorite on the Redpath Chautauqua circuits that reached into the midwestern ethnic farming pockets containing Germans, Irish, Poles, and Swedes. On the Redpath circuit, the play was always presented in English, however.

The evolution of drama that took place on the chautauqua circuit between 1912 and 1916 — from the "reading" to Shakespeare to other plays — indicated that a change toward a certain sophistication in taste had taken place in rural areas of the country. Through the circuit chautauqua, many rural peoples experienced for the first time plays and other attractions that heretofore had not been available to them. When the circuit chautauqua took the chance of introducing Shakespearean plays and other Broadway productions to Main Street, it took a major step towards becoming a form for mass popular entertainment. By the entrance of the United States into World War I in 1917, the circuit chautauqua movement had dropped the veil of strict morality and had abandoned its former emphasis on adult education.

DRAMATIC READERS

After 1912, the readers of dramatic and humorous literature became increasingly overshadowed by the demand for drama and comedy. Yet many of the earlier circuit readers — Day, Amsbary, Bunny, Flowers, Gilligan, Manlove, Nye, Ratto, Read, Rice, Sandburg, Taggart, and Willis — continued on the program, although the length of time allotted for their individual performances was reduced. Aware of the movement toward drama on the circuit, many readers began selecting their performance cuttings from popular Broadway plays. Others served in supporting roles when a dramatic company needed "extras."

Gay Zenola MacLaren was an ever popular circuit chautauqua reader and "actress" and an example of how the chautauqua reader could turn dramatist. MacLaren was born in Howard, South Dakota, before the turn of the century. As a young woman, she became intrigued with elocution while watching readers at the nearby Lake Madison permanent chautauqua assembly. Early in the 1900s, MacLaren moved with her family to Minneapolis, where she was enrolled in the Manning College of Music, Oratory, and Dramatic Arts. She recalled that "it was understood, however, that I was not to be allowed to go into dancing classes or take part in stage plays. I was to be seriously trained for the Chautauqua platform."

Upon graduating from Manning College, MacLaren traveled to New York City to acquire additional training in elocution. While there, she contracted with the Star Lyceum Bureau as a reader. During one of her lyceum engagements, Mark Twain happened to hear her read and was impressed with the performance. Twain himself was a popular lyceum and permanent chautauqua lecturer and had appeared any number of times at Lake Chautauqua, New York. Twain recommended to Reverend Vincent that MacLaren be brought to Lake Chautauqua to perform as a reader. In 1910 she signed her first contract with the Redpath Lyceum and Chautauqua Bureau, agreeing to appear as a reader on Redpath Lyceum and Chautauqua tours for two years.

MacLaren recalled that during the first several seasons of lyceum and chautauqua work, the Redpath agency constantly "cautioned [me] against using the term [play] in conjunction with my recitals. In spite of my stubborn insistence that I was giving a play, I would hear myself introduced as giving a reading." By the time the dishonor associated with the words *play* or *drama* had ended on the circuit, MacLaren had become known as the "Girl with the Camera Eye" because of her

Gay MacLaren, the "Girl with the Camera Eye," could recall complete plays and literary selections without referring to a script. MacLaren Collection, University of Iowa.

ability to repeat word for word the lines of the characters she portrayed in Broadway plays. A 1916 promotional statement noted the following: "She attends the production of a modern play five times and without having read the original book or dramatization can go upon the Chautauqua platform and give a recital of the production, impersonating every character. In preparing her recital she attends only great productions and sees only the interpretation by the best actors."

Another popular "chautauqua reader" and dramatist was Edna Means. Means began around 1910 as a chautauqua girl working with children. During the months in which chautauqua did not tour, she took Chautauqua Literary and Scientific Circle home study courses in literature, drama, and delivery techniques. In 1913, Means began to move toward being a chautauqua reader by taking the place of several readers who had canceled their program appearance. By World War I, Means had achieved the status of being, at least in circuit publicity, a "featured reader and dramatist." Even though chautauqua was much more entertainment-oriented than it had been before 1913, it was still important that a performer had a "message." A 1916 promotional statement for Means explained, for example, that "while entertaining her audiences, she seeks also to leave behind a message of helpfulness and worthwhileness.... Miss Means has a wonderful voice, a charming personality, and an unusual mastery of her art."

While coming into her own stardom as a reader, Means took on an understudy by the name of Conrad Nagel. Born in Keokuk, Iowa, Nagel had attended chautauqua as a boy and as a result had become fascinated with the dramatic arts. While attending college in Des Moines, he worked as a tent boy during the summer months on the same Redpath chautauqua circuit as did Means. During Nagel's free moments, Means tutored him in elocution and acting. From time to time, Nagel was called upon to read before audiences, and on several occasions he and Means performed short dramatic pieces together. Upon graduating from college in 1914, Nagel left chautauqua and went to work for the Princess Stock Company of Des Moines. The following year he joined the New York City branch of the Keith Vaudeville Circuit.

The Versatility of the Music

Although large orchestras and bands continued to be touted as major headline entertainment on circuit programs after 1912, they were gradually displaced by a greater number of smaller musical groups. This change occurred because of the expanded offerings of full-staged circuit drama. In order to accommodate and transport the large theatrical companies, the bureaus had to reduce personnel and equipment in other program areas. Because the large bands and orchestras containing thirty or more players took up the majority of transportation space, it was in this area that the bureaus decided to reduce the numbers. The major chautauqua orchestras such as Kryl's Orchestra and Band, Thaviu's Great Orchestra, the Schildkret's Hungarian Orchestra, and Hugh McNutt's All-American Band, however, were kept with the same number of performers they had retained in former years. But in general, the bureaus did not encourage or add large bands to their chautauqua programs after 1912.

The versatility of musical companies and bands was encouraged by the circuit bureaus. Frequently, when a musical group appeared on a program, it was coordinated in such a way that it would be available to provide music for a play or an opera. The bureaus thus had fewer entertainers to transport and saved money in salaries. A 1913 promotional statement for Thaviu's Band, for example, indicates how his band was integrated into the operatic production of the *Lovely Galatiea*:

> When twilight soothes and the heart is out for joy, the full glory of the great band will appear. A musical extravaganza of surpassing splendor by twelve Grand Opera Stars accompanied by the entire band. They will render Thaviu's adaption of the opera Lovely Galatiea, and the chorus effects will surprise and inspire with beauty and power. Handsomely staged and sparklingly [sic] in artificial lights, this scene will leave nothing to be desired.

The 1914 and 1915 Britt Chautauqua presentation of *The Bohemian Girl* provides another example of how different musical companies were used in the name of efficiency. The entire opera was presented by the Hinshaw Singing Band Opera Company, "composed of ten singers," and "the Hilder Orchestra of five musicians."

More than anything else, the employment of smaller musical groups and the versatility required of them promoted a distinctive variety of music on the chautauqua program. There were duets, quartets, sextets, operettas, and full-staged operas. Moreover, an increasing number of foreign ensembles were being included on the program. Chautauqua audiences were fascinated by foreign-born performers and usually enjoyed their music as long as it was presented in English. Circuit bureaus that experimented with presenting music, including operas, in foreign tongues quickly abandoned the practice.

The variety of music presented on the circuit program introduced audiences to styles of music that most of them would never have experienced if it had not been for chautauqua. Some of the singers and musical performers who appeared before them were from prestigious and well-known production companies.

OPERA COMES TO MAIN STREET

In 1915, the same year the Redpath bureau gambled on the play *The Servant in the House*, the bureau also decided to tour Alice Nielsen of the Metropolitan and Boston opera companies on its southeast circuit. Nielsen traveled from engagement to engagement in her own railroad car, the *Mayflower*. The former owners and residents of the *Mayflower* included Presidents Roosevelt and Taft, Lillian Russell, and Sarah Bernhardt. When Nielsen was to travel into a town for a chautauqua engagement, prior publicity was released to local papers about all of the famous people who had been connected with the *Mayflower*. By commenting on these names in advance of her arrival, the newspaper would draw attention to her arrival and, of course, the chautauqua program. Born in Nashville, Tennessee, Nielsen made her opera debut in Naples, Italy, and later, in the early 1900s, sang with Caruso in London. During her first year on the chautauqua circuit in 1915, she traveled to more than 100 towns. The following year Nielsen's Operatic Company was transferred to an Ohio branch of the Redpath chautauqua circuit.

Taking Nielsen's place on the southeast circuit was Julia Claussen, who was associated with the Royal Opera Company of Sweden. Claussen came to the United States directly after a group that she was touring with in Europe was halted by the Germans. After a series of successful Redpath Chautauqua engagements in 1916, she left the circuit and joined the New York Metropolitan Opera. That same year Leonora Sparks, setting aside some time from her busy schedule at the New York Metropolitan Opera, appeared with President Taft on the eastern Community Chautauqua circuit. She was promoted as being the most important "Prima Donna Soprano for the [New York] Metropolitan Opera Company" to appear on any chautauqua program.

Roena Gates Clements, a former chautauqua girl, recalled the conditions under which she became acquainted with the well known opera singer Harriette Henders: "On the night of [a] play one girl showed up. She was about 20 years old, I expect. Her name was Harriette Henderson. And how she sang! What a beautiful voice. There was no rehearsal ... She graduated from Simpson [College] and later sang in the big opera houses in Europe and the Metropolitan in New York City [under the name Harriette Henders]." In addition, the opera great C. Pol Plancon sang before chautauqua audiences in the East accompanied by the Aida Instrumental Quartette.

The performance of the husband and wife team of Estelle Gray and Mischa Lhevinne, which featured various combinations of piano, violin, song, and dramatic reading, was a popular circuit feature between 1913 and 1917. During the winter months, the duo performed at the New York Metropolitan Opera. A 1915 chautauqua brochure explained that their performance would be "humorous, pathetic, thrilling and always inspirational." Others associated with the New York Metropolitan Opera who appeared before chautauqua audiences as part of Redpath's Oratorio Artists included Elsie Baker, Mary Stoddard, and Frederick Wheeler. The voices of many "chautauqua opera stars" could at that time also be heard on scratchy-sounding Victor Records played on hand-cranked Victrolas.

MORE VARIETY

The number and variety of musical numbers offered on any given circuit program was astounding. A 1914 Britt Chautauqua brochure, for example, detailed the "musical numbers" featured on its program. Aside from the three operas and four "big" bands, the program included the following entertainers:

(1) The Ethiopian Serenaders, under the direction of jubilee manager Howard C. Washington, in "the Ethiopian Musical Episode and Evolution of the Negro Race from the year 1408 to present time."

(2) The Hawaiian Singers and Players

(3) The Stelzls, "A Family of musicians, German born and educated abroad.... They are a combination of skilled musicians and entertainers."

(4) The Boileau Concertiers, an instrumental sextet.

The musicals featured on the 1914 midwestern Redpath-Vawter circuit were identified and described in advertising as follows:

(1) The Chautauqua Six are coming with a fine assortment of musical surprises. This is a sextet of handsome and talented young ladies....

(2) The Regniers come with music, story, makeup, cap and bells.

(3) The Orpheans are coming. This is one of those well balanced male quartets....

(4) The Beach trio, as the name implies is made up of three girls.

(5) And Ferrantes Hungarian Orchestra, too!

Literally thousands of different types of musical groups marched across the chautauqua stage between 1912 and 1917. In addition to those already mentioned, there were the American Ladies Orchestra, the Beulah Buck Quartette, the Fisk Jubilees, the Metropolitan Grand Quartet, the New York City Marine Band, the Tyrolean Alpine Singers and Yodelers, and so many more. The enormous assortment exposed chautauqua audiences to popular live entertainment and, in doing so, fostered a tolerance and an appreciation for something not readily available elsewhere.

Ethnic Images

The circuit chautauqua bureaus used three dominant images when commercially presenting ethnic entertainers. First, they were presented as entertaining in such a manner as was consistent with popular Anglo-American stereotypes about "primitive people." Second, ethnic performers were generally described as having been culturally enlightened through "Christian pursuits" or a "college education." Third, the substance of their performances contained nothing that could be construed as offensive or controversial to the chautauqua audiences.

BLACK ENTERTAINERS

Chautauqua audiences were always dominantly Anglo and generally were made up of ethnic groups who had come from northern Europe. The bureaus did not actively screen who attended their programs, but in the South, some chautauqua boosters and business people were members of the Ku Klux Klan and on several occasions attempted to bar blacks from attending programs. Black circuit lecturers were not included on programs in towns where the Klan had a strong foothold. If the chautauqua bureau misread the attitudes of a town and included a black speaker on the program, the Klan occasionally tried to organize a boycott. This sort of bigotry did not result, however, if blacks appeared as jubilee singers performing in the stereotypical roles of romantic plantation days gone by.

A 1914 Britt Chautauqua brochure, in promoting the Ethiopian Serenaders as directed by Howard C. Washington, himself a black, stated directly that the performance was designed to fulfill the expectations of chautauqua audiences:

> Mr. Washington has been associated in the jubilee business for the past nine years and has made a special study of what the Caucasian audiences would expect and enjoy in a musical program rendered by an Ethiopian company....
>
> He presents the Ethiopian Serenaders in the Ethiopian Musical Episode and Evolutions of the Negro Race from the year 1408 to the present time....
>
> Space will not permit us to use any of the many commendations awarded to these great artists, as each one is a College and Musical College graduate and also a graduate of one of the schools of the Southland.

The management takes pride in offering not only the greatest Ethiopian Organization in the musical world but an organization of young cultured ladies and gentlemen.

After their introduction to America at the 1893 Columbian Exposition in Chicago, the Kaffair Boys became a popular lyceum attraction. When the fair closed down in October of that year, the Chicago Redpath Lyceum Bureau managed to place the Kaffair Boys, as well as several other groups of foreign origin, under contract. The Kaffair Boys were featured on various Redpath circuit chautauqua programs until 1917. The "Recital by the Kaffair Boys in Flashing Jungle Costume," with the accompanying lecture by their manager J. H. Balmer, was described in a 1915 Redpath-Vawter brochure as follows:

[Mr. J. H. Balmer] painstakingly trained them [the Kaffair boys] in the art of song, and entertainment, and made a tour of England. Repeated appearances were made before the Queen.... Typical songs of the various races are given in native dialect, but the major portion of the programs are in English....

It's a long jump from the jungle to the Chautauqua platform, but the Kaffair boys are some jumpers. It is just nuts for them to entertain a crowd. Their faces beam with delight for the fact that they are not dodging reptiles and lions, but singing to civilized men and women.

Jubilee groups that were popular chautauqua attractions, especially after 1912, included such companies as the Booker T. Washington Tuskegee Singers, Fisk Jubilee Singers, Ralph Dunbar's Maryland Jubilee Singers, and the Tuskegee Black Performers. Typical of how all of these jubilee companies were advertised was a statement about the Booker T. Washington Tuskegee Singers, named after the great black leader, that was contained in a 1915 Lincoln Chautauqua program brochure. Building on a romantic Southern stereotype of plantation life in the "ol' South," the brochure promised that these singers would provide a "program of old-fashioned plantation melodies, folk songs and dialectical readings.... This company, made up of highly educated, earnest, young college men who know how to sing, enjoys the reputation of being the best company of colored singers on the road." As with the Ethiopian Serenaders and Kaffair Boys examples, the Tuskegee performers were promoted in such a way as to suggest that they were educated and cultured and "safe" for chautauqua audiences to see and hear.

BLACK ORATOR LAURENCE C. JONES

There were very few black speakers featured on circuit chautauqua programs, but Booker T. Washington appeared at several early 1900s permanent chautauquas. Because of his great fame in the field of education, the Redpath bureau tried to get Washington to travel with its circuit on several different occasions. His duties as chief administrator of the Tuskegee Normal and Industrial Institute made it impossible for Washington to commit himself to a two- or three-month schedule away from his school. As a result, each time the Redpath Bureau made an offer he declined. He did speak, however, from the circuit platform on several occasions as a "day feature" or "special one-day attraction."

Sharing Washington's vision concerning the importance of vocational education and training for blacks was Laurence C. Jones, another black educator. Jones, originally from St. Joseph, Missouri, attended the State University of Iowa. After his graduation in 1907, he traveled into the South and began the Piney Woods Country Life School for blacks in Mississippi, which was eventually chartered in 1913. Although the school provided instruction in a number of subjects to the men and women that attended, Piney Woods was primarily a vocational school in agricultural practices and technology. In 1914, Jones, along with his wife, traveled with the Redpath Chautauqua and talked to circuit audiences about his school. While with the Redpath Chautauqua in Des Moines, Jones saw a State University of Iowa classmate by the name of W. O. Finkbine. Finkbine and his brother, as it turned out, owned 800 acres of land next to the several-acre Piney Woods tract. The brothers made a gift of the land to the school.

Jones toured with the Redpath circuit until the end of World War I, using the money he made by lecturing to help support his school. Moreover, a sympathetic ear in the chautauqua audience would sometimes emerge and directly assist the school with financial or other needs. A 1915 Redpath promotional brochure noted that Jones "realized that his education had placed a racial obligation upon him. His 'eyes had seen the glory of the coming of the Lord.'" His chautauqua speech, "A Voice from the Black Belt," broached the importance of vocational and agricultural education for blacks. The South was not ready for the type of message that Jones was preaching, however, and the majority of his lectures, while on the Redpath circuit, were given in the North. Even northerners had to be cautiously approached. Chautauqua promotion assured audiences that Jones did not

> preach social equality, neither does he discuss the rights and privileges of the negro. He realizes that his people are a primitive folk and that, like all primitive people, they are better off amid primitive surroundings. He urges them to stay away from the city, to stick to the soil.
>
> He has taught the farmers the folly of raising ten cent cotton to buy fifty cent bacon and dollar corn. He has gone into the fields and taught the farmers how to select seed corn....
>
> This young Iowa negro is the "young Booker Washington."

Black jubilee singers and South Seas performers were always a special worry to the circuit chautauqua manager. Not only did special accommodations have to be made for these ethnic groups, but sometime cultural practices had to be, when possible, restrained. More than one circuit manager had to round up Hawaiians, for example, who had stripped to the nude and jumped into a nearby pond or river. Social customs also led to travel provisions for these ethnic groups that were different from those for entertainers of Anglo-European or Oriental extraction.

In *The Little Professor of Piney Woods*, Laurence Jones, through biographer Beth Day, related how he was treated while touring with chautauqua:

> The summer tour [of 1915] was a resounding success. At the same time, it was shadowed by the old bugaboos of travel — the denial of restrooms, the trouble getting tickets; the refusal of food and hotel service....
>
> He had to spend the night in a box car and another [night] in jail after a demoralizing "vagrancy" arrest by an overzealous policeman who thought all people of color should carry passports after dark. And this was the North.

Special accommodations for ethnic entertainers usually meant supplying bedding for sleeping in a boxcar or on the ground beneath the stars or occasionally in the main tent or a smaller one.

SOUTH SEAS PERFORMERS, "NATIVE AMERICANS," AND THE "CIVILIZED SAVAGE" METAPHOR

The strategy used in the promotion of South Seas performers was similar to that used in publicizing black entertainers. A romantic image of the South Seas was infused with comments indicating that the performers who appeared on chautauqua from these areas were "civilized savages." The Hawaiian Singers and Players, for example, were described in a 1914 Britt Chautauqua promotional piece as being "genuine full blooded Hawaiians, finely educated and finished in music [who] are capable of weaving out the sunshine, the wish of the murmuring seas, the haunting melodies of the Ukelele."

Another popular chautauqua musical company, simply referred to as the Raweis, was comprised of a father, mother, and son from the Maori tribe of New Zealand. The Raweis were promoted on the basis of performing their "tribal songs in English," accompanied by a film called *From Cannibalism to Culture*. The film clearly made the point that Anglo-cultural "enlightenment" was essential for the betterment of "primitive people." Basically, the film was a before and after glimpse of the senior Rawei's life after he was adopted and educated by an English missionary. According to Redpath publicity, the film showed how Rawei was "transformed from South Sea savagery to a gentleman of Christian culture and wonderful entertainment talents."

There were few Native American performers who appeared on circuit programs prior to the war. When "American Indian" acts were included on the program, they were performed by Anglos dressed as Native Americans. The Story of Tahan, the "White Savage," was promoted in a 1912 brochure as an "Indian Lecture in Costume." In his presentation, "Things I Saw and Did as a Savage," Dr. Griff as the "White Savage" described for chautauqua audiences how he had been captured and raised by "Indian savages" and later transformed into a "Christian minister" through the influence of "white man's education and kindness." A Redpath promotional flier described the eloquence of Dr. Griff in presenting his story: "THE STORY OF TAHAN, the White Savage, and of the Red Man as told in the poetic picturesque eloquence of the Indian and the perfect English of the white man, is Homeric in its simplicity and strength.... The Indian dress he wears is a trophy of war and was the dress of an Indian Chief Tahan killed in battle."

The "civilized savage" metaphor was used by the bureaus to promote non–Caucasian performers (or Caucasians acting in these roles) throughout the entire history of circuit chautauqua. The attractiveness of the image for circuit audiences was that it was both alluring and safe. These entertainers were cast in the "primitive" roles that popular stereotypes of that time dictated. Yet at the same time, they were presented as having been educated and enlightened about appropriate cultural mannerisms and etiquette. The irony or clash of these two parts of the metaphor created a "safe" situation for Anglo-dominated chautauqua audiences. College-educated black jubilee singers performing Southern plantation songs, "trained" African Kaffair portraying native ways (in English), the civilized Native American (even when not really an American Indian) as a reminder of the American frontier, and Rawei as a "gentleman of Christian culture" talking about cannibalism reinforced the notion that these cultural groups were only a generation or two away from savagery.

Most of those sitting in the chautauqua audience considered themselves and their ancestors to be part of the "civilized Christian" world. As Robert Wiebe noted, this was an important perceptual status because by World War I, the world in the American mind had been separated into two parts: "Above lay the civilized powers, principally Europe and the United States; below fell the subjects of their imperialism in Asia, Africa, and Latin America. If some nations straddled the line — Turkey, Japan, even Russia — by and large the nature of the division drew them either up or down." The general ethnic backgrounds of chautauqua audiences placed them in the top layer of Wiebe's scheme. Chautauqua audiences, curious about other cultures, but not wanting to feel threatened as "civilized people," could relate comfortably to the "civilized savage" metaphor.

Junior Chautauqua and "Entertainers"

COSMOPOLITAN NATURE OF THE PROGRAMS

As the chautauqua program became more entertainment oriented and cosmopolitan after 1912, so too, did the chautauqua activities and programs designed for children. The nature walks, outdoor activities, and "playing Indian" characteristic of the earlier children's activities were expanded by the inclusion of varied play festivals. Because older children in urban areas generally had more time on their hands than those living on a farm, the children's program went out of its way to invite older urban children to participate in chautauqua activities. In fact, the phrase "Children's Program" was abandoned in most circuit promotion and replaced with either "Junior Chautauqua" or "Youth Program."

In addition, there were features added to the youth program that aimed at providing young adults with a global perspective of various regions and cultures. The following segment pertaining to the junior chautauqua was printed in all 1914 and 1915 Redpath brochures:

> Here is where the young folks from six to fourteen years of age get in on a mighty good time....
>
> This year there will be what they call Story Travels and Character Sketches in addition to the Festivals of Play.... We will all go around the earth nearly, and get to see the most curious people....
>
> The first trip is going to see American Indians right in their homes.... Old Savage Ravancha, a chieftain, is going to tell the youngsters about the clothes his people wear, also about how these aborigines do things....
>
> Then we will get into an airship and go across the Pacific Ocean to Japan. When we get there a fellow named Yone Santo is going to tell us Japanese stories....
>
> Next day we are off to Holland ...
>
> Next to Sweden ...

By 1915, the Lincoln Chautauqua Bureau's "Junior Chautauqua" was expanded to include something for both young persons and adults: "Every morning at 10:00 o'clock there will be original play features for the young people, with something on the side for the grown-ups, such as round-table discussions, demonstrations of home parties and neighborhood plays, introducing new ideas for the consideration and benefit of parents and teachers."

FESTIVAL ACTIVITY

By 1914, many of the larger circuit bureaus had an organized preprogram play festival activity for children. A chautauqua girl or festival director usually arrived several days in advance of the day that marked the start of the program in a community and organized a play festival utilizing local children of various ages. In addition, he or she often organized a children's festival parade to greet the first day's chautauqua talent upon their arrival; sometimes the children's parade would accompany them down Main Street to the chautauqua grounds.

The play festival activity was gradually incorporated into the adult evening programs by most of the circuit bureaus. The reason for this was economic. Almost any boy or girl who tried out for a part in the festival play was "carefully selected" to participate. Once the play festival was made part of the adult program, a greater number of parents and adults attended because they wanted to see their child or children perform on chautauqua. Overall, the play festival activities were an effective device for drawing attention to chautauqua programs and stimulating ticket sales. The play festival, as an activity and part of the adult program, was commonly included on most circuit programs until the late 1920s.

Despite the careful planning that went into preparing the play festival, things sometimes went awry. In her diary about chautauqua life, Roena Clements recalled one such incident. After working all day with the youth in preparation of a play festival, she had a problem with one of the professionals.

> The leading man got *drunk*. Since he was unable to appear, Josh Lee of Oklahoma who was to be on the program later that night volunteered to give a reading that had won a national honor for him in a public speaking contest sponsored by the Women's Christian *Temperance* Union! It was well received and was most appropriate for the occasion. Josh Lee was later elected United States Senator from Oklahoma.

ECLECTIC ENTERTAINMENT FOR PEOPLE OF ALL AGES

Beginning in 1913, a greater number of magicians, cartoonists, impersonators, "savages," and foreigners were featured in the morning and early afternoon time slots, sometimes on the youth program and other times on the adult program. Essentially what was begun was the practice of blurring the lines of demarcation between what was specifically for adults and for children. The chautauqua bureaus would build on this convention to the degree that by the 1920s there was little difference between most adult and youth programs. In turn, one feature could be advertised in a manner that would attract both adults and youngsters. Although Shungopavi, the Medicine Man, was advertised, for example, as part of the youth program, a 1913 Redpath-Vawter program brochure announced, "Fathers, mothers, children, grandparents, aunts, uncles and cousins ... will want to see and hear Shungopavi, the Moqui Medicine Man." Despite the fact that Shungopavi was an Anglo appearing as a Native American, the promotional statement noted that he would take "his hearers to the very borders of the dark and awful secrets of tribal mystery."

Magicians, illusionists, and impersonators were also popular features that transcended the boundaries of age. Joining the ranks of the earliest chautauqua magicians such as Edwin Brush and the Floyds were names that were well known to late 1800s and early 1900s lyceum and vaudeville circuits. Edward Reno started as a magician on the lyceum circuit in 1881 and within several years also performed before vaudeville and permanent chautauqua audiences. Assisted by his wife, Madame Reno, he started touring with the Redpath circuit in 1912. One of his acts, most popular with the children before whom he appeared, was described in a 1913 chautauqua brochure: "One of his performances that never fails to amaze audiences is known as the 'dove trick.' He burns a piece of common paper and a dove rises phoenix-like from the ashes. He apparently tears the dove in two, only to find that he has two doves in his hands. He throws a glass of water into the air, and it changes into a dove and flies away."

Another of Reno's "assistants" was "Mister Duck," a large white duck that he pulled from his hat at the beginning of his performance rather than the more standard rabbit. In another routine referred to as "from the stewing pan into the water," Reno placed Mister Duck into a stewing pan with a fire beneath it. The duck would jump from the pan, draw water from Reno's pocket, and put the fire out by spitting on it. While in a town waiting for their chautauqua program to begin, Reno and Madame Reno, accompanied by Mr. Duck, would walk up and down Main Street pulling coins out of the ears of children.

Carl Rosani, a magician, was described by vaudeville veteran Joe Laurie, Jr., as being a "vet of vaude that played all over the world." By 1900, Rosani was performing before both vaudeville and permanent chautauqua audiences. He began working for the Redpath Chautauqua in 1912 and stayed with the bureau for the next 14 years. Rosani was known on the circuits as the "Wonder Worker and Novelty Entertainer" because he did more than just magic during his act. A 1912 Redpath brochure described his act in the following manner:

> Among the accomplishments of this versatile genius might be mentioned his balancing act with whips, plates, balls, pipes, sticks, bowls, bottles, glasses, hats, swords, tops....
>
> Rosani is a master of an art which he terms Chapeaugraphy which consists of the impersonation of some twenty-five great characters by simply placing on his head an ordinary rim of felt for a hat and changing its shape....
>
> In finger silhouette productions, Rosani is par-excellent. By the

manipulations of his hands alone he throws upon the screen pictures of animals, figures and faces....

Bring the children and enjoy this fine performance.

After the chautauqua and vaudeville circuits began to fold during the late 1920s, Rosani organized his own touring company which traveled throughout the world. In the 1930s, Rosani performed at Buckingham Palace and before Joseph Stalin in Russia.

The ever-popular impersonator Halwood Manlove began his circuit chautauqua career as a reader in 1910. By the early 1910s, however, Manlove had clearly made the transition from being a reader to being the "Man of Many Faces." He especially centered the attention of his act on ethnic impersonations. As early as 1913, he was promoted in the following way: "Manlove carries with him a full line of grease paints, wigs and make-up material and with the aid of these, changes very quickly into Irishman, Swede, Jew, Dutchman, Frenchman, Italian, rube, old man, maniac, grouch, silly kid, tramp, dude, and what not."

Thomas Elmore Lucey was another preferred impersonator on the chautauqua trail. His physical image was described in one circuit publicity piece as being one that "resembles a composite photograph of Sol Smith Russell, James Whitcomb Riley and Edwin Booth." Like Manlove, he used a variety of makeup supplies and costume changes in presenting his impersonations of Mark Twain, James Whitcomb Riley, Edgar Allan Poe, Abe Lincoln, Bill Nye, Edwin Booth, and others.

Ethel Hinton, known as the "Little Humorist" on the circuit, performed various dialect and impersonation routines before audiences. Ralph Bingham, as the "Fun Maker," continued to be a featured impersonator for his "merry soul, as merry as 'King Cole' of old" routine. The circuit programs introduced many other performers and acts to chautauqua audiences of all ages, including, among many others, the magic of Loring Campbell, humorist Leon Cope (who began chautauqua in 1904 and retired from it in 1929), Albert and Martha Gale in "Songs and Stories of the Redman," Garretta and his birds, the "Man with the Joy Face" Thomas McClary, Pamahasika and his Pets, and humorist-reader Charles Rose Taggart from "droll Vermont."

Beyond the Rural Heartland

When the demand for circuit chautauqua began to extend beyond the reaches of the rural Midwest after 1912, the condemnation of urban politics, business, and life-styles so characteristic of earlier programs was quickly replaced with entertainment, self- and community-improvement presentations, and cultural-awareness features. After 1913, the chautauqua program began to be promoted as a sort of vacation and "cure all" for whatever problems an individual or a community might face. The lecture as a form of entertainment, a means of improvement, and a channel of information about other cultures; the evolution from Shakespeare to Broadway play productions; the presentation of "big city" musical attractions; and the broadening of the features on the youth programs all attest to the fact that circuit chautauqua before World War I was well on the road to becoming a form of mass media entertainment and an important channel of information about world events for thousands of Americans.

As the Redpath-Vawter "Chautauqua Psalm," featured in most of the bureaus' program brochures published between 1913 and 1917, stated:

> The ordinary run of life entails many problems. The Chautauqua is built for joy; and joy is a good thing for my family.
>
> My hands have labored long and steadily. I will give them a little rest at Chautauqua. At the same time I shall get the brain tonic of the wholesome enthusiasm there.
>
> All my friends and neighbors will be there. It is a wonderful place for sociability. It is a picnic a week long; and I need the picnic.

V

"Making the World Safe for Democracy": Chautauqua Goes to War

At a time when circuit chautauqua was becoming a successful commercial enterprise, war broke out in Europe in August of 1914. President Woodrow Wilson, reflecting a popular American stance, attempted to direct the country in such a way as to avoid involvement in the war overseas. Wilson's "neutrality" stance was defended by statesmen Secretary of State Bryan and Congressmen Champ Clark and Robert L. La Follette in congressional debates, magazines, and in newspapers articles. Although these men were popular chautauqua orators, the troubles in Europe and resulting German imperialism were surprisingly not a prominent topic on the chautauqua platform.

Even after the sinking of the *Lusitania* in May of 1915, which was followed by Bryan's resignation as secretary of state, and the German attacks on the *Sussex* and other American ships in 1916, the European war was a taboo circuit chautauqua topic. Americans throughout these years, of course, were concerned and troubled about what was happening overseas. As the sentiment of the country gradually moved toward an active preparedness stance in 1916, President Wilson pushed through Congress a series of measures that, within reason, made the country ready for war "if attacked." By the election of 1916, according to Arthur S. Link, the "opinion in the country as a whole agreed that the administration's program provided 'reasonable' preparedness for the uncertain years ahead."

Silence on the Platform

From 1916 until 1917, circuit chautauqua programs did not focus on the issues pertaining to the war or preparedness for several reasons.

First, when the war broke out in Europe in 1914, the country took a wait-and-see posture. The general popular belief was that the United States had no critical interest in the war. The president had issued a formal proclamation of neutrality in the summer of 1914 that he followed with personal appeals through newspaper and motion pictures media that Americans remain "neutral in both thought and action." For any chautauqua bureau actively to introduce any aspect or issue pertaining to the war on its 1914 or 1915 program would have resulted in the disfavor of President Wilson and his secretary of state, William Jennings Bryan.

Second, even though chautauqua by 1915 had become popular in urban centers on both coasts, its most supportive and financially lucrative area continued to be in the rural Midwest, where pockets of German-Americans had made their homes. Although German-Americans could and did identify with the message of the *Melting Pot*, at the same time, they were wary of national syndications and politicians who pushed the need to prepare for possible war against their homeland. Many German-Americans had parents, brothers, sisters, or other relatives who resided in Germany. Aside from the German-American factor, the vast majority of farmers and workers in the Midwest desired neutrality and were skeptical of Wilson's posture of "watchful waiting."

On the other hand, there were those of various ethnic backgrounds living in urban areas who had been convinced by the president that some degree of preparedness was necessary. Because of the standardized nature of circuit programming and advertising, many of the same features presented in rural areas were also presented in urban centers. The circuit bureaus avoided the potential of alienating either rural or urban factions by simply not dealing with issues about the war or preparedness. Even after resigning as secretary of state because of the president's movement toward preparedness, Bryan was barred from discussing the issue on the circuits.

Third, as the chautauqua program became more oriented toward providing information and entertainment, it increasingly avoided anything controversial, especially issues that would alienate segments of its audience. Lectures or debates about preparedness and whether the country should enter the war were simply too controversial. The promotional image adopted by the circuit bureaus after 1912 stressed how it functioned as a "modern" form of entertainment (and to a lesser extent education) but also stated that the movement itself was "undenominational" and "nonpolitical." Chautauqua lecture features between 1912 and 1917 were dominantly characterized as "funny," "humorous," or "sensational"; circuit lecturers no longer promoted causes. Another example illustrates this point even further. The Redpath bureau featured a suffrage debate on its 1915 northeast circuit, which caused a great deal of animosity between those on opposite sides of the issue. As a result, the suffrage debate was deleted from the program by late summer.

Chautauqua Goes to War

Despite the circuit chautauqua bureaus' efforts to remain neutral on the issue of war, when President Wilson declared war against Germany in April of 1917, chautauqua, too, "went to war." The circuit bureaus' rapid response to the president's announcement, which presented chautauqua as part of the war effort, indicated two things. First, the chautauqua bureaus had anticipated the president's declaration and had been actively involved in their own efforts of preparedness. The many program features that in one way or another dealt with the war effort and the promotional materials claiming chautauqua's place in fighting the war, that appeared as early as May indicated that all of this had been planned and, in some cases, executed prior to the declaration of war. Second, the highly publicized events that occurred in the beginning months of 1917 had finally aroused Americans to a point of supporting the decision to enter the war against Germany and had legitimized such discussions for the circuit chautauqua program.

In the first months of 1917, Germany responded to Wilson's proposal for a negotiated peace in such a manner that the president, his cabinet, and even some congressional pacifists were outraged. Beginning on February 1, Germany announced that all ships, belligerent and neutral, found in a zone around Allied powers would be sunk. By the end of the month, the Zimmermann note, which outlined a plot to align Mexico and Japan with Germany if the United States went to war, was in the hands of the president. Wilson released it to the press on March 1 for publication. On March 18, German submarines sank three American ships without warning with a heavy loss of life. By April 6, the president and both the House and Senate had construed recent events in such a way that they could declare war on Germany because Germans had "attacked" the United States. Wilson's declaration of war

After President Wilson declared war, the 1917 and 1918 chautauqua programs became patriotic in purpose. The front page of the 1918 Lincoln Chautauqua boasted American troops. Redpath Collection, University of Iowa.

against Germany passed both the House and the Senate with huge majorities.

Circuit chautauqua rhetoric throughout the duration of the war highlighted America's (and especially chautauqua's) commitment to bring an end to the war. This was to be accomplished by having Americans work and struggle together in bringing about peace. Chautauqua was presented as the rallying point for the struggle. In fact, the "real patriots" in the war effort were identified in Lincoln Chautauqua Bureau promotional material as being those who attended chautauqua. President Alonzo Wilson of the Lincoln Chautauqua Bureau wrote in a 1917 brochure:

OPPORTUNITY FOR PATRIOTIC SERVICE

During these stirring times of patriotic responsibility, when every loyal citizen is called upon to serve the flag and country, it is with the fullest realization of their opportunity for genuine patriotic service that the Lincoln Chautauqua enters upon this season. There comes to the Lincoln Chautauqua organization a feeling of exaltation in entering upon this year's work, because of the greater importance of chautauqua endeavor at this time, and of the patriotic significance which will be placed upon the Lincoln Chautauqua program wherever it may be presented....

It becomes the rare privilege of the Lincoln Chautauqua, in cooperation with the local committee, to inspire patriotism, instill loyalty and arouse every man, woman and child to a keener sense of love of flag and duty to country....

Let there be no wavering step in the world of civic and commercial endeavor. It has been emphasized in the press and by our nation's leaders that among the real patriots today are those who with calm assurance go about their business duties, conserving resources, inspiring confidence, building character and upholding community welfare. Churches, schools and institutions for community betterment, such as the chautauqua, are confronted with opportunity for real service at this time.

Then let us make the Lincoln Chautauqua in your town a real factor for the promotion of patriotism and the propagation of higher American ideals, molding the sentiment of the public along lines that will make the people of the community better citizens and if need be — better soldiers. The Lincoln Chautauquas will render real service in their propaganda of patriotism.

Although some members of the tent crews and even some performers actually left chautauqua to enlist in the armed forces, under a ruling by the secretary of war both chautauqua and lyceum personnel were exempt from the draft because of the "educational nature" of their work.

A promotional section contained in 1918 and 1919 Redpath-Vawter program brochures called "Let's All Pull Together" praised community effort, as well as chautauqua's, toward ending the war:

Here is a town that not only refuses to stand still, but insists on going forward.... They have responded nobly. They have raised their full quota by subscriptions to Liberty Bonds, War Savings Stamps, Red Cross and War Camp Community Service. Many have given sons, brothers or sweethearts to their country's service.... The community must have the Chautauqua for its educational and inspiring qualities. It is not to be regarded as a burden to be borne but as a benefit to be secure.

The "War Tax"

Ironically, at the same time chautauqua was being praised for fulfilling its patriotic duty by the federal government, in April of 1917, a newly created 10 percent amusement tax was applied to chautauqua tickets—both season and individual admission. The managers of the larger circuit chautauqua bureaus confronted their senators and congressmen in May of that year. They argued that chautauqua was "an integral part of national defense" and an educational movement and, as such, not subject to the amusement tax. There was some validity to the managers' argument about defense in that the federal government in 1917, 1918, and 1919 did use the chautauqua platform to promote the Red Cross, sell liberty bonds, and provide information about the war. The argument that chautauqua was an educational activity, however, was on shakier ground.

More than half of the circuit chautauqua programs on any given circuit were oriented purely toward providing fun, relaxation, and entertainment. A 1917 Redpath brochure, for example, identified the following reasons why individuals should attend chautauqua:

>PAY YOUR DEBTS
>
>YOU OWE it to your BOYS and GIRLS to give them a week's fun at Chautauqua.
>
>YOU OWE it to your WIFE to give her a Chautauqua vacation from the routine of house work.
>
>YOU OWE it to YOURSELF to get the recreation, inspiration and entertainment which the Chautauqua program affords.

In a 1918 open letter to chautauqua patrons, a Midland circuit manager described the purpose of chautauqua in the following terms: "RELAXATION of the mind from the cares of business and public affairs is as important as recreation of the body. While war is uppermost in all our minds ... it is well, however, to have occasional relief from the strain. One restful place to which the burdened may turn in these times of stress and national peril, is the Chautauqua." The Evening Star Bureau even went so far as to suggest that its program was a cure for just about anything and everything a person might encounter: "Its wholesome message can have but one possible influence on the community. That influence is for inspiration, progress, unity of effort, better homes, better crops, better men and better citizenship."

To counter any negative impressions that the word *amusement*, when associated with chautauqua might conjure up in the minds of local sponsoring committees, the circuit bureau managers all agreed to call this tax a "war tax." Between 1917 and 1920 when ticket prices were mentioned in conjunction with the tax on circuit chautauqua promotional materials, tickets, and contracts, the phrase "war tax" was used.

Lectures

THE PATRIOTIC LECTURE

The oratory heard from the chautauqua platform from 1917 until the signing of the armistice in 1919 fulfilled a variety of valuable social and political functions. Various first-hand accounts of the war were offered through the lectures delivered by Allied soldiers. Red Cross nurses delivered speeches about the medical treatment being given to troops overseas. Various government representatives sold war bonds from the chautauqua platform. In addition to the lectures given to circuit audiences by the soldiers and nurses who "had been there," analyses about how the war was influencing domestic, political, and economic policies were also provided by some chautauqua speakers. In addition, some of the more popular inspirational speakers persisted on the circuit, as did those delivering travelogue lectures.

Despite the eclectic nature of chautauqua rhetoric during the war years, the majority of the speeches heard on the circuit dealt in one way or another with the war and patriotism. Even President Wilson underscored the importance of circuit chautauqua's assistance to the war effort. In a letter to Montaville Flowers, president of the International Lyceum and Chautauqua Association, dated December 14, 1917, Wilson wrote:

> It has been on my mind for some time to thank your organization for the very real help it has given to America in the struggle that is concerned with every fundamental element of national life. Your speakers ... have been effective messengers for the delivery and interpretation of democracy's meaning.... Let me express the hope that ... the people will not fail in the support of a patriotic institution that may be said to be an integral part of national defense.

This letter was subsequently reprinted in literally thousands of 1918 and 1919 circuit chautauqua program brochures.

The most highly publicized and popular lecture feature on the 1917 and 1918 circuits was returning soldiers from the war. Most of these soldiers incorporated motion pictures and slides into their presentations. The majority of the lectures provided by soldiers were promoted in an electrifying and graphic manner. Lecturer Lieutenant H. Manning, for example, was said to have been "thrown into battle of the Somme July 16, 1916, where he 'lived a lifetime in two months'—gassed and dangerously wounded with shrapnel—saved by his corporal who gave his life in the effort." The speech he delivered before 1917 and 1918 circuit audiences was titled "The War from an Officer's Viewpoint" and was accompanied by government war pictures of "torpedo boats, submarines, cavalry, fire, gas, etc., in action on the battle lines." The abuses encountered by Allied soldiers while in the hands of the enemy were intensely and forcibly described in Alfred H. O'Connor's presentation of a "Survivor of the Somme." Before 1917, 1918, and 1919 Midland chautauqua audiences, O'Connor told time and time again how "a German soldier struck him so violently on the chin with the butt of his musket that he was left for dead."

Private Ernest Powell was advertised in Redpath chautauqua publications as telling "a tale of gripping interest" about "how he was captured near St. Julian and carried to a great German prison camp at Glessen. How he was forced to work on farms, in mines and caverns. Of brutal treatment by German guards and German civilians." A relation of Florence Nightingale by the name of Sergeant George E. Nightingale was noted for his presentation of "Two Years in the Devil's Playground." In this speech, he described his twenty-two-month ordeal behind enemy lines and explained how the "German enemy jeopardized DEMOCRACY and the rights of civilization." And at the conclusion of his speech, Nightingale requested "loyal Americans and chautauquans" to "buy liberty bonds." Laurence Jones traveled with the Redpath circuit, primarily in the Midwest, throughout 1917 and 1918, selling liberty bonds and soliciting support for the Red Cross from "all races."

Private Peat's lecture "Two Years in Hell and Back with a Smile" also dealt with overseas war experiences in the hands of the enemy. The Redpath Bureau presented Private Peat in promotional statements as follows:

> He was gassed at Ypres and survived to later see his company, ammunition exhausted, surrounded and captured. He lay fifty-two hours on the battlefield—"My shoulder smashed, my lung punctured, ribs caved in and a few other trifles busted and dislocated."

For months his right arm hung limp — his right lung is gone, but his indomitable spirit and irresistible humor have been untouched.

After the war, Peat turned ardent pacifist and presented various speeches from the circuit platform about the "atrocities of war — any war."

Allied journalists and photographers who had covered the war overseas were also sometimes featured as lecturers on the chautauqua program. Journalist Irvin S. Cobb was introduced in a 1918 Alkahest Chautauqua brochure as follows:

> It is with pleasure and satisfaction that we are able to announce the coming to our chautauqua of America's most famous war correspondent, his name is practically a household word with all the readers of the *Saturday Evening Post.*
>
> He has had the privilege of the battle front for the past three months and has been in the front line trenches. His experiences are right up to the moment. ...
>
> He is also known as one of the greatest humorists of the day and is more sought after in New York and eastern cities that any other after dinner speaker.

As the promotional statements for both Cobb and Peat suggest, chautauqua tried to be a serious source of information about the war, but somberness was balanced with humor and entertainment.

Red Cross nurses who had served overseas were frequently hired by circuit managers to speak about the medical treatment injured American soldiers received in Europe. Mary K. Nelson, an American Red Cross nurse supervisor in France, described to 1918 and 1919 chautauqua assemblies the nature of the medical treatment given the first group of American soldiers wounded in the battle of Chateau-Thierry in 1917. Laura Roser, a Red Cross nurse, was hired by the Redpath bureau to speak about the types of medical treatment provided by European Red Cross stations to American soldiers. Roser's presentation was accompanied by colored slides and movies.

According to a 1918 program brochure, American ambulance nurse Harriet Bird Warren was said to have served in the front-line hospitals "where they bring the wounded right from the battle line.... [She] "has a story of the war from an entirely different view point ... It is so thrilling, so tragic, so instructive and so full of facts not generally known." The statement continues by noting that Warren specialized in plastic surgery while in the Red Cross overseas and that "many a wounded soldier whose face was distorted, mangled and crushed by bombs, gases and shells, owes to this Ambulance nurse the fact that his face was brought back into shape and a hideous countenance was, through her skill, avoided for the remainder of his life."

It was important that those lecturers, whether they were soldiers, journalists, or nurses, who discussed the war overseas from the circuit platform had "been there." Chautauqua audiences wanted first-hand narratives of what was occurring in Europe. In fact, there were so many individuals returning from the war overseas who had an experience they wanted to share on chautauqua that the circuit bureaus had a wide variety from which to choose. The lectures given by these individuals, in conjunction with their pictorial presentations of battles, artillery, and medical treatment of injured soldiers, were an important source of information for chautauqua audiences about what was occurring overseas. Although brief film clips of the war could be seen in populated areas, in rural areas where the movie house and radio virtually did not exist, the chautauqua program was the main avenue of "seeing" and learning about the European war. And most of the individuals who attended the program knew at least someone, frequently a family member, who was fighting or had died overseas.

DOMESTIC MATTERS AND SCIENTIFIC CURIOSITIES

Although overseas events dominated much of the chautauqua rhetoric between 1917 and 1920, some of the earlier popular circuit orators continued the same messages they had delivered before countless pre-1917 circuit audiences. Lincoln McConnell, the "apostle of sunshine and better living"; J. H. Cyclone Davis, known as the "Opie Read of Politics"; "Gattling Gun" Fogleman; community experts Nels Darling, John E. Aubrey, Edward Ott; and Bryan, Conwell, Gillian, Read, and others persisted on the circuit into the 1920s.

Various scientific and technological innovations were brought to the attention of the American public during the war. Beginning in 1917, the same year the country entered into the overseas conflict, chautauqua programs began featuring lecturers with academic and practical expertise in science to discuss technological innovations.

Hilton I. Jones, known on the circuits as "Hi," left a professorship of chemistry at Wesleyan University in South Dakota to join the Redpath chautauqua in 1917. In his lecture "The Harp of the Sense, A Study in Vibrations," Jones discussed the relationship between sound, electric, and light waves. Through his lecture, Jones introduced thousands of people sitting in chautauqua tents to scientific innovations that would change the world within their generation. When electricity was not available locally, he used a portable generator powered by a Model T Ford to work his apparatus that demonstrated how the airwaves could carry not just sound but images as well. The following year, the bureau insisted that Jones change the title of his lecture to something less academic and easier to comprehend. From 1918 until the end of his career with chautauqua in the late 1920s, Jones' lecture was referred to in promotional materials as "Science Made Plain."

Before joining the Redpath Chautauqua in 1915, Montraville Wood was an electrical engineer and aerial postmaster for the United States Post Office; he had gained some fame as being the first pilot to fit a plane with a gyroscope. Wood would demonstrate his gyroscope before circuit audiences and apparently requested audience members to "tame it." Harry P. Harrison recalled that the gyroscope apparatus "measured about two feet wide, weighed twenty-eight pounds, revolved like a maniac on the loose and could quickly get the best of any bold spirit who accepted Wood's challenge to mount the stage and wrestle with it. Watching the contraption rise bodily, get on its feet and turn around, many people thought it not only spectacular but perhaps a bit supernatural."

Using his knowledge about the gyroscope in conjunction with his other experiments in sound waves, Wood developed the "hearing torpedo" that was subsequently purchased and used by the United States Navy, first in World War I and then again in World War II. The use of his invention by the navy starting in 1917 centered a great deal of publicity on Wood. Not coincidentally, that same year Wood became a "headline" attraction on the Redpath-Horner circuit. He was promoted in a 1917 Redpath-Horner brochure as follows:

> Professor Wood is the inventor of the "hearing torpedo" about which many illustrated articles have appeared in the prominent magazines and scores of the largest city papers. By means of a special contrivance on which the torpedo is poised delicately and subject to sound waves produced from a small wooden rattle (representing the sounds coming from the propeller of the ship), the demonstrator is able to explain to his audience the principles of his invention.

Wood also did various demonstrations with the ultraviolet ray before circuit audiences. He would write the names of audience members on the wall of the tent with the ray, and these names remained visible some minutes. Circuit members considered Wood as much a magician as a scientist.

For chautauqua patrons who still cooked by kerosene and used kerosene lights, lectures and demonstrations with electric and scientific innovations were fascinating. As demonstrations involving electricity became more and more common to chautauqua, advertisements for electricity were more frequently seen in the program brochure. A local utility company in one 1917 brochure took out an advertisement that simply stated "COOK WITH ELECTRICITY." Another promotional statement for the use of electricity that appeared in a 1918 chautauqua flier read:

> In the beginning there was light.
> FREE LIGHT
> Let me demonstrate the
> DODGE AUTOMOBILE
> and
> FREE LIGHTING AND COOKING SYSTEM

The war also drew popular attention to the new and exciting phenomenon of the airplane. Circuit bureaus frequently hired returning military pilots to provide air exhibits for their patrons. But because the demonstration could not be confined within the tent and could be seen from a distance, the event also was used to draw attention to the chautauqua. Prior to the actual air demonstration, a lecture was customarily provided by the pilot. A 1919 chautauqua brochure, for example, promised a lecture by the "famous air-fighter" Lieutenant Milo Miller, followed by a demonstration. To assure the reader that the lecture-demonstration would occur as promised, the brochure noted: "Two machines, battle-planes have been ordered, One of these machines will be kept in reserve at a central point and will always be ready in case anything should go wrong with the first machine. ... Expert mechanics will be on hand at all times to forestall engine troubles and to make sure that the machine is in constant shape." The air show was usually scheduled right before the afternoon program intermission, and it lasted from 15 to 20 minutes.

DOMESTIC AND FOREIGN ISSUES

A wide variety of national and domestic issues were addressed from the circuit chautauqua platform while America was involved in the war.

The topics were varied and included such matters as the "proper place" for women in the modern-day world, the causes and consequences of crime, socialism versus democracy, and growing worldwide instability and its impact on America. Richmond Mills delivered "The Battle Ground of the Nation" before more than a hundred circuit audiences between 1918 and 1920. Speaking at a time during which American women were seeking jobs and volunteer activities outside of the home largely to assist the war effort, Mills maintained that the "proper place" for women was "in the home." He usually concluded his remarks with the statement that "women must love their babies more than their poodle dogs or the grist of the divorce courts will be fed." On the other hand, Dr. Nan Sperry, assistant labor commissioner of Missouri, viewed women as part of the American industrial force and discussed ways in which "to better the conditions of women in industry" before 1917 and 1918 circuit audiences.

About 1916, Reverend Sylvester J. Dowling began lecturing on the chautauqua circuit about causes of crime, which he outlined as follows: "(1) The parental negligence. (2) Faulty education. (3) Immoral atmosphere in the home. (4) The privilege of choosing companions at a critical age. (5) Evil training at home." He also advocated temperance with regard to the use of alcohol because, as he stated, "head and shoulders over all else in the beginning of crime is intoxication and intemperance.... Intoxication and immorality are twin sisters. Where one goes the other follows and you seldom find them apart." Dowling was a friend of Billy Sunday's, and occasionally the two of them got together to review arguments that could be used against the consumption of alcohol.

A North Carolina preacher by the name of Frank Dixon began delivering a speech called "Man Against the Masses" in 1912 on the Redpath Chautauqua circuits. The speech was basically an outline of the negative consequences socialism would have on the American way of life. Only after the introduction of D. W. Griffith's film *The Birth of a Nation* in 1915, however, did Dixon become a Redpath Chautauqua "headliner." The film was loosely based on a book by Dixon's brother, Reverend Thomas Dixon, entitled *The Clansman*. The Redpath bureau of course tried to cash in on the popularity of the Dixon name and frequently reminded circuit audiences that Frank Dixon was "the brother of that famous author, Thomas Dixon, upon whose *The Clansman* 'Birth of a Nation' is based." At the close of World War I in 1919, however, the demand for Dixon's "Man Against the Masses" on the chautauqua circuit quickly diminished.

Former Judge Ben Lindsey of Colorado, who first began on the chautauqua circuit in 1909 by describing "his fight against corporate greed and industrial injustice," restructured his lecture so that by 1917 "corporate greed" was defined in terms of suppliers of ammunition. He was said to have had "implicit faith in America, American institutions, American patriotism, and the American people" in bringing about an end to the war. Other "big names" on the earlier circuit platform also adjusted their speeches to produce a "message" appropriate for the times. Bryan adapted the theme of the "Prince of Peace" to suggest that Americans needed to have faith both in themselves and in God to bring about an end to the war. Russell Conwell expanded the various scenarios of "Acres of Diamonds" to include the stability of democratic institutions and traditions. "Democracy," he at times proclaimed, "is the acres of diamonds we all long for."

Many circuit lecturers examined the impact that the war was having and would possibly have on America, democracy, and the world. War correspondent Raymond B. Tolbert in his lecture "The Hour of Democracy" provided, as noted in 1917 and 1918 Redpath promotion, a "graphic summing up of world conditions and our relation to them," offering this message:

> The great war has shaken society to its foundations. While the guns at the front were churning up the soil of France, they were also upheaving the social and industrial structures of the nations. Out of this war is to emerge a new social order. The strength of democracy must stand further tests. We must understand the forces at work, the forces that are bringing such changes to pass, and then applys [sic] intelligent political and industrial action.

An earlier populist advocate and former congressman from Minnesota, J. Adam Bede, discussed before 1917 and 1918 Redpath audiences how "the civilization of Europe is tottering" and why the country "needs a strengthening of our faith in our democratic institutions." And Reverend Samuel Parkes Cadman changed the focus of his chautauqua lecture after 1917 to assess the possible moral, political, and economic state of the world at the close of war in the "Re-created World."

TRAVELOGUES

The travelogue lectures featured on the circuit chautauqua from 1917 until 1920 frequently assessed the political or economic stability (or instability) of other countries. Mohammed Ali, a native of East India, was described as combining "native Oriental keenness of perception and subtleness of wit and humor with a perfect command of the purest English" when surveying "conditions, political, social and religious in India." On a 1918 Standard Chautauqua program, Homer A. Hulbert, who was advertised as having been "in the employ of the Korean Government," provided a travelogue lecture on Korea. It was said to provide and explain the "stirring scenes which directed the attention of the whole world to the Far East."

Morris Gershon Hindus, who was Russian born and university educated, in addition to having been a postgraduate at Yale, lectured on the 1918 and 1919 Lincoln Chautauqua circuits about his country. According to Lincoln promotional fliers: "He acquaints you with the Russian peasant and portrays the terrible conditions there — tyrannies of church, state and nation — in words too graphic that his scenes and characters seem to live before you. He gives a glimpse of the lives of exiles in Siberia and paints a word picture of the future Russia." Other travelogues that were presented on the circuit chautauqua programs between 1917 and 1919 dealt occasionally with social and political conditions in China, Japan, and Mexico. After the war concluded in 1919, however, these countries became a central focus of the chautauqua lecture, especially in the consideration of their potential economic impact on the United States.

Music and Patriotism

As with other elements of the program, the way in which many of the music performances were advertised reflected the importance of patriotism as an advertising appeal. The names and promotional statements of musical groups that had appeared on programs before the war were changed to reflect this consideration. The "nine clever and versatile lassies" of the Dunbar White Hussar Band, formerly referred to as Dunbar's Ladies Orchestra, were described in 1917 and 1918 promotion brochures as having the "'stuff' in them to make you want to go to war.... These [were] the same girls who delighted the soldier boys in the encampment." The members of Dunbar's White Hussar Band were now described as being "all American" and committed to the "cause of democracy." The music of the Class Royal Grenadiers was said to provide not only "classical excellence" but also "patriotic airs."

The popular prewar circuit feature known as the Pilgrim Girls was referred to as the Liberty Maids Quartet in a 1918 Redpath Bureau

The Liberty Maids Quartet dressed in "patriotic costumes" and radiated "patriotism, refinement and culture." Redpath Collection, University of Iowa.

promotion. A 1918 Redpath flier described them as "pretty young ladies in patriotic costumes [who] radiate patriotism, refinement and culture." The Niles Hussar Band joined the Lincoln Chautauqua circuit in 1914 and was promoted largely on the basis of performing songs of foreign origin. In 1917, the name of this band was changed to the All American Niles Hussar Band. The band was promoted as performing numbers that would "not offend American propriety and custom." Thaviu's Great Orchestra abandoned the classical pieces, many of German origin, upon which its reputation had been established for "patriotic numbers."

NEW FACES

Although chautauqua talent was exempt from the draft, vaudeville performers and Broadway actors were not. What this meant was that the new names and faces coming from vaudeville and Broadway to chautauqua were largely women.

The Mildred Morrison Concert Party, consisting of all females, joined the Lincoln Bureaus in 1917 and was promoted as presenting a "well-balanced program of high merit." The Old Fashioned Girls, a musical act complete with "hoop skirts, hand mitts, curls and 'bunnitts'," signed with the Standard Chautauqua Bureau in 1918. The Althea Players, an ensemble of six "experienced" female violin players, joined the 1918 Vawter-Redpath circuit after having performed before vaudeville audiences.

The Red-Headed Quartette appeared in 1917 on the Redpath Chautauqua program for the first time. They were noted as being "unusual — strikingly unusual — because they are all red-headed." Ruth Gordon, the well-known film actress and screenwriter, was one of these redheads. She was singled out in the program brochure and described in the following way: "A perfect vocalist and an accomplished actress, she can sing the complete role of Faust, Il Trovatore, etc., or if you prefer she will sing you a Red Head Song that will stir her audience with rippling smiles and pent up laughter." Gordon had joined the Red-Headed Quartet in vaudeville in 1916. The year before joining this group, she had begun to attract public attention by appearing with Maude Adams in the Broadway production of *Peter Pan*. In 1918, she returned to Broadway to appear in the production of *Seventeen* with Gregory Kelly. Gordon continued her association with Broadway into the 1930s until she began to make her transition into film.

SOUTH SEAS AND OTHER COMPANIES

More and more South Seas bands and musical companies were included on circuit chautauqua programs of the war years. The chautauqua bureaus' supply of foreign bands from Europe was seriously interrupted by the war. Nonetheless, chautauqua audiences liked hearing and seeing something different and something foreign. To fulfill this demand, the bureaus turned largely to the South Seas as a source for foreign musical numbers. Various South Sea groups appeared in "native costume" before literally thousands of chautauqua audiences between 1917 and 1920. Commonly, these performers played the instruments "unique" to their country and were said to represent "the best" of their cultural heritage.

As had been the custom in promoting South Seas islanders before the war, the bureaus used a cultural stereotype that presented South Sea islanders as a primitive and bewitching people. The Midland Chautauqua Bureau introduced Kealakai's Hawaiians to 1917 circuit audiences in the following manner: "The haunting minors of the Hawaiian Ukeleles have taken the country by storm. We are glad to present one of the best of the original Hawaiian companies so our patrons may sit under the witchery of these weird and enchanting melodies of the South Sea Isles in all their native beauty." Introduced to Redpath audiences that same year were the Royal Hawaiians, also known as "The Aloha singers of a vanishing race." In 1918, the Hawaiian Quintette was promoted in a Vawter brochure as follows:

> HAWAIIAN music has started the whole world whistling and humming the haunting, lilting strains of the tropic islands and has sounded the most bewitching note in the history of instrumental music.
>
> A pathetic, lovable, melancholy people, the Hawaiians have woven into their music the story of their race, their joys and sorrows, their sufferings and triumphs, their loves and hates, their innermost thoughts and life.

The widespread popularity of the Waikiki Hawaiian Singers and Players was noted in the following 1917 promotional statement released by the Redpath bureau:

> The talking machine companies are finding great difficulty in supplying the demand for records of Hawaiian music, both instrumental and vocal. Therefore, it is to be doubted if a more popular offering will be made in the chautauqua this season than The Waikiki Hawaiian Singers and Players, a company that was a feature attraction at the Panama-Pacific International Exposition at San Francisco last season.... Their music is weird and haunting. The Waikiki Company appeared for one whole year at the big exposition in San Francisco and has since remained in the States. They appeared for a long chautauqua tour the past summer over one of the big Circuits and will tour from coast to coast in the Lyceum this coming season. They play and sing, using the instruments of their native land, appearing in native Hawaiian dress.

Despite wartime travel restrictions, there were several European musical groups that were brought to the United States to perform on circuit chautauqua. The Croatian Tamurica Orchestra apparently came, according to 1917 and 1918 Midland chautauqua promotion, "from the heart of the great war zone in Europe, just south of Austria" to perform before chautauqua audiences. Also introduced to American circuit audiences by the Midland Chautauqua Bureau were the Venetian Troubadours, who were advertised as appearing in "their elaborately decorated costumes" and singing songs of their homeland. The Redpath-Vawter Chautauqua Bureau was not to be outdone by the Midland Bureau's Venetian Troubadour feature. The Venetian Trio, brought to this country in 1917 by the Redpath-Vawter circuit, was said not only to appear in costumes native to their homeland but to change into Southern plantation costumes and present "Dixie Land in song and story."

The Redpath-Vawter Bureau presented "It's Bonnied Scotland in Sweetest, Earnest Song" by Knight MacGregor on its 1918, 1919, and 1920 programs. MacGregor was promoted as performing his songs "dressed in appropriate Scottish costume, with a brogue as rich and liquid." Loseffs' Russian Quartette was a feature attraction on the Evening Star program between 1918 and 1922. The quartette was advertised as providing "a combination of life and enthusiasm and cover[ing] a wide range of music, from the wild, fantastic folk songs of the Russian peasants, through the most exquisite and difficult airs of the old masters, to that modern music termed 'popular but not trashy.'"

The Rudolph's Swiss Singers and Players, appearing in "national costume," were promoted in 1918 and 1919 Standard Chautauqua brochures as "using the unique instruments of their native land." Many of the ethnic groups that were brought to this country after 1917 by the circuit chautauqua bureaus were professional touring groups. The presence of South Seas islanders, Croatians, Russians, Venetians, and other ethnic groups (German groups were notably absent) on the chautauqua stage exposed audiences to a breadth of cultural customs not likely to be seen on Main Street nor, in some instances, even in larger metropolitan areas. The majority of the foreign companies performed their numbers in English, but if a group performed in any other language, there was always someone present to explain what the words of the song meant.

BLACK (AND WHITE) JUBILEE AND NATIVE AMERICAN MUSIC

As before the war, circuit chautauqua bureaus continued featuring black jubilee singers as a major part of their programs. During the war, the circuits also began to feature, albeit on a limited basis, some "real" Native Americans in Native American musical numbers. Also, as had been the case prior to 1917, much greater emphasis was placed on jubilee singers (as well as many other types of musical groups) than upon Native American performers on the chautauqua program. The main reason that chautauqua bureaus downplayed Native American performers was that they did not want to be associated with Wild West shows. In fact, there was never a "cowboy" act, much less a "cowboy and Indian" routine, on the adult chautauqua program. Occasionally, however, there was a "let's play cowboy and Indian" segment on the children or youth program offered through chautauqua, but this occurred very infrequently after 1916.

Whereas a program entitled "Indian song and folklore" received one short promotional line in a 1918 Redpath-Vawter brochure, the same brochure devoted an entire page, including a picture, to advertising the Williams Jubilee Singers. The statement for the Williams Jubilee Singers read as follows:

> Your feet will tap time with the rollicking plantation melodies and you will marvel at the sweetness and power of such camp meeting tunes as "It's Me" and "Every Time I Feel the Spirit," sung with that spirit of religious fervor and primitive pathos which is peculiar to the American Negro....
>
> Your entire being will respond when these dusky artists sing the stirring patriotic songs of America and you will thrill with the tenderness of those old, old songs we love so well, such as "Swanee River," "Nelle Gray" and "My Old Kentucky Home." How those old melodies do push back the years and bring to us all of those tender memories that live in the heart of age.

In 1919, the Williams Jubilee Singers were so much in demand by circuit audiences that Redpath-Vawter management decided to have the group appear on the program both in the afternoon and in the evening.

Other black jubilee groups commonly appeared as headline features on many of the chautauqua circuits. The Booker T. Washington Singers, the At Home Plantation Singers, and the Dixie Jubilee Company were all very popular chautauqua entertainers. Black jubilee groups were usually presented in chautauqua advertising as recreating something akin to the plantation days in the South before the Civil War. The promotional image was essentially the same one that had been used before World War I. The promotional statement for the Dixie Jubilee Company in a 1918 program brochure makes this point: "The popularity of the company has been something extraordinary. The organization presents a program of negro music, including jubilees new and old, camp meeting songs, plantation songs, comic darkey songs, negro melodies and lullabies, songs of sentiment, river songs of the old slave days."

By the time the country had actually entered into the overseas war, it was beginning to become customary to integrate Caucasians with blackened-faces into the jubilee groups that toured with chautauqua. There were several reasons why this occurred. First, by doing this, the circuit bureau could hire smaller jubilee companies and add other performers when needed. A smaller company meant that there were fewer people who would need transportation and lodging. This was an important consideration when the transferring of war troops limited the availability of train travel. Second, the introduction of this practice had already begun and was popularly welcomed on the vaudeville and Broadway stage and, to a lesser degree, in silent films.

In a 1992 interview, Leah Spratt, who had regularly attended chautauqua each year as a girl in Cameron, Missouri, recalled how Caucasians were combined with the black jubilee company while performing on the stage:

> There would be five or six minstrel singers on stage at the same time. Some were white, usually the men at each end, with black cylinder grease on their faces. They played the banjos and sang. The singers on each end would tell jokes back and forth. Occasionally, the minstrels would play the bones by placing two dried bones between their fingers and rapping them back and forth.

As with the jubilee companies, the depiction of Native American performers was developed in such a way as to capitalize on a popular caricature of their image. As chautauqua bureaus attempted to provide popular mass entertainment, there was less emphasis placed on actual Native American traditions. Native American performers, especially after 1917, were essentially products of then popular media art forms. Chief Caupolican was promoted in a 1918 brochure, for example, in the following manner:

> [Chief Caupolican] appeared in leading theatres throughout America, where he was recognized as a star in the vaudeville world. Caupolican's story of his people is essentially, however, a chautauqua product.... He presents a lecture entertainment in which song and story and

oratory is cleverly woven into one of the most striking chautauqua productions of the present age.

There are other examples of Native Americans appearing as popular entertainers on chautauqua. Indian soprano Princess Watahwaso or "Bright Star" of the Penobscot Tribe was a featured performer on the 1919 Redpath program. According to the publicity, she had "had training under the masters in musical art and besides is a born entertainer." Princess Te Ata, or "the Dawn," performed songs native to her "people" on the 1919 White-Myers Chautauqua program. The Caucasian husband-and-wife team of Albert and Martha Gale performed before numerous Lincoln Chautauqua audiences in an act called "Songs and Stories of the Redman." The Gales were advertised as providing a "carefully developed interpretation of Indian life, illustrated with real Indian tepees, totem poles, and Indian dress, with Indian songs and music."

The strategies used in promoting jubilee and Native American performers after 1917 indicate that chautauqua was moving toward providing its audiences with forms of mass entertainment. "Black" jubilee companies were not made up entirely of blacks in many instances, and they were no longer intended to represent happy-go-lucky plantation slaves who sat around all day in idyllic bliss. Nor did Native American performers have tribal ties and some vast cultural wisdom and folklore to share with chautauqua audiences. Both ethnic groups were promoted based on popular media expectations perpetuated by vaudeville, Broadway, silent shorts, and chautauqua itself. In a broader sense, the way the chautauqua program came to be packaged and promoted is not dissimilar to what has occurred with modern-day television.

THE POPULARIZATION OF OPERA

By the time the country entered World War I, there were many theatrical and opera companies willing to tour with chautauqua. The longer silent film features, in conjunction with the increasing number of movie houses being constructed across the country, were drawing audiences away from theatre and the vaudeville houses. Despite having the opportunity to bring in the big names associated with either theatre or opera at that time, the chautauqua managers decided to focus on opera in their programs. The reasons why the circuit chautauqua bureaus favored opera over drama can be summarized as follows.

First, the chautauqua bands (although frequently ill-equipped to do so) could play the musical scores for the operas. Second, the operatic scores chosen for chautauqua programs usually had only two or three lead performers. Other circuit performers were drafted into the production when needed. Third, and most important, operatic productions required the transportation of far fewer personnel, props and costumes than did Broadway theatrical productions. Basically, then, the operatic productions were far less hectic, expensive, and time consuming for the chautauqua bureaus.

Despite the many precautions taken on the part of the bureaus to insure the availability of railroad transportation for their programs, once the country had actually become involved in the war, the transporting of troops and war equipment meant long delays in the moving of chautauqua personnel and equipment. During this period all of the larger chautauquas had to purchase trucks and busses to ensure that their programs could be transported from one town to another. The Chicago branch of the Redpath Chautauqua Bureau, for example, purchased 18 motorized vehicles in 1918 for the express purpose of moving its programs.

Many of the operas that were presented from the chautauqua stage were in actuality cut-down versions of the original. Complete operas, with four or five acts, were too long for the chautauqua program, which prided itself on versatility. As was the case with longer or "questionable" plays, lines, characters, and complete acts were cut from operatic productions. In 1917 the Redpath Bureau sent out the then well-known Howard Tooley Opera Company to perform Gilbert and Sullivan's *Mikado*. Tooley and band leaders Ralph Dunbar and Sandor Radanovits edited the play to reduce it from five to two acts. It was closer to the truth than audiences probably knew when the Redpath Bureau described the opera in a 1917 brochure as "travesty in thin mask. Tragedy in masterful strokes."

The Redpath production of the *Mikado* featured an all-star cast for that time. Arthur Aldrich came directly from his Broadway portrayal of the *Mikado*'s Nanki Pooh to play this same role before Redpath audiences, Broadway performer Edward Andrews appeared in the part of Ko-Ko, and Bertha James Gilbert played the role of Yum-Yum. Single admission tickets to the Redpath production of the *Mikado* cost 75 cents. Also in 1917, the Western Redpath Chautauqua Circuit featured the Montague Light Opera Company on its program. The company performed excerpts from a number of recent Broadway features, including the *Mikado*, *Red Mill*, *Madame Butterfly*, *Robin Hood*, and the *Pied Piper*.

In 1918, the Redpath bureau toured in the East with two operatic productions that had come straight from Broadway: the *Chocolate Soldier*, based on George Bernard Shaw's *Arms and Man*, and Gilbert and Sullivan's *HMS Pinafore*. Next to the *Mikado*, *HMS Pinafore* was the most frequently featured opera production on all of the chautauqua circuits. The Redpath production of *HMS Pinafore* featured Arthur Deane in the role of Captain Corcoran. Deane had played this role in the original production of the opera in London.

The first operatic productions seen from the chautauqua stage were a long cry from Broadway and the New York Metropolitan Opera House. The cast of the New York production of *Bohemian Girl*, for example, numbered into the hundreds. The Britt Chautauqua Bureau's presentation of this opera on its 1916 and 1917 tours, on the other hand, boasted having "ten singers" and "five musicians" perform the complete production. By 1918, however, most of the larger chautauqua bureaus, including the Ellison-White, Lincoln, Peffer, and Redpath, began engaging professional New York opera companies and producers.

De Wolf Hopper was hired by the Redpath bureau to head his own opera company. He began his stage career in the mid-1880s as a comedian and musician on the vaudeville stage. By the early 1900s, he was appearing in major musical and play productions on Broadway with such notables as Ethel Barrymore, Sidney Drew, Tyrone Power, and Mack Sennett. Beginning in 1910, Hopper's name became associated both as a director and performer with a series of opera revivals that appeared on Broadway, including Gilbert and Sullivan's *Patience*, *HMS Pinafore*, and the *Mikado*. In 1915, Hopper, along with other well-known actors, actresses, and directors such as Billie Burke, Louise Dresser, Douglas Fairbanks, Lillian and Dorothy Gish, and William S. Hart, signed with the Triangle Film Corporation which had been formed by D. W. Griffith, Thomas H. Ince, and Mack Sennett.

Dramatic Arts

THEATRE TAKES A BACK SEAT

Although fewer play production companies toured with circuit chautauqua between 1917 and 1919 in comparison to the years immediately before and after the war, some drama was featured on the programs. *Uncle Tom's Cabin* and *The Melting Pot*, which had been popular circuit plays before the war, continued to be promoted as main features on many chautauqua programs. After 1917, however, the advertisement of *The Melting Pot* no longer focused on how immigrants to America had become "100 per cent American," as had been the case before the war. Rather the play was said to have answered an important question in the minds of many Americans concerning the loyalties of foreign-born Americans while the war was going on.

In the process of answering this question, the playwright Zangwill was transformed into an American prophet. As a 1919 chautauqua brochure noted of *The Melting Pot*:

> Full of interest that is vital and virile and appealing is Zangwill's prophetic vision of America's future. It visualized the hope of democracy on these shores.
>
> It is intensely patriotic and is especially appropriate at this particular time. The products of the melting pot have been tried in the refining fires of the great war and have stood the test. In the American army were men of every race and nationality. There were Italians who even fought better than did their kin on the other side of the Alps. There were Germans who licked the everlasting daylights out of the Germans across the Rhine. Why? Because these men were products of the great American Melting Pot. They had come under the influence of American ideals and American institutions.

Examples of how the circuit bureaus used their theatrical talent in multiple ways were many. The Glenn Wells Players presented "farcical playlets" and constituted a musical company on the same 1918 Lincoln Chautauqua program. The Cambridge Players, under the direction of Elias Day, performed in a production of *The Rivals* and did a feature called "music and reading" before 1918 Midland Chautauqua audiences on the same program. The Cambridge Players, however, left the Midland circuit to join the Evening Star bureau in 1919 because they were contracted to perform only as "dramatic artisans."

The success of the circuit play productions before 1917, first Shakespearean comedies and then several Broadway comedies, encouraged the circuit bureaus to offer Broadway play productions on their programs during the war when feasible. The major feature play chosen by the Redpath-Vawter bureau for its 1917 season was the Broadway play by Roi Cooper Megrue and Walter Hackett called *It Pays to Advertise*. William Keighley directed the play for the bureau, and it was so well received by Redpath audiences that it continued to be promoted as a "Redpath feature" for the next four years.

By 1919, other circuit companies had begun regularly featuring *It Pays to Advertise* on their programs. The plot of the play, as noted in a Redpath brochure, was a

> familiar story of the rich father and idle son. The father makes a wager with his stenographer that she cannot induce the son to go to work. She succeeds in getting him interested in a business proposition. He forms a partnership with a fellow who believes with all his heart and soul and amazing nerve that it pays to advertise.
>
> The father is a soap manufacturer and the young fellows enter the same field, flooding the territory with ads of their soap. The ad campaign was a tremendous success but the young enthusiasts forgot to make soap. The public demands the new soap and the youngsters force the soap trust to buy them out at an enormous price.

Another comedy coming from the Broadway stage to chautauqua was the production of *The Rivals*. A 1919 Evening Star program brochure described this play in the following manner:

> Captain Absolute is in love with Lydia Languish, a sentimental young girl. The Captain, being quite wealthy, finds that his gold is a hinderance to his love making. Lydia has told her aunt, Mrs. Malaprop, that she will not marry a man of riches. Capt. Absolute on hearing this, assumes an "alias" and woos Lydia under the name of "Beverly" who is suppose to be a poor ensign. Under these circumstances he easily wins Lydia's heart.
>
> One screams with delight over the love affairs of Mrs. Malaprop and Sir Lucius O'Trigger, which is complicated by the mischievous maid, Lucy. One of the hearts broken almost, by this playful intrigue of the Captain's is his old friend, Bob Acres, an awkward country boy, who is in love with Lydia.

Among the other comedies that made their way from Broadway to chautauqua between the years of 1916 and 1920 were *Peg O' My Heart*, *Broadway Jones*, *The Perplexed Husband*, *Romancers*, *The Pleasure Seekers*, and *A Pair of Sixes*. Despite the limitations encountered during the war in producing plays for chautauqua audiences, it was clear to the bureaus that there was a demand for drama, especially comedy, on the circuit. As transportation restrictions eased after the war, an increasing number of major Broadway productions appeared on the chautauqua program. By the mid-1920s, theatrical productions were the single most desirable feature on the circuit chautauqua program.

THE READERS AS THE QUEEN OF THE DRAMATIC ARTS

The dramatic art form that was most frequently featured on the chautauqua program between 1917 and 1920 was the dramatic reader. Beginning as a novice reader on the Redpath circuit before 1917, Katherine Ridgeway became the front-cover headline attraction on the 1917, 1918, and 1919 Redpath-Vawter Circuit Chautauqua program brochures. At this point in her career, she was described by one Redpath manager as being at "the pinnacle of her profession and ... acknowledged by all to be America's greatest reader." Ridgeway's most popular circuit readings were cuttings from the *Christmas Morning at Home* and *Colored Lochimnvar*.

Ridgeway, as the "Queen of the Chautauqua Platform," caused some controversy and gained some notoriety on the circuits by beginning or ending her program with a cutting from *Not Understood*. She used the piece as a way to protest the war in Europe and raised the ire of many chautauqua audiences. The segment that she used most often from *Not Understood* was as follows:

> Oh, God, that men could see a little clearer,
> Or judge less harshly where they cannot see—
> Oh, God, that nations would draw a little nearer
> One another. They'd be nearer Thee—
> And Understood.

A vast number of readers appeared on circuit chautauqua programs during the years in which the country was involved in World War I. Jeannette Kling, as did Gay MacLaren, read segments from *The Regeneration* to countless chautauqua audiences. Actor William Sterling Battis, known as the "Dickens Man," read various Dickens pieces to circuit audiences. Promoted as being a "master interpreter," V. S. Watkins presented one-man plays on the Redpath-Horner circuit. According to a 1918 Redpath brochure, he impersonated "each character with remarkable realism. No difficulty [was] experienced in distinguishing between the different characters." Before joining the Redpath-Horner circuit chautauqua, Watkins had been a drama critic for *The New Dramatic Mirror*. As a member of the Redpath-Horner circuit, he not only read before circuit audiences but also was part of the coaching staff which trained readers and actors. Before circuit audiences, Watkins presented various selections from the current Broadway comedies, including *Bought and Paid For*, *The Fortune Hunter*, *Bambi*, *Efficiency*, and *Rip Van Winkle*.

Everett Edward Kemp, known to circuit audiences as "The Man with the Million Dollar Laugh," was promoted as being able to make his audience "forget where it is and go with him on long and wonderful trips through the lands of the book he is interpreting." Kemp had joined the Redpath Chautauqua bureau around 1910 and was immensely popular with chautauqua audiences by the time of the war. His main circuit reading was a selection from Harold Bell Wright's *That Printer of Udells* which was usually followed by a cutting from an original Kemp piece called *The Man with the Bone-Colored Whiskers*. Kemp had originally developed and performed in *Whiskers*, a vaudeville skit involving a "fat man, a thin man, and a fall." After chautauqua folded, Kemp became involved in radio broadcasting and later television work.

Elias Day started working for the Redpath Chautauqua Bureau in 1908 as sort of a jack-of-all-trades in the area of the performance arts. He was the production manager of the *Cambridge Players* for a short while in the 1910. He intermittently assisted band leaders and play producers in staging and editing their programs. In addition, Day spent hours each summer coaching young men and women in the art of reading as part of his job as a coordinator of the youth activities. As a reader, he was best known for his renditions from Poe's *The Raven*, a self-created monologue called "Colonel Fayerweather of Frankfort, Kentucky, suh," and *Cohen on the Telephone*, taken from a popular Broadway monologue.

The president of the School of Speech Arts in New York City, Henry G. Hawn, performed before many circuit audiences. Noting his academic and professional training, a 1918 Redpath brochure suggested that this background enabled "him to fully grasp the ideas of the author in his literary interpretations." His reading was from *The Soul of Things*. Another academic who appeared before circuit chautauqua audiences was Cotton Noe, the head of the Department of Education at the University of Kentucky. Reading frequently from the selections of Mark Twain, he was billed as the "Mark Twain of Kentucky" in White-Myers circuit publicity.

The many selections taken from fashionable Broadway productions by the circuit readers indicate several things. First, chautauqua audiences wanted exposure to up-to-date drama and demanded that the bureau provide it. Second, although the bureaus were frequently limited in offering drama productions because of travel restraints, they accommodated the desire for such productions through the selections performed by the reader. Chautauqua reader Edwin Whitney, for example, was advertised in a 1918 Ellison-White program brochure as being "a whole play company at once" in his performance of the play *Turn to the Right*. The vast majority of the circuit readers during the war years took their circuit readings from Broadway plays.

IMPERSONATORS SOUND OFF

Although the art of impersonation had always been aligned with reading on the chautauqua program, after 1917 it became quite clearly more ostentatious and distinct from reading performances. Impersonators merged their character portrayals with the creation of "sounds" and were frequently accompanied by music, hand bells, and chalk talks. This entertainment feature was usually advertised in such a manner as to appeal to both adults and children. And in an attempt to entice youngsters to these features more directly, a greater number of children, especially young girls, appeared as impersonators on the chautauqua program. Edna Francis Thomas began her career in 1918 at the age of 12 as an impersonator on the Midland Chautauqua program. She impersonated "different sounds" and was accompanied by Mr. Poluhni's "organ chimes, swiss hand bells, musical glasses, etc."

The Alice Schroder Company, which featured Alice Schroder accompanied by her mother on the piano, was a major attraction on circuit chautauqua programs. Schroder began her association with chautauqua at the age of 11 in 1917 as an impersonator and a "magnificent whistler." Her performance, according to a 1917 brochure, was said to be of interest to "grownups and children alike ... She instantly wins the attention of her audiences, and holds their undivided interest until the end." Elsie Mae Gordon, another well-received young impersonator on the circuit, revealed the secret of how to be a successful imitator in a 1918 chautauqua pamphlet as follows: "Just by studying life with open eyes and open heart, then telling it all simply and naturally."

Not all of the impersonators who appeared on the circuit program between 1917 and 1919 were young females accompanied by their mothers or some other adult (usually a relative). Tom Corwin was highlighted time and time again in the Standard Chautauqua advertising. He was described as having the ability to imitate just about any imaginable sound. As a 1918 Standard Chautauqua brochure noted:

> He imitates the sawmill, turning lathe, hub and spoke factory, drinking from a quart bottle, and imitates a bunch of half dozen

dogs fighting. Still funnier is his imitation of John at Grandpa's on the Fourth of July, rocking the baby to sleep, graduating from College, and the funniest of all will be the imitation of the railroad and Ohio River steamer whistles, man and boy running hogs out of the cornfield, the landing of the side wheel steamer, and the taking of the cow and the calf ashore.

Impersonator Jessie Rae Taylor provided various ethnic and character sketches before hundreds of chautauqua audiences. Her performance was aimed at entertaining those in attendance, as was suggested in a 1918 brochure:

> She never attempts to show you what she can do—on the contrary, her entire effort is always toward entertaining you—making you forget the sordid realities of every day life.
>
> One moment she is before you as "Grandma" a lovable body, in the next as an adorable child with bright, sunny curls, telling you of her escape in a high clear treble; then as "Grandpa" the genial old philosopher and story teller, with trembling limbs and wrinkled sallow skin, or as "Uncle Zebe" the faithful old ante-bellium [sic] negro, with a fund of quaint anecdotes.

Some of the more notable impersonators who had joined circuit chautauqua before 1917 made their acts more in keeping with the patriotic spirit of the times. Beginning in 1917, for example, John B. Ratto was featured as providing a "patriotic review" of the "great world notables, past and present" that included George Washington, Abraham Lincoln, and President Woodrow Wilson. Impersonator Halwood Manlove was described as "an educator" who instructed audiences about the Allied war leadership through the use of "make-up" and "appropriate stories."

The Junior Chautauqua

THE PAGEANT AND PATRIOTISM

As with other aspects of the circuit chautauqua program, the youth programs focused on the importance of being patriotic and the self-sacrifice that was needed to end the war. The youth pageant was the most customary means of instilling the importance of being patriotic among the young involved with chautauqua. Typical of how the circuit bureaus attempted to inspire youngsters (and their parents) to be patriotic was the way in which the Lincoln Chautauqua handled its 1918 production of *Columbia's Awakening*. After rehearsing all day under the direction of the bureau's youth director, those children selected for inclusion in the play presented it as the opening number of the chautauqua. The bureau, of course, made sure that almost any child wishing to participate in the production got some part in it.

A 1918 Lincoln brochure explained the patriotic significance of the play:

> There never has been greater need for concerted effort along patriotic lines than now. We must impress upon the people and particularly the boys and girls, the significance of these times in which they are living and their opportunity for service. This play was written for the exclusive use of Lincoln Chautauquas and has a vital message for all true Americans. We consider it one of the especially strong patriotic features of the program and urge that it be given your fullest co-operation....
>
> The Youth's Chautauqua program has been built with the idea of attaining the highest possible efficiency along the lines of patriotic endeavor.

Another youth pageant production frequently presented from the chautauqua platform was *America Yesterday and Today*. In circuit promotion, the play was described as being "symbolic of live issues which stand for the best in history, in patriotism and in real community building." The *Liberty Torch* and *The Spirit of 1776* were patriotic youth pageants that were frequently presented on 1918 and 1919 chautauqua programs. Both plays stressed the historical importance of patriotism to the well-being of American social and political institutions. Occasionally, musical numbers were presented on the youth programs in conjunction with the presentation of the pageants. For example, the "American Girls Americanism" accompanied the presentation of the *Liberty Torch*, which was part of the 1918 Redpath-Vawter Junior Chautauqua.

"AGGIE AND SCI"

A promotional statement issued by the Midland Chautauqua in 1917 and again in 1918, promoted a pair of puppets named "Aggie" and "Sci." Through the antics of "Aggie" and "Sci," children were told why it was necessary for them to sacrifice to feed "all the little children and

their fathers and mothers in Belgium, France and starving Armenia."
The significance of this youth program was explained as follows:

> JOLLY GOOD FUN FOR YOUNG PATRIOTS
> EVERYONE CAN SERVE HIS COUNTRY
> CHILDREN need play even if war is serious business. But my! how much more fun it would be to know that while playing you were serving your country too!...
>
> DRILL AND PLAY... . This year [the Junior Chautauqua] will be better still ... and they will probably play "Soldier" and drill just like "real soldiers." Won't that be fine! And don't forget the Wienie Roast!
>
> "THE GOOD FAIRY, THRIFT." And right here is where you can help our good government in these war times.... Do you know that you can help stop waste? Well, you can. And more than that, by this beautiful, bright, jolly play about the "Good Fairy, Thrift" you can help to show your town folk where they can do something, also.

MAGIC AND WONDERMENT

As had been the case in the years before 1917, magicians and illusionists continued to be favorite features on the circuit chautauqua youth programs. Many of the earlier circuit magicians continued to present essentially the same routines they had offered before the war. Appearing on the youth programs were Reno the Great and Madame Reno with "Mister Duck" in tow, Edwin Brush as the Man of Mystery, the husband and wife team known simply as the Floyds, and Rosani as the Wonder Worker. Eugene Laurant came into the chautauqua limelight during World War I as a magician. Laurant had appeared on various lyceum and vaudeville programs before 1900. Although he had joined the Redpath Chautauqua Bureau early in the 1910s, it was not until the war that he came into his own as a magician on the Redpath circuit.

Laurant won great fame among chautauqua audiences by flying from engagement to engagement when time was of the essence. When not traveling by plane, he came in his decorated van which had painted across the sides "Laurant and His Show of Wonders, Redpath Chautauqua." Laurant presented a wide variety of magical feats before chautauqua audiences. He carried with him a human skull which, once in place upon a table on the stage, appeared to answer questions that he asked of it. In an act called the "Phantom Bride," Laurant seemed to

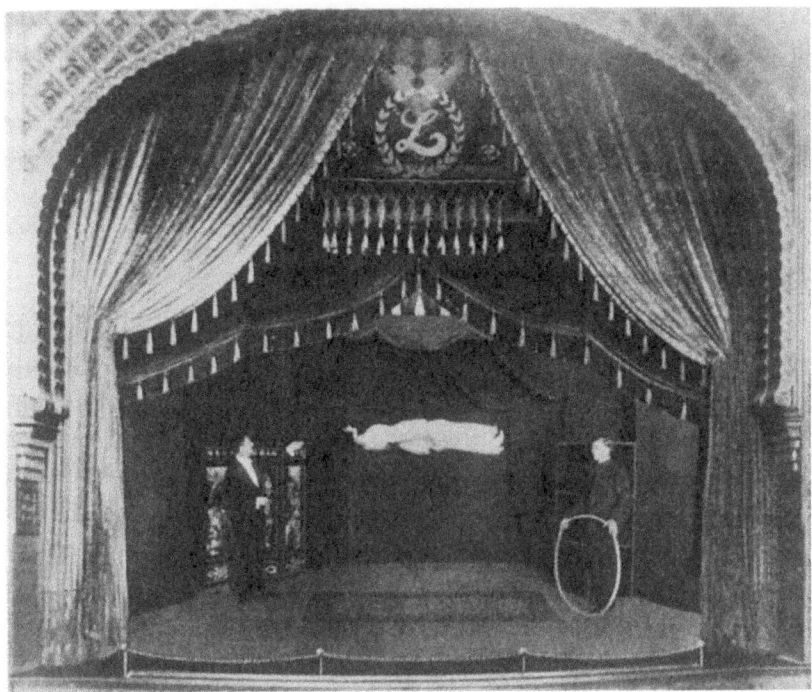

Eugene Laurant was a popular circuit magician who flew from chautauqua engagement to engagement. In his act "The Phantom Bride," he appeared to make the bride float off into thin air. Redpath Collection, University of Iowa.

make his assistant, the bride, float off into the stage curtain. He would have a clown step into a box and make him seemingly disappear and then reappear. Laurant transported much more intricate and massive stage equipment than any of the other magicians who appeared on chautauqua. He also incorporated far more assistants, anywhere from three to five, into his routines than did any other circuit magician.

A trend that was started before the war and was continued throughout the period was to have the various performers and features that made up the regular program advertised in such a way as to motivate not only adults but children to attend. As already noted, programs such as "Songs and Stories of the Redman" by Albert and Martha Gale; Chief Tahan, the "White Savage"; Chief Caupolican tales; stories by Princess Watahwaso and Princess Te Ata; impersonators Edna Thomas and Alice Schroeder; and the production of *Robin Hood* were all promoted in this manner. Children were also enthralled with airplane and scientific demonstrations provided through the circuit chautauqua.

Occasionally, a short moving-picture feature was incorporated into the morning segment of the youth program. But by the time of the war, circuit chautauqua managers were becoming more and more aware that motion pictures would eventually become stiff competition for the circuit programs. As a rule, film features were avoided unless they accompanied a speaker or demonstration.

The Nineteenth Amendment

Early in 1919, the 66th Congress proposed the nineteenth amendment to the Constitution, which would allow women to vote. Between 1919 and 1920, the states debated whether to support the amendment. The circuit bureaus quickly picked up the issue of women's suffrage again and promoted it in such a way as to stir up interest not only in the issue but also in chautauqua programs. Not wanting to offend patrons, however, none of the bureaus took a public stand on the issue.

The Redpath Chautauqua Bureau, as did the other large bureaus, hosted "Women's Days" in conjunction with its 1919 and 1920 programs. Banners promoting various suffrage speakers were frequently hung along Main Street, and a small tent was set up outside the main gate from which suffrage literature could be distributed. In an attempt to liven up a program, the chautauqua superintendent took a straw vote among the audiences as to whether they were "for or against women having the vote."

Some of the suffragettes who appeared on chautauqua before the war reappeared to rally the cause of women's suffrage. Although she was busy with the Hull House settlement in Chicago and international peace politics, Jane Addams appeared on chautauqua several times in 1919 in support of the vote. Jeannette Rankin was the most vocal suffragette on the Redpath-Chicago circuit and spoke about the issue every chance she got. Anna Howard Shaw, a physician and Methodist minister, appeared several times with Addams and Helen Keller on the Redpath circuit.

Debates over the suffrage issue were popular with chautauqua audiences, especially those in the Midwest. In one such debate on the midwestern Redpath chautauqua, Helen Todd, who was associated with Jane Addams' Hull House and was a major factor in the passage of the amendment in California, squared off against Lucy Price, who was said to be a "large factor in defeating the Equal Suffrage Amendment" in Ohio. Audiences were asked to vote for or against the amendment after the debate. Once the Susan B. Anthony amendment was finally ratified in August of 1920, the suffrage issue lost its general appeal as a crowd pleaser. One former suffrage advocate and promoter of the newly created League of Women Voters, Mrs. Percy Pennybacker, did join the 1921 Redpath circuit, however, to discuss "How Should You Use Your Vote, Now That You Have It?" The proposal and eventual passage of the nineteenth amendment in many ways symbolized a gateway into the 1920s. It represented a fundamental shift in American thinking about the role of women in society.

Chautauqua as a Gateway Into the 1920s

Circuit chautauqua programs between 1917 and 1920 reflected an American desire to make "the world safe for democracy" in the face of the German enemy. Many lecturers exposed the evil and cruel nature of the enemy, using lantern slides and moving pictures to highlight their tales. Youth programs educated youngsters (and some parents) about democracy, conservation, and ways in which those less fortunate in the war could be helped. Other program elements such as music and plays were either used to appeal to the patriotic side of circuit audiences or were modified so that there would be no hint of "un-Americanism" in the feature. From the perspective of the circuit manager, the best way to be a loyal American and support the war effort was to purchase a chautauqua ticket.

Although circuit chautauqua presented itself as having an important national mission during the war, the program was also oriented toward entertainment and promised to provide a break from the worries and problems associated with the war. The dramatic readers, foreign musicians, jubilee singers, informative lecturers, impersonators, and operettas were avenues for "relief from the strain." Although noncommittal over women's suffrage, the bureaus provided a platform from which the issue was widely discussed. Chautauqua also brought an awareness to audiences about modern scientific and technological innovations, many of which would profoundly affect their lives for a decade.

Despite chautauqua's balancing of the serious issues and problems with entertainment and relaxation, the impact of the war could not be erased from the American mind. The "war to end all wars" resulted in 130,000 Americans dead, uncollectible debts of about $18 billion, and frightening new international alliances. As the 1920s progressed, Americans wanted to forget the war and foreign entanglements. They wanted to strive for the impossible, to return to the calm days of isolationism that had been left behind, something that President Warren B. Harding would in 1920 call "normalcy."

VI

The Post–World War I Era: From "The Hand at the Nation's Throat" to Comedy

The vast majority of Americans by 1920 no longer supported President Wilson's vision of maintaining post–World War I order and peace through the League of Nations. Wilson had unveiled his League idea as early as 1916 in a draft of the Democratic platform. Basically, the blueprint for the League reflected the president's desire to have a group of nations plan and work together in an effort to secure and enforce world peace. Much of his League plan became an integral part of the 1919 Treaty of Versailles and had been negotiated at the Paris Peace Conference in June of that year. In the United States, the treaty was initially received with mixed reviews but was overall favored. Some thought it not harsh enough, others believed it too harsh, and various groups of German-Americans, Italian-Americans, and other American ethnic groups believed the pact was not suitably beneficial to their homelands. Nonetheless, the general public sentiment toward the treaty throughout most of the summer of 1919 was generally supportive.

Henry Cabot Lodge and the League of Nations

As the summer of 1919 turned into fall, the positive feeling toward the Treaty of Versailles and the League eroded. The constant and highly publicized criticism raised by Senator Henry Cabot Lodge, chairman of the Senate Committee on Foreign Relations, about the treaty raised doubts. Lodge's condemnation of Wilson's peace proposal was based upon the belief that the League provision would undermine American sovereignty and entangle the country in further European matters.

Lodge's position was supported to varying degrees by isolationists such as Albert Beveridge of Indiana, William Borah of Idaho, Hiram Johnson of California, Elihu Root of New York, Robert La Follette of Wisconsin, former president Theodore Roosevelt, and Wilson's former secretary of state, William Jennings Bryan.

To counter the Lodge movement, President Wilson began a trip across the country by rail early in September of 1919 in an attempt to win public support for the treaty and to keep the League of Nations provision entirely intact. While out West, the president was taken ill and had to cancel the remainder of his tour. Once back in Washington, President Wilson suffered a debilitating stroke during the first part of October. While he was recovering, the Senate debated the Treaty of Versailles and attached a series of reservations and restrictions to it. When the treaty was put to a Senate vote on November 19, 1919, Wilson insisted that it should be passed only as originally proposed and ordered Senate Democrats not to vote for it with the reservations. The Senate failed to ratify the treaty. The treaty was put to a Senate vote again in March of 1920, with several additional modifications. Once again it failed to pass.

The card-playing and cigar-chewing Warren G. Harding ran for the presidency in 1920 and defeated Wilson. He was sworn into the office of the president in the spring of 1921. During Harding's campaign he had promised the country that it would return to something he coined as "normalcy." In July of 1922, under the Harding administration, the Congress of the United States unceremoniously passed a joint resolution simply declaring that the war was officially over.

Disarmament and Chautauqua Rhetoric

Despite the highly publicized debate in the United States Senate over the Treaty of Versailles and the League of Nations, the 1919 and 1920 circuit chautauqua programs did not as a rule really get into the particulars of the controversy. Several circuit orators, however, did discuss the broader issues pertaining to disarmament, defense, and preparedness. During the 1919 and 1920 chautauqua seasons, Thomas Brooks Fletcher advocated peacetime universal military service for men from the Redpath platform when there was enough audience interest in the topic. Before the war Fletcher had been promoted as a "community expert" on the circuits, and the titles of his two most well-liked lectures about the subject were the "Tragedies of the Unprepared" and "Martyrdom of Fools." With a little imagination, the titles for both of these lectures could be readily adapted to the discussion of conscription.

Because of the difficulty in predicting how much interest any given chautauqua town might have in the topic of universal military service, Fletcher arrived a day early for his scheduled appearances to determine what interest there might be in this subject. Redpath publicity did not explicitly detail what Fletcher's "Tragedies of the Unprepared" or "Martyrdom of Fools" were about. In fact, there was so much latitude in the promotion of these presentations that if there was enough interest in the issue of universal military service that was what Fletcher discussed; otherwise, the presentations simply focused on community improvement.

Some of the lecturers who spoke from the chautauqua platform about the necessity of arms limitations during the early 1920s had supported Lodge's assault on the Treaty of Versailles. Senator Oscar W. Underwood of Alabama (the author of the first federal income tax bill and the Underwood Tariff Bill), William E. Borah and David Jordan, president of Stanford University, were occasionally featured on chautauqua programs as being the "spokesmen of disarmament."

The most popular speaker about the issue of disarmament on the chautauqua circuit who supported the League of Nations was Private Harold Peat, a Canadian soldier. He had already won recognition as a circuit speaker during 1918 and 1919 with his presentation of "To Hell and Back with a Smile." In 1920, Peat began delivering the "Inexcusable Lie" on the Redpath circuit, which summarized his position on disarmament. He always concluded this speech by telling members of the audience that they needed to support "the idea of Wilson's League of Nations to assure world peace and stability."

Throughout the 1920s, Peat was constantly referred to in chautauqua promotion as the "one man League of Nations" and a "crusader against war." Occasionally, when Peat was scheduled to appear on a program, members of the local American Legion tried to pressure the sponsoring committee to cancel his lecture on the basis that it was "un-American." If the bureau, in turn, was approached with this request, it alerted the local newspaper that "undue pressure" was being placed on the sponsoring committee to cancel a "major chautauqua feature." The publicity that the program received from the American Legion's action, if mentioned in the paper, usually resulted in more interest in the program. In the early 1920s, Peat published a book entitled *Private Peat*, which focused upon his war experiences and appealed to readers to support the League of Nations. Peat also used the chautauqua platform to promote his book, which became a best-seller in the United States and in Canada.

Although several notable figures talked about armament on chautauqua, overall there was little attention directed toward the particular issues that grew out of the League controversy. Circuit chautauqua failed to focus on the particulars for several reasons. Within months after the signing of the armistice on November 11 of 1918, the American people began losing interest in hearing or reading about topics pertaining to the treaty or the League. Chautauqua bureaus found that those elements of the program dealing directly with the war could not draw substantial audiences to the chautauqua tents in the 1919 and 1920 seasons. This trend was also evident in other forms of media. Lillian Gish, for example, recalled that D. W. Griffith's British-subsidized propaganda film, *Hearts of the World*, which premiered in New York City in March of 1918, became less and less of a box office attraction after the armistice. By the end of 1919, there was such a glut of war stories being sent to popular periodicals and so little reader interest in them that publishers began sending out warnings to authors not to submit manuscripts dealing with the war.

Bolshevism in America

Although Americans had tired of thinking about the war, they remained concerned about "foreigners." Foreigners, both within and outside of the country, were frequently viewed in the popular press as posing a threat to American institutions and ambitions. A movement began in the United States during 1919 to rid the United States of the foreign menace, especially those who called themselves Bolsheviks or Communists or were so labeled. The movement began largely as a result of an announcement made at the March 1919 meeting of the International Conference on Communism. During the conference, it was revealed that money was being transferred to New York for the purpose of spreading bolshevism throughout America. The story was picked up by the American press and printed in almost every major newspaper in the country.

Indecision on the part of many Americans concerning the threat of bolshevism was put aside when Eugene Debs, the well-known American-born socialist labor leader, publicly announced his support for the

Bolshevik Revolution. Moreover, in September of 1919, the editors of the *Russian Socialistic Federation*, Leon Trotsky and Nikolai Burkarin, led a group primarily made up of Slavs that met in Chicago and founded the American Communist party. An American-born Communist by the name of John Reed, who was afraid that Communism would fall exclusively into the hands of foreigners, established at this same meeting the Communist Labor party. Its membership consisted primarily of American workers.

The United States economy was affected by the transition from a supply and demand wartime economy and the enormous loans made to Europe. In 1919, the country experienced a rapidly growing inflation rate, with salary increases lagging far behind. Average Americans became more and more frustrated with the postwar economic situation and disillusioned with the government's inability to do anything about it. As a result, thousands of Americans joined the Communist party in 1919 and 1920, and a series of strikes, largely concerning wages, were initiated across the country. The government and big business singled out bolshevism as the cause of unrest within the country.

In January of 1919, the Seattle shipyard strike closed down the city. Seattle's mayor ended the strike and publicly proclaimed that it was the work of the "Bolshevik influence in America." On September 8, the Boston police force walked off the job because of the dismissal of 19 policemen who had joined the American Federation of Labor. Two days later, on September 10, steel workers issued a call to strike on September 22 if higher wages were not forthcoming. Wilson's newly appointed attorney general, A. Mitchell Palmer, publicly denounced the strike as the work of Bolsheviks. In the fall of 1919, under the leadership of John L. Lewis, the United Mine Workers struck for higher wages. The mine owners and operators charged that Moscow, under the direction of Lenin, was financing the strike.

Another major factor in the history of American red scare politics was A. Mitchell Palmer. Immediately after having been appointed attorney general in March of 1919, Palmer began a series of raids on "enemy aliens," with the assistance of the Justice Department's J. Edgar Hoover. The first major raid occurred in November and resulted in the arrest of more than 200 members of the Union of Russian Workers. Acting under Palmer's orders, the majority of these Russians, all reportedly Bolsheviks, were deported that December.

In January of 1920, over 4,000 alleged Communists were arrested in a cross-country raid that involved 33 cities. In April, Palmer revealed that a revolutionary plot was under way to overthrow the government of the United States and would begin on May 1, 1920. When May 1 came, nothing happened. But during the same month, Nicola Sacco and Bartolomeo Vanzetti, both Italian aliens and admitted anarchists, were arrested for robbery and murder. Both were eventually convicted and executed. They were cited by Palmer as examples of the threat all revolutionaries posed to the country.

At about the same point in history when the Treaty of Versailles and the League of Nations were being debated in the Senate, many Americans were afraid of the so-called "foreign menace" and were beginning to think that the country was on the verge of a revolution. Not surprisingly, the focus of the country shifted from the arguments over alliances with Europe and disarmament to persons, places, or movements that threatened the security of America. The unrest that started to occur in 1919 and lasted into the early 1920s was reflected in circuit chautauqua rhetoric.

Chautauqua Rhetoric in the Postwar Era

"HAND AT THE NATION'S THROAT"

The lecture titles included in chautauqua programs of this period reflect a public uneasiness about foreigners both within and outside of the country. Featured on the chautauqua programs were such menacing titles as "America's Tomorrow?" "The Hand at the Nation's Throat," "Lawlessness," "Pending Perils and Problems," "Problems of Peace," "Hour of Democracy," and "The Riddle of the Russian Revolution." A statement made by David Vaughan in his presentation of the "Hand at the Nation's Throat" summarized much of the thinking represented by these speeches: "America's greatest problem [is] large groups of foreigners."

The majority of circuit speeches that dealt with the potential of foreign takeovers of American institutions focused specifically on bolshevism. From the early 1920s Redpath platform, Frank Tolbert presented the following scenario to hundreds of chautauqua audiences: "Communism in Russia is robberism; it tolerates imprisonment, persecution and execution without trial.... There is no government." Dr. Joseph Clare, former pastor of the British-American Church in Petrograd, lectured on "The Riddle of the Russian Revolution" before Redpath audiences. His speech was promoted as an "eye witness" account of the Russian Revolution, including "the hoisting of the red flag of the revolutionists, the nights of terror, the downfall." A lecture by Ralph Dennis, a former United States vice consul in Moscow, was promoted in 1920 Redpath brochures as providing listeners with a choice of "Russia, Or America; Which?"

Congressman Homer C. Boblitt presented a lecture entitled "Bolshevism in Russia and America" on the 1919 and early 1920s Vawter-Redpath circuit. The speech dealt with "causes, aims, and methods of Russian Bolshevism, and their meaning to the United States." Count Ilya Tolstoy, who looked remarkably like his father, Count Leo Tolstoy, appeared on various circuit chautauqua programs denouncing socialism and "the disease of bolshevism." In a 1923 brochure, Tolstoy was promoted in the following manner:

> Count Ilya Tolstoy is well known to Americans through his writings and his famous lectures. His perfect command of the English language; sympathetic understanding of all phases of American life, and his noted facility of expression, enable him to bring his audiences his message in a manner to leave lasting impressions.
>
> Count Tolstoy's story of conditions in Russia, his analysis of Bolshevism, and personal experiences make a lecture thrilling, interesting and educational, as well as enjoyable.

The circuit bureaus even recruited "reformed" socialist Alexander Schwartz to speak out against bolshevism. In a 1923 brochure, the tragic story of Schwartz and his wife was outlined. They had both been socialists when they had left San Francisco to travel to Russia in order to attend the Second Congress of the Third International Conference. Upon arriving in Russia, Alexander Schwartz

> was apparently prepared to overlook the anarchy and wholesale murder because he was assured that the horrors were merely the necessary prelude to the dawn of happier conditions of life than the people of Russia had ever known. It was in these circumstances that this American and his wife entered Russia. They were not there as unsympathetic spies, but as friends. What has happened? The husband has just made his escape from the reign of terror and is returning home to his children after burying his wife in Reval — another tragic victim of long, solitary confinement in a Bolshevik prison, where she has suffered the pangs of hunger.

Schwartz related this and other stories about bolshevism to chautauqua audiences in a lecture entitled "A Tragedy in Popular Government."

TRAVELOGUE AND WORLD INSTABILITY

The majority of travelogue speakers who were featured on circuit programs after the war examined foreign affairs in terms of American economics and trade. In a travelogue about China, one lecturer predicted that the country would soon be "an industrial rival of other nations and a power to be considered in national and international affairs." Homer A. Hulbert, a former adviser to the emperor of Korea and a featured travelogue speaker on the White-Myers program, presented the "Far East Question" to many early 1920s audiences. The lecture centered on "the struggle between nations and between races for dominance of territory and trade" in Asia. Explorer Dr. Gabriel Maguire, promoted in Redpath materials as the "first white man up the Congo after Stanley came out," presented a travelogue called "With an Irishman Through an African Jungle." Although Maguire described his experiences as an explorer, he also commented on the availability of natural resources in Africa and the difficulties that they would pose for that continent once "civilized" nations began to compete for them.

By 1920, Ruth Bryan Owen, daughter of William Jennings Bryan, was an established circuit travelogue lecturer. Her presentation entitled "Modern Arabian Knights" was given on various Redpath-Vawter programs throughout the early 1920s. She was promoted as providing an eye-witness account of the changes and dangerous situations occurring in the Middle East: "when Jerusalem fell; when General Allenby marched on foot at the head of the British forces through the Holy City, Ruth Bryan Owen was there." And another lecturer, known only as W. L. Mellinger, explained to 1920 and 1921 chautauqua audiences why and how Mexico could be a potential threat to American interests. He was quoted as saying that in Mexico, "we know that new regimes were created and overthrown in a day, that her cities and towns were devastated for years and that some of our American boys fell while trying to unravel the triangle."

THE FARM BLOC

The extent to which the fear of bolshevism gripped the country was also evident in the area of farming. As crop prices fell increasingly behind the pace of inflation during 1919 and 1920, there was a renewed interest, primarily in the midwestern states, in revitalizing an earlier farm movement known as the Nonpartisan League. The Nonpartisan League or Farm Bloc, as it was commonly called, had developed out of various farm movements of the late 1800s. It essentially became a national organization that concentrated on establishing state control over utilities, insurance, transportation, and other aspects of industry and business. In 1919, there were about 200,000 members in the League, with Minnesota, Montana, and North and South Dakota making up about half of the total membership and Colorado, Idaho, Iowa, Kansas, Nebraska, Oklahoma, Texas, Wisconsin, and Washington making up the remainder. Most of the "Bloc" states were also the biggest supporters of circuit chautauqua. In fact, the desirability of state-controlled utilities, business, and transportation had been a major underlying theme of many of the early 1900s chautauqua orators such as Bryan, Clark, and La Follette.

As the fear of bolshevism, socialism, and communism spread throughout the country after the war, the Farm Bloc, as was the case with striking urban workers, came to be viewed as a part of a great foreign conspiracy. In 1919, for example, a publication entitled the *Red Flame* that was sponsored by a group of Minnesota businessmen was started with the goal of exposing the Nonpartisan League as being part of a bigger socialistic plot. Another organization by the name of the Independent Voter's Association came into being in 1920 with the express purpose of fighting the agenda of the "socialist" Nonpartisan League. The association distributed thousands of pamphlets which, among other things, charged the League with having direct connections with Lenin.

The increasing momentum of the Farm Bloc, coupled with the claims being raised about its connections with Russia, focused public attention on the issue of organized farming. On the chautauqua circuit, a variety of speakers discussed the issue. Congressman Homer C. Boblitt, who also delivered "Bolshevism in America and Russia" on the circuit, provided his perspective on the topic in a speech called "Is Farming a Business?" In light of his other circuit speech, it was not surprising that Boblitt stressed the importance of the traditional family farm over the "socialistic tendencies that are already destroying farming."

Speaking out in favor of the Nonpartisan League, and frequently on the same program on which Boblitt appeared, was W. E. Daly. Promoted as "A REAL DIRT FARMER WHO TALKS IN PLAIN TERMS OF PRACTICAL THINGS," Daly presented to 1922 and 1923 Redpath audiences his "great dream of the greatest business on earth — farming — being organized and handled as efficiently as any big business." Another presentation called "What's in the Farmer's Mind," by John F. Conner, was promoted as presenting a "balanced perspective" about farming to chautauqua audiences. The speech was described as addressing the following questions: "Is the farmer a profiteer? What is the situation that has brought him uppermost in the headlines of the press? What is the destiny of this big giant, the 'Farm Bureau?' Do you understand the crisis in the farming industry? Do you know 'what's in the farmer's mind?'"

In general, the lectures that dealt with the direction which agriculture should take, as heard from the chautauqua platform during the early 1920s, were generally favorable to organized farming. This was especially true of those speeches dealing with the issues that were presented in the Midwest.

The Response to Unrest

AMERICAN DEMOCRACY

In addressing the complexity of social, economic, and political problems within and outside the country, the answer that chautauqua provided was that Americans needed to renew their faith in the tenets of democracy — that is, American democracy. Basically, this was the theme of Grandville Jones' lecture "Back to the Constitution," which was regularly featured on the early 1920s Redpath circuit. Jones usually closed the speech with the following phrase: "And this is Americanism — just liberty and the love of it; just union and the practice of it; just reverence for God and the confession of it." On the cover of a 1923 Swarthmore Chautauqua brochure, the following list of Harry Foster Burns lectures was presented. In each lecture title, democracy is presented as overcoming some problem:

1. "Democracy Solving the Housing Problem"
2. "Democracy and International Relations: Cooperation vs. Competition"
3. "Democracy Overcoming Industrial Conflict: Human Ends vs. Dividends"

Midwestern Congressman James Bromwell was featured on several 1922 Evening Star Chautauqua programs for his delivery of the

"Renewed America." He was described in a 1922 Evening Star brochure as follows:

> He is a voice crying aloud in eloquent terms for the regeneration of our beloved America, and her salvation from the surging tides of destructive propaganda that threaten her very existence.
>
> One of the ablest orators of the times, a keen student of public affairs, a zealous patriot, and withal a tender and true friend of man, James L. Bromwell is more than a lecturer. He is a vital force for the purification of American life and his words strike electric fire to burn out the germs of death.

"100 PER CENT AMERICAN"

One of the promotional images that was evident in chautauqua advertising between 1919 and 1923 was a scenario that suggested that if the country could somehow make itself "100 per cent American," then the factors that undermined American democracy and traditions could be obliterated. Trying to understand what was meant by "100 per cent American" was like trying to figure out what Harding meant by "normalcy," however. Both statements, taken at face value, were ambiguous, but somehow "Americans" knew what they symbolized. The "pure" American theme was commonly expressed in circuit rhetoric dealing with solutions to postwar problems. The ideal was squarely embodied, according to circuit publicity, in the former Colorado governor George A. Carlson. He was described in Redpath brochures as being "a simon-pure, 100 per cent American [who] is opposed to any and all 'isms' which threaten the foundations of democratic institutions."

John Palubicki, a priest, delivered a speech titled "Enthusiasm for American Ideals" before many early 1920s Redpath audiences. A statement advertising his lecture noted that it was "a thoroughly patriotic lecture — an argument and plea for one hundred per cent Americanism. The message embodies [sic] in this great lecture seldom fails to cause a rift in the clouds, and a golden ray of enthusiasm sweeps the troubled hearts, fresh and strong resolutions are vowed, that no matter what sacrifices are to be made, it is all for America." In a similar manner Congressman J. Adam Bede, who was now associated with the Ellison-White circuit, argued in his lecture called "Americanism" that "purer patriotism" was necessary for the "very survival" of the United States."

Another perspective presented from the circuit platform was that to protect American institutions, it was necessary to share democratic ideals with other countries and to provide economic and political assistance in some instances. This was the fundamental theme expressed in two popular early 1920s chautauqua speeches, "America's World Leadership" by Charles H. Brough and Robert S. MacGown's "The Individual and Society." The underlying assumption in both presentations was that by bringing about social and economic stability in other parts of the world, America protected its own self-interests. James E. Bromwell also echoed this sentiment in one of his many chautauqua lectures when he told Redpath audiences that they needed to "renew their faith in America and share it with the rest of humanity."

Edward Trefz, an assistant food administrator under Herbert Hoover during World War I, appeared periodically on chautauqua from 1919 into 1923. His presentations usually made the point that it was necessary for Americans to "feed the needy of the world" because this action would "thwart further challenges to democracy." A former adviser to the emperor of Korea explained to Redpath audiences why he thought it necessary for the United States to get involved in "the Chinese Eastern Railway situation, the Siberian situation and China, Japan and Korea." The reason he offered was that these countries would be of critical importance to "world politics and commerce and democracy." The lecturers who viewed American stability in global terms reflected some of what Wilson had been trying to achieve with the League of Nations.

Financial Troubles Begin

AMUSEMENT TAX

Although chautauqua programs fared well between 1917 and 1919, the war had a negative impact on circuit operations which became more evident as the 1920s progressed. The amusement tax, or "war tax" as it had been referred to during the war, continued to be applied to all season and single-admission chautauqua tickets despite that fact that the armistice had been signed. Frustrated by this situation, the owners and operators of the seven leading chautauqua bureaus met with President Harding (himself a former circuit sponsor and lecturer) in the spring of 1921 to protest the tax. The president was sympathetic to their plight but could not promise an exemption from the tax for chautauqua.

In 1922, however, largely through the lobbying efforts of President Harding, assisted by the International Chautauqua and Lyceum Association, the tax was finally reinterpreted in such a way as to apply only to season tickets. Single admissions were exempted completely from the tax. President Harding followed up this action with a letter dated December 6, 1922, to Dr. Paul N. Pearson, president of the International Lyceum and Chautauqua Association, assuring all concerned of how important chautauqua was to the country:

> It has been to me a personal satisfaction, as well as an intellectual and spiritual opportunity, to be numbered among the lecturers who have carried the message of Chautauqua throughout the country. Indeed one may with much confidence say that this splendid educational movement has found its greatest intellectual beneficiaries among those who ... have known the eagerness with which the people, to the number of many millions annually, seek illumination of public questions and the broadening of community vision....
>
> Chautauqua has served to reveal the individual American community to itself at its best. It has been a voluntary, inspirational service in which men and women have given the best they have in them for the sake of the social interest. The confidence of intellect and authority which you have brought together here suggests a certain parallel to the intellectual movements in which the universities of Europe were founded.... It justifies, indeed, expression of the wish that this beginning might point the way toward a new advance into the light of understanding by which alone we may safely lay our course in such times as those in which we live.

The amusement tax affected chautauqua in several other ways in the post–World War I era. When the tax had first been applied to chautauqua ticket sales in 1917, local sponsoring committees raised questions about the educational and cultural nature of chautauqua when it was subject to an amusement tax. Circuit managers countered by explaining to sponsors that it was not an amusement tax but a "war tax" and was required to support the war effort. Once the war ended and an "amusement tax" was still being applied to chautauqua tickets, backers revived their earlier doubts about the value of circuit chautauqua.

The growing popularity of tent chautauqua during the war years encouraged the many small fly-by-night medicine shows, circuses, and carnivals to work the term *chautauqua* into their name. The word *chautauqua* lent a flavor of respectability to the small traveling show. These traveling shows did not need a contractual agreement with a community as did chautauqua. Because small traveling "chautauquas" did not require a contract, potential sponsors, when approached about chautauqua, questioned why they had to provide a guarantee when other "chautauquas" and amusements did not demand it. Moreover, the situation that all circuit chautauqua bureaus faced after the war was the competition from the many new and available forms of popular entertainment. In order to compete, the bureaus had to promote their programs largely on the basis of providing enjoyment and fun. But because of this promotional direction, the circuit bureaus had greater difficulty trying to convince potential sponsors that chautauqua was "educational" and not like the carnival or medicine show.

Sensitive to these criticisms and doubts about circuit chautauqua, Keith Vawter in an open letter published in 1921 Redpath brochures tried to diminish the importance of the medicine show and carnival by explaining why chautauqua was so much better than either. He wrote, "The old time medicine show is gone — the worst of the street carnivals are nearly gone ... because the Chautauqua has led the people away from such coarse horse-play." Vawter's view was far from the reality of what was actually happening. The small traveling shows did cut into the bookings of the larger circuit chautauqua bureaus.

POSTWAR INFLATION

Postwar inflation not only caused alarm in the steel, mining, and shipping industries but also in bureaus operating chautauquas. Throughout the 1920s, the circuit bureaus constantly faced spiraling personnel, travel, and hotel costs. This problem was compounded for chautauqua owners. They could not practically increase the contractual guarantee in view of the disapproval being raised at the local level about the existing guarantee. In order to meet expenses, the owners and operators of chautauqua circuits tried a number of ways of dealing with the situation. Several owners, for example, tried to operate their chautauqua company as a not-for-profit corporation to avoid paying the amusement tax placed on ticket sales.

The incorporation scheme tried by the Ellison-White Chautauqua Bureau provides an example of how this was supposed to have worked. The owners of the Ellison-White Bureau tried to place the ownership of the bureau in the hands of local sponsoring committees on a not-for-profit basis. The idea behind this plan was that local committees could create a better circuit by reinvesting profits back into the corporation. In exchange for the Ellison-White name and operation, the corporation would purchase the bureau's existing equipment and contract agreements. Of the twenty or more sponsoring committees approached about this arrangement, not one was interested.

"Straight from Broadway"

Many important social, economic, and political postwar issues were addressed on the circuit chautauqua platform. But by 1922, circuit chautauqua programs were dominated by plays, not oratory. The primary purpose of early 1920s circuit chautauqua, as stated time and time again in advertising materials, was to provide its audience entertainment, gaiety, and fun. This aim was primarily accomplished by making available to its audience "straight from Broadway" comedies and slapstick plays. What the bureaus faced by 1922 was similar in circumstances to what the lyceum bureaus had experienced in the late 1860s after the Civil War. After the immediate post–World War I issues had been ironed out, Americans simply wanted to forget the war and any problems associated with it. Not only circuit chautauqua, but also theatre, vaudeville, and the movie industry turned their attention toward comedy and slapstick.

The motives for attending circuit chautauqua programs centered upon the needs to be entertained, interact with friends, and forget the ordinary worries of everyday living. An Evening Star Chautauqua brochure of the early 1920s, for example, promised that its program would evoke "clean, wholesome, laughter — provoking entertainment" and "make you forget your problems." A 1922 Redpath-Vawter advertising brochure specifically noted these reasons for attending the program:

REASONS WHY I am going to take my car and drive over to chautauqua this summer

Because

I am sick of war, strikes and labor unrest. I want to hear, to discuss, to decide how to act....

I want to get out of the rut. As in running my car, so in running my life, I do not want to get stuck on the road because of "low clearance." I want to take in the relaxation that refresh and refine and inspire me to fuller speed ahead

Because
> I want the sociability of it all — old neighbors to chat with — new friends to shake hands with — human things of human interest, that happen in human's lives to talk about.

That drama was the dominant means of entertainment on the chautauqua circuit throughout the 1920s can be explained by any number of reasons. During the war, the connection between chautauqua audiences and Broadway had been maintained predominately through opera. Opera companies traveled from New York and toured with the chautauqua companies. Audiences wanted something new after the war, especially something that would allow them to see the "stars" who appeared on the chic film features. Many of those who acted in the films of that day worked back and forth between theatre, film and, to a lesser extent, opera.

Circuit managers, already fearing that film would lure audiences away from the chautauqua tent, were reluctant to provide movies as part of their regular program. Theater was a safe way to bring the stars of the cinema to chautauqua without drawing further attention to the film media. By contrast, hundreds of lyceum theaters across the nation, beginning in the 1920s, were featuring various silent films on their Saturday and Sunday programs.

The easing of travel restrictions after the war also made it more feasible for the chautauqua bureaus to transport large theatrical companies as they had done before 1917. Moreover, the competition that the moving picture industry was posing to large urban theatre and opera production companies made it possible for the chautauqua bureaus to place well-known dramatic companies under contract. In fact, the amounts paid for these companies were in many instances lower than what the bureaus had paid for comparable companies before the war.

By 1922 the cost of a ticket in New York City to attend a movie production by a big-named producer like D. W. Griffith or Mack Sennett ran anywhere from $2 to $3, approximately the same amount required to attend a well-known dramatic or operatic production. For about the same sum, on the other hand, a person could purchase a week-long pass to a chautauqua program, enabling him or her to see anywhere from 4 to 5 Broadway productions and other program features. The price of individual chautauqua tickets to Broadway productions usually ranged anywhere from 75 cents to a dollar. Chautauqua promotional materials always reminded readers that they were "getting Broadway drama [and opera]" at a bargain price: "Imagine, Broadway right here on Main Street and tickets at ridiculously low prices."

WILLIAM KEIGHLEY AND COMEDY

William Keighley, the Broadway producer who was hired by the Redpath bureau in 1912 to direct its circuit plays, turned out a number of well-known plays for the Redpath bureau into the mid-1920s. His "chautauqua" productions included, among others, *Abraham Lincoln*, *Smilin' Through*, *Nothing but the Truth*, *So This Is London*, *Romeo and Juliet*, and *It Pays to Advertise*. With the exception of *Abraham Lincoln* and several other plays he directed, the vast majority of Keighley's work for the Redpath Bureau involved comedies. The Keighley-directed *Nothing but the Truth* performed by the Broadway Players, for example, was described in a 1920 Redpath brochure as involving "a bet of $10,000, a twenty-four hour truthteller, and some of the funniest situation comedies ever contrived."

The most popular Keighley-produced comedy on the early 1920s circuits was Winchell Smith and John Hazard's play *Turn to the Right*. The play had enjoyed a successful Broadway run since 1916 before appearing on the Redpath circuit in 1922. Initially, this play had been introduced to circuit audiences in 1918 as a reading by Ellison-White's Edwin Whitney, who portrayed all of the characters in the play. The play basically traces the plight of a "country bumpkin" who raises enough money selling jam in the "big city" to pay off the note on his "poor old" mother's cottage. The country bumpkin is assisted by two ex-convicts who foil the attempt of a "rapacious money-lending" deacon to steal his "hard earned money." In the end, each of the ex-convicts finds a "good country woman" who "makes an honest man" out of him.

The "country bumpkin" in the Redpath production of *Turn to the Right* was played by Canadian-born actor Eugene Lockhart. Lockhart acted various roles in other Keighley-Redpath productions, including *It Pays to Advertise*, *Nothing but the Truth*, *Peg o' My Heart*, *Smilin' Through*, and *Applesauce*. In 1923, Keighley also produced the *Meanest Man in the World* for the Redpath circuit, with the popular Redpath illusionist Halwood Manlove in the lead role.

There were many additional Redpath "comedy hits" taken "straight from Broadway" to the chautauqua stage. George Cohan's *Broadway Jones*, which was performed on the 1923 Redpath circuit, was described in a promotional brochure as involving "spending so much money on Broadway everybody called you 'Broadway' Jones. Going broke on Broadway. Marrying a woman twice your age — and homely as blue Monday." The play *A Pair of Sixes* was featured on the Redpath-Vawter circuits. The plot of *Sixes* was said to evolve around "two equal partners in a pill making venture. The theme runs along smoothly enough until a dispute arises as to what has given the product its wide popularity. One claims it is the color, the other maintains it is the chemical contents. A row results. And then the fun begins."

The *Witching Hour*, introduced to Redpath-Vawter audiences beginning in 1923, probed the uses and abuses of mental telepathy and involved "two pretty love stories, and a hint of a third." At the conclusion of the play, those present were asked by the producer to think about the "possible dangers and misuses" of mental telepathy. The Redpath-Horner chautauqua circuit that operated out of Kansas City, Missouri, featured *The Elixir of Youth* on its program that same year. The play was advertised as having "witty lines, ludicrous situations, funny characters" which traced "the discovery of a substance supposed to transform old age into youth." Other fashionable comedies that made it to the Redpath circuit in the 1920s included *The Bubble*, *The Temporary Husband*, and *Six Cylinder Love*.

The Redpath bureau generally set the pace for introducing Broadway drama and comedy to circuit audiences. There were, however, some exceptions. The J. Hartley Manners' play *Peg o'My Heart*, which had opened on Broadway in 1912, was first introduced to the circuit by the White-Myers Chautauqua Bureau in 1920. The comedy was promoted by the White-Myers bureau as having something for everybody: "It so thoroughly pleases everyone who sees it, men as much as women, children as much as grown people [and] it has not yet been shown in the pictures." Another then current Broadway drama with which the White bureau, this time through its western branch controlled by Roy J. Ellison, acquainted circuit audiences was a comedy called *Cappy Ricks*. The Oscar-winning film actor Dean Jagger began his professional training under the direction of Elias Day, who produced this play for the Ellison-White Bureau. When the play toured the circuit, Jagger accompanied it working as a stagehand and, if need be, as an extra.

SERIOUS PLAYS

All of the circuit chautauqua programs after 1920 were unquestionably dominated by dramatic comedies. Despite this drive toward the laughable, there were several chautauqua productions that can safely be classified as serious or historical drama. *Uncle Tom's Cabin*, from its first appearance on the circuit in 1904 to its last in 1929, was always a well-received play. After World War I, however, a major change did take place in terms of who portrayed the slaves in the play. Prior to the war and even until the armistice, dramatic roles calling for blacks were generally played by either black thespians or jubilee singers who doubled as actors. In the 1920s, such roles were depicted mainly by Caucasian actors in grease paint.

The reason that this change occurred was largely to accommodate the players of the New York theatrical companies. More often than not, the minor players belonging to a dramatic company were Caucasian and were paid on a per performance basis. In order to entice well-known road companies to tour with chautauqua, the bureaus had to make sure that their actors and actresses worked. So when lesser-known plays or old dramatic standbys like *Uncle Tom's Cabin* appeared on the program, the roles were played by the members of the larger companies. This meant that Caucasians had to play roles in grease paint when the situation warranted it.

Whereas Harriet Beecher Stowe's *Uncle Tom's Cabin* examined the issue of slavery in relationship to the events leading up to the Civil War, John Drinkwater's *Abraham Lincoln* presented the dilemmas faced by President Lincoln in trying to bring a close to the war. Keighley directed this play first for Broadway in 1919 and then brought the production to the Redpath circuit in 1922. Another serious play that was popular on the early 1920s circuits was *The Shepherd of the Hills,* based upon Harold Bell Wright's book by the same name. The play was the feature attraction on the Standard Chautauqua System program in 1922.

In 1922, the White-Myers Chautauqua Bureau introduced the book *Polly of the Circus* to its circuit audiences in the form of a play. The play was advertised as pitting the "morality or stupidity" of "narrow-mindedness" against the power of "true love" in the following manner:

> POLLY, an equestrienne of tender years, is injured when her horse falls in the circus arena. She is carried unconscious into a parsonage.... The parson undertakes to care for the little girl until she is recovered sufficiently to resume her vocation. But Cupid plays an immense part. The girl wins her way into the parson's heart, falling deeply in love with him herself.
>
> NARROW-MINDED members of his congregation criticize the minister severely for having Polly in his bachelor home — and finally they drive her away, her heart bleeding. But when the circus strikes the village again, the minister claims Polly for his wife, never again to let her go.

The importance of having drama on the chautauqua program can be assessed from several vantage points. Chautauqua "brought the best of Broadway" to its audiences by making it accessible and affordable. These audiences responded well to drama, as then Broadway actress Louise Tredwell observed in the October 23, 1923, issue of the *New York Times*: "[The circuit chautauqua audience] does not drop in ... because it is the play to see — and criticize; it comes early, often before the actors, to see the one play, in all probability, that it will see during the entire year, and it comes to enjoy it." Circuit chautauqua productions prepared many actors, actresses, directors, and others for later careers in radio, film, professional drama, and television.

Chautauqua directors were required to work under adverse conditions, and in doing so, they developed versatile directing skills that would later assist them in the movie-making industry. They also learned how to make actors and actresses out of musicians and tent crew members, how to use grease paint in transforming the college-boy musical company into a jubilee group and how to adapt and edit scripts to accommodate a wide variety of American audiences. Various staging techniques, lighting, and equipment, in addition to novel and innovative approaches to play writing and acting, were all undertaken on the chautauqua stage.

Fading from Center Stage: Opera, Readers, Impersonators, and Magicians

OPERA

As drama became fashionable on the chautauqua circuit, the full-length opera productions that had once been a regular part of the program were pushed aside. Beyond the reasons already provided as to why this occurred, it should be also noted that most of opera stars featured on chautauqua had ties with Europe, and once the war had ended, many of them returned home or were engaged in European tours. These artists included the Swedish-born Julia Claussen of Sweden's Royal Opera, Carmen Pascova, Mischa Lhevinne, Estelle Gray, and C. Pol Plancon.

The opera that was incorporated into the circuit program after 1920 was usually presented in the form of operettas or short excerpts, taken from current New York opera productions. Condensed versions of longer operas might last anywhere from 20 to 40 minutes on the circuit program and sometimes were used as "fillers" between main features. The Ferguson Light Opera Company, for example, was promoted as performing passages from such operas as the *Mikado, Maytime, Floradora, Princess Pat, Robin Hood,* and *Martha* between "the big attractions" on the Standard Chautauqua program. The Neapolitan Grand Opera Company was advertised in a 1924 Redpath-Horner circuit brochure as executing "short pieces from grand opera" between program changes.

Three major operettas that were frequently produced on the chautauqua circuit during the early 1920s were the *Mikado*, the *Mascot*, and especially *Robin Hood*. The *Mikado* was a popular feature on a variety of chautauqua programs both during and after the war. The *Mascot* was presented exclusively on the White-Myers programs, and *Robin Hood*, written by Arthur Pryor, was a favorite on the Redpath circuits. The Keighley-directed version of Pryor's *Robin Hood*, as it appeared on the Redpath program in 1922, was advertised as appealing to a variety of ages and interests:

> You older people — if your children do not know "Robin Hood," if they haven't seen the genial Tuck and the strutting Sheriff, and thrilled as Maid Marian fled to Robin's arms in green boughed Sherwood — you are depriving them as much of their happiness as if you deprived them of Tom Sawyer. And you are losing as much yourself, if you fail to renew your own youth again at Robin Hood's everlasting fountain of springtime and loyalty and good fellowship!

All three of these operettas had been taken from popular late nineteenth-century Broadway productions bearing the same name, with the *Mikado* experiencing a revival in the early 1920s. Each of these musicals had by 1923 served as the basic plot for one or more silent films. *Robin Hood*, for example, had been transformed from an opera into a "short" as early as 1912 by Eclair Production Company and then again released under the United Artists label in 1922, starring Douglas Fairbanks. By featuring one of more of these three particular operettas on their programs, the circuit bureaus were subtly attempting to compete with the growing interest in film.

READERS

The dramatic reader feature, like opera, also lost its former central prominence on the circuit program. Many of the notable dramatic readers such as Everett Edward Kemp, Gay MacLaren, Edna Means, and Katherine Ridgeway appeared on chautauqua into the 1920s, but usually with much less regularity and allotted performance time then had once been the case. On the whole, readers were no longer main feature attractions. And as each year of the 1920s passed, fewer and fewer readers were included on the program. In 1921, the Redpath-Vawter bureau, for example, featured Bertha Kuntz Baker as "America's greatest interpretive reader" and Fern Cashford's twenty-minute performance of *Humoresque* on the same program. By the following year, neither Baker nor Cashford appeared on the Redpath program. After 1925, the dramatic reader as a chautauqua feature was all but nonexistent on the circuit program. Having been displaced in chautauqua, Kemp went into radio work, MacLaren married Redpath band-leader Al Bachman and continued her work as a reader by performing before permanent chautauqua groups, and Means and Ridgeway became instructors in the dramatic arts.

As had been the case with several earlier readers, some artists read from their own writings and published works. The major difference, however, between the author-reader who appeared on the program during the 1920s and those previously featured was in the contract arrangement. The earlier readers such as Opie Read, Bill Nye, and Strickland Gillilan signed a season-long contract with the bureau which, among other things, detailed how many readings were to be given, where, and when. The literary artists who read before chautauqua audiences after 1920 had only a day-by-day agreement with the bureau. As in the case of other performers, this was a desirable arrangement for the circuit chautauqua bureaus. By this time, the economic situation for the circuits was bleak, and their audiences could lose interest in a reader almost overnight.

Carl Sandburg, after almost a decade of absence from the chautauqua circuit, returned to it in the early 1920s. Featured in Redpath brochure as "America's most distinctive poet," Sandburg was promoted on the basis of reading from his own works. The selections from which he was to read were simply identified as an "American Folktale" and "Stories About Lincoln." Sandburg at this time was probably using chautauqua audiences as a sounding board to gauge his own works. In 1926, he published *Abraham Lincoln: The Prairie Years*, the first of two volumes of a multivolume biography about the president, and in the following year he published an anthology of American folklore called *The American Songbag*.

IMPERSONATORS

There were few impersonators featured on the circuit chautauqua programs after 1920. Generally, less than 5 percent of the entire circuit program was devoted to impersonations by this time, whereas 10 to 15 percent of the earlier program had been devoted to this feature. The impersonator's performance was generally condensed to accommodate drama and was squeezed in during scene changes and intermissions. Impersonators might perform for only 15 to 20 minutes, a marked contrast to the performances an hour or more in length requested of them on the circuit prior to 1920. Ethnic humor continued to be used on the chautauqua circuit. Children as impersonators, on the other hand, had almost entirely lost their appeal for chautauqua audiences.

Throughout the entire 1920s, both Jessie Rae Taylor and Joseph Regnier did the same ethnic impersonations they had done before the war. Joseph Regnier had been first hired by the Ellison-White Chautauqua Bureau in 1915. Throughout the war and during the entire 1920s, he was promoted by the Ellison-White and later by a "Redpath" circuit as portraying "the colored cook, the Irish janitor, the stately old colonel of the South or the Italian fruit vender." In the 1920s, Redpath's Jessie Rae Taylor appeared before chautauqua audiences impersonating the exact same characters—"Uncle Zebe," "Grandpa," and "Grandma"— as she had done for so many years. In fact, after Taylor left chautauqua, she performed at various permanent chautauqua assemblies throughout the United States until retiring in the 1950s.

In 1923, a vaudeville entertainer by the name of Clarence Nash was hired by the Chicago branch of the Redpath Chautauqua Bureau to tour as an impersonator. Among other characterizations, Nash impersonated a duck with a lisp reciting "Mary Had a Little Lamb." Nash appeared on both the adult and youth programs offered by the Redpath circuit. His association with the Redpath circuit lasted until it was sold in 1926. During the late 1920s, Nash pursued a career in radio broadcasting both as a reader and an impersonator. After hearing Nash perform his duck routine over the radio sometime in 1933, Walt Disney offered him a job. He was hired to depict the voice of a duck in the 1934 film *The Orphans' Benefit* that featured Mickey Mouse. The duck tries to get through a recital of "Mary Had a Little Lamb" despite the razzing he gets from the other characters in the cartoon. By the end of 1934, Nash as "Donald Duck" made his official debut in a cartoon called "The Wise Little Hen."

MAGICIANS AND ILLUSIONISTS

The feats of magic and illusion also faded from the chautauqua circuit after the war ended. Those magicians and illusionists who did appear were frequently the old troupers who had been with circuit chautauqua since its beginning. The "Great Illusionist" Alton Packard, who had begun his stage work before 1900 as part of the Redpath Lyceum Bureau, was with chautauqua each season until the movement ended. His friend and colleague, "Master Illusionist" Edwin Brush, who had also appeared every season on chautauqua since its inception in 1904, was considered a "headline attraction" throughout most of the 1920s. In 1923, Redpath director Keighley placed him in the leading role of the play the *Meanest Man in the World*, which continued on the Redpath program for several years.

As late as 1924, Edward Reno was still appearing on the circuit with "Mr. Duck in the stewing pan" and doing the "Famous Dove Trick" that had been introduced to chautauqua 15 years earlier. Professor Floyd and Mrs. Floyd also endured on the chautauqua circuit. Known as "Master Magicians and Illusionists" of "mystery and mirth" throughout the 1920s, they were promoted as providing a "new version of the old trick of 'taking rabbits from your hat.'" The husband and wife team had joined the Redpath circuit in 1909 and continued working in chautauqua until the Great Crash in 1929. After leaving circuit chautauqua, the Floyds booked engagements at permanent chautauqua assemblies. Other "old timers" in the field of magic that continued to be associated with the circuits after the war included the Campbells, and Laurant.

The little attention that circuit chautauqua bureaus gave to opera, readers, impersonators, magicians, and illusionists after World War I was indicative of changing American tastes in the fields of popular education, culture, and entertainment. Several reasons can be identified as to why this transformation was taking place. First and foremost, the people who had attended chautauqua for so many years had grown weary of these types of features. The availability of movies and the increasing number of sideshow carnivals made these once novel attractions appear more conventional. Second, many of the best chautauqua performers in these realms were getting older and had lost touch with what contemporary audiences wanted. Still others had retired or died or had left chautauqua work to pursue careers in film (and later radio). Whatever the reason, American ideas about culture, education and entertainment were changing.

The Musical Variety Continues

Many of the same musical companies that had been with circuit chautauqua before and during the war continued to be circuit features in early 1920s programs. The practice of appealing to a wide variety of musical tastes in programs, and sometimes within a particular feature itself, continued. A 1921 Redpath promotional statement about the Adananc Quartette, for example, noted that the company would delight the "sensitive ears of the critic," as well as the "average attendant of our average concerts." Joe Du Mond's Male Quartette was described in a 1922 Redpath-Vawter brochure as "catering to the best musical tastes.... They sing all manner of songs, some high brow, some low brow, some dignified, some comic, some sentimental.... They are a bully bunch of boosters."

The George Tack Orchestral Troubadours (formerly referred to on the circuit as the Royal Dragoons) were featured on 1921 and 1922 Redpath-Vawter programs as furnishing "musical comedy favorites that make you forget cares and worries in the joy of being alive." The Colonial Players and Singers performed popular and classical numbers on the 1923, 1924, and 1925 Redpath programs. Their selections included such numbers as "Annie Laurie," "Old Kentucky Home," "Comin' Thro' the Rye," "When You and I Were Young, Maggie." The Redpath-Vawter bureau also included the "banjo picking Mitchell Brothers" on its 1923, 1924, and 1925 programs. The Mitchell Brothers were described in one Redpath brochure as hailing from way down Tennessee where possums and banjos grow wild, and where banjo music has its true home."

VOCALISTS

Vocalists were also promoted as satisfying an assortment of musical interests. Included in the 1922 White-Myers program was the Howard Russell Song Review, which was said to be "at once popular, humorous and elevated." The Evening Star program of 1922 featured the Old Home Singers, who were promoted as providing "Music with Soul" that would stir "tender memories of days when the heart beat young." The performance of Jo King and Her Harmony Maids promised, according to a 1922 Redpath-Vawter program brochure, to "fill the cup of pleasure to the brim."

In 1922, the Redpath Bureau toured the S. de Zanco-Smith-Oster Trio on its midwestern circuit. So awe-inspiring was the vocal lead of

Banjo music became more popular on circuit chautauqua programs after World War I. Author's collection.

this company that it was reported that when he sang, "The accompanying symphony orchestra stopped in amazement in the middle of one of Oster's songs and sat mute to the end in musical rapture." Other vocal companies that regularly appeared on the circuit programs after 1920 included the Allpress All Star Company, the Cambridge Singers, French soprano Madame Dora De Phillippes, the Musical Merry Makers, the National Male Quartet, the Plymouth Male Quartet, and the Zedler Symphonic Quintette.

ETHNIC FEATURES

Ethnic groups performing songs and music native to their heritage had always been in demand for chautauqua engagements, as long as the group could perform the number in English. The post–World War I period was no exception. The Ben Davies Welsh Quartet, which had first appeared on the 1914 Redpath-Vawter program and had disbanded because of wartime commitments, rejoined the Redpath circuit in 1923. A story frequently related to chautauqua audiences was how Ben Davies and some of his band members survived the sinking of the *Lusitania* in May of 1915. Davies and his band were often introduced to 1920s circuit audiences as "the Survivor of the *Lusitania* and His Welsh Quartet."

The Gondoliers Musical Program, "straight from Italy," was promoted in a 1921 Redpath-Vawter brochure as presenting Italian music so impressive that "Eyes and Ears alike will be filled with the spirit of romance, of joyous song and the festive gaiety of a moonlight boating party." The Blanchard Costume Singers and Highland Lassies sang native Scottish songs to Redpath-Vawter audiences in 1923 and 1924. Fink's Hussar Militaire and Loseff's Russian Orchestral Quartet appeared in "full military costume" when performing music reflective of their homelands. The Croatian Tamburica Orchestra continued to be featured by the White-Myers Bureau as playing "slavic tunes with native instruments."

Entertainers from the South Seas were in as much demand after the war as they had been before 1919. The promotional appeals used to entice people to the tent to hear South Seas performers were essentially the same ones that had been used before and during the war. South Sea islanders were stereotyped as somehow being mysterious and enchanting. The Philippine Quartette in 1922, for example, was advertised by the Evening Star bureau as delivering the "mystery melodies of the far east done with grace and bewitching charm." By the mid-1920s, chautauqua programs had even gone so far as to include cross-over ethnic musical acts. South Sea native and black jubilee images were merged into one in the performance of the Filipino Jackies. According to 1923 and 1924 Redpath promotion, the group was a "combination musical company of south seas islanders and black jubilees." Redpath publicity for the company promised that "their entertainment will leave a memory of native costume, flashing black eyes, gleaming white teeth, and music — music from their very souls."

During the 1920s, almost every circuit program had at least one or more jubilee group. Not all of these groups were comprised of blacks. Moreover, the trend that had been initiated during the war of having Caucasians made up in grease paint perform as jubilee singers became openly highlighted in circuit advertising. The group called the All College Glee Club and Black Face Minstrels joined the Redpath-Vawter chautauqua in the summer of 1922. The company was advertised on the basis of its versatility: "As a white glee club their singing captivates with its blending of trained voices in melodious rhythm. As black face minstrels they bear off the palm, with gorgeous costume colors effects and snappy minstrel stuff." The following year, 1923, the name of the All College Glee Club and Black Face Minstrels was shortened to the White and Black Minstrels in Redpath advertising.

Despite this trend, there were some all-black jubilee companies that performed before circuit audiences throughout the 1920s. The Jackson Jubilee Singers were the main program attraction of the 1920, 1921, and 1922 Evening Star program. This all-black group was lured away from the Evening Star bureau by the Redpath organization late in 1922. The following year the Jackson Jubilee Singers performed "plantation songs, jubilee chants and negro spirituals ... haunting melodies from Southern cotton fields, weird superstitious hymns and gay pranks" before hundreds of Redpath audiences. The Booker T. Washington Singers, the Tuskegee Jubilees, and the Fisk Players, also companies comprised of all-black entertainers, performed intermittently throughout the 1920s on the chautauqua circuit.

The Diversity of Exhibitions for Community Youth

After 1920, the chautauqua programs that the youngsters could participate in were far more diverse than they had ever been. More features on the adult program were advertised in a manner to attract children and young adults. Promotional materials about plays, operas, and musicals frequently included statements such as "there will be something for everyone" or "people of all ages will enjoy this." In fact, so much of the overall chautauqua program after 1920 was devoted to attracting audiences of all ages that many circuits phased out specific programs for children. Moreover, circuits that did retain the youth programs advertised them in such a way as to almost always promise that there would be something worthwhile for adults who attended.

CHAUTAUQUA TOWN

The youth program, like other features of the program, had to compete with readily available motion picture features, carnivals, circuses, and medicine shows. In an effort to get children and young adults involved in the week-long chautauqua activities, several circuit bureaus came up with the idea of "Chautauqua Town" or "Junior Town." In order to participate in Junior Town, a child had to have a season ticket. Through participating in Junior Town, the children involved presumably learned something about civic affairs and leadership.

A 1922 Redpath-Vawter ad described the Junior Town activity in the following manner:

> The Honorable Mayor SO and SO, ah, ha. See him sit up there and lord it over the common people who elected him! And the councilmen, Mr. SO and SO, and So and So. My what a lot of town business they have to dispose of.... And one of these fine days they will be able to make their elders seem altogether like excess baggage.
>
> Everything that goes to make up a town from the high jinks at the top to the poor old Dog Catcher, will appear in the officiary....
>
> Every youngster who has cut his or her teeth, is eligible to join in the Junior Town Movement. All you need to do is to coax your dad to buy you a Season Ticket.

PUPPETRY

Ventriloquism, as a feature, was added to youth programs during the early 1920s. The most well-known ventriloquist on the circuit was Edgar Bergen. Bergen was appearing in vaudeville and lyceum acts in and around Chicago until he was "discovered" by a Redpath manager. In 1922, he started touring with the Redpath Bureau and continued appearing each season on chautauqua until 1929. From chautauqua, Bergen went to New York's Palace Theatre and played there in 1930, 1931, and 1932, until the Palace closed, symbolically marking the end of vaudeville. During his first season with chautauqua, Bergen appeared only on the morning segments of the youth program. In the following year, he was featured not only in the morning but, because so many parents enjoyed his act, also on the afternoon adult program.

During his first two years on the Redpath circuit, Bergen used two

Edgar Bergen, with Charlie McCarthy and Effie Klinker, as he appeared on the 1922 chautauqua platform at the age of nineteen. Redpath Collection, University of Iowa.

dummies — Charlie McCarthy and Effie Klinker. Chautauqua audiences loved the antics of Charlie McCarthy but never could warm up to Effie. After the 1923 season, Bergen never used Effie again while performing before circuit chautauqua audiences. By the mid-1920s, Bergen and "Charlie" were considered chautauqua "headliners" and appeared on all segments of the program.

According to Bergen's daughter, Candice Bergen, his circuits represented a "moment in time when life is at its most lighthearted and spirits their most carefree, a moment Edgar — not a carefree man by nature — gazed back on many times."

So popular was Bergen with children and adults alike that the Redpath bureau engaged several other ventriloquists. Al Baker and "Dummy Dennis" were hired by the Redpath bureau in 1923 to work its midwestern circuit. Baker had appeared with "Dennis" in various eastern vaudeville and lyceum programs before joining the Redpath chautauqua. Not only was Baker a ventriloquist, but he was also a magician who delighted children. A 1923 Horner-Redpath promotional brochure noted:

> Al Baker loves kids. At Chautauqua he meets them. After the show they can learn a few things about magic and even, if he is a good boy that day, meet Dumb Dennis.
>
> Mr. Baker is a resident of New York and during the Winter is in constant demand. He takes his vacation on the Chautauqua. And then too, Dennis is getting to be a big boy now — and New York is no place for a kid like him, he is hard boiled enough now. Just wait until you see — and hear him.

Other ventriloquists that worked the chautauqua circuit during the early 1920s included Frank Guy Armitage and Lucy Elmore. Noted puppet artist Paul Clemans also joined the circuits in 1923 and was featured for telling the story of *Jack and the Bean Stalk* with marionettes.

CHAUTAxUQUA AND THE CIRCUS

Children of any time are fascinated by a circus. Although some circuit bureaus advertised that certain aspects of their youth programs were like a circus, the practice was basically shunned. The managers and owners who constituted the International Lyceum and Chautauqua Association tried whenever possible to disassociate chautauqua from the circus. The early circuit movement was dominantly associated with popular education and culture, not the pure entertainment of a circus. Therefore, if circuit chautauqua wanted to keep itself "pure" in the public eye, it could not be in any way associated with the circus. Even the canvas tents that circuit chautauqua used were purposely tinted a different color than those used by the circus.

As the chautauqua circuits oriented their programs more toward entertainment, however, the circuses were better able to compete for their audiences. More than one circuit manager cursed a Barnum and Bailey or some other circus for following their chautauqua into a town and setting up as close as possible to their grounds. Harry P. Harrison, for example, noted that in "Norwich, New York, in 1921, Elsie Baker and William Durieux were in the middle of their concert when a Sells-Foto parade blared past. Half the audience ran to look at the elephant and maidens on horseback." In extreme cases, where competition between chautauqua and a circus became too much to bear, differences were settled by crews with fists and clubs.

In 1922, a "toned-down" version of *Polly of the Circus* was presented on the White-Myers youth program. Unlike the adult version, this rendition did not raise questions about the morality of having a young circus girl stay with a single minister. Instead, the program promised young participants a "chance to go to a chautauqua circus." The chautauqua circus was said to feature animal acts, clowns, and acrobats. The owners of the White-Myers bureau were severely chastised by the International Lyceum and Chautauqua organization for the presentation of this program. The White-Myers Bureau did not rebook *Polly of the Circus* for the 1923 season on either the adult or youth program.

The Call of the 1920s: Entertainment and Comedy

After a brief interlude in which so-called foreign designs on the country were exposed and discussed and during which the flag of democracy was waved, circuit chautauqua programs concentrated on fun and entertainment. The lecturer, reader, opera, magician, and illusionist were fading from the program. In the postwar era and all through the remainder of the 1920s, Americans wanted to be entertained and entertained through drama. Chautauqua made Broadway productions available to them at "a bargain price." Many of those associated with circuit drama of this period — actors, directors, and crews — received the training they needed to later go into careers associated with modern-day forms of electronic mass media.

VII

The Jubilee Year and the Vestiges of Hope

The Chautauqua Institute in New York began making preparations in the fall of 1923 for its "Golden Jubilee," to be held the following year marking fifty years of continuous operation. In the spring of 1924, the owners of circuit chautauqua bureaus through the International Lyceum and Chautauqua Association sent a letter to the New York institute congratulating "Mother" Chautauqua for its educational and cultural accomplishments. The owners also took note that 1924 marked a "Jubilee Year" for circuit chautauqua in that the movement had begun 20 years earlier. Circuit publicity agents went to work publicizing that fact. In the towns that circuit chautauqua visited in 1924, various anniversary celebrations were observed. The tents were filled to capacity in 1924; ten to twelve thousand towns hosted a program and thirty to forty million Americans attended one or more programs that year.

Chautauqua Success

WHAT MADE CIRCUIT CHAUTAUQUA SUCCESSFUL?

The circuit chautauqua movement was successful, at least until the mid–1920s, for several reasons. First, the programs it offered were effectively promoted and met the needs of the marketplace. Second, the circuit bureaus were adept at adjusting their programs and marketing strategies as the audiences they served changed. Last, circuit chautauqua always had a "message" or cause with which its audience identified. In the beginning years, the movement was successful in fulfilling the rural midwestern yearnings for popular education, culture, and assurance that agrarianism was central to the destiny of America.

As circuit chautauqua began to serve a more heterogeneous audience after 1913 — rural and urban, eastern and western — in addition to its already established midwestern following, the programs addressed community and individual matters of success and started to feature "big city" entertainment. When the United States formally entered World War I, circuit chautauqua served as an important information source about the events taking place overseas and also provided some diversion from day-to-day problems. After the war, chautauqua presented not only deliberations over the impact foreign influences were having on America but also Broadway comedies.

Circuit chautauqua is a tangible part of early twentieth-century American social history. The vast majority of Americans by 1924 had attended one or more chautauqua programs. For several decades, many towns had routinely prepared each year for the coming of the chautauqua. "Chautauqua season" was an American ritual that came after spring planting and before fall harvest. Although circuit chautauqua had visited large urban centers, including the cities of Atlanta, Chicago, Kansas City, and New York, it always remained more of a rural phenomenon than an urban one.

Yet the movement bridged the gap between rural and urban peoples by bringing a little of each to the other. By 1924, circuit chautauqua had democratized American culture; it was the traveling fulfillment of Zangwill's play *The Melting Pot*. As President Coolidge expressed in a letter to Elmer Willis Serl, superintendent of the Swarthmore Chautauqua, dated August 29, 1924, the movement "has been a fine liberalizing element in our community life, and I can hardly express a better wish for it than it may continue in the future to follow the same ideals."

The promotional materials of 1924 also presented various explanations as to why the circuit chautauqua movement was apparently so successful. Shannon White of the White-Myers Bureau provided one such explanation from an economic standpoint: "At Chautauqua, people get huge pleasure. At a ridiculously low price, they hear superb music and stirring lectures and see a first rate New York play.... People welcome Chautauqua as a schoolboy welcomes Christmas. They want thrills. Not only because thrills are delightful but because there is something ennobling in them."

The Redpath Chautauqua Bureau published a booklet called *Twenty Years of Chautauqua Progress, 1904 to 1923*, which was widely distributed in 1924. The booklet began with a section called "A Bit of History" that outlined what Keith Vawter had accomplished to make

This booklet was widely distributed by the Redpath Bureau in 1924, the "jubilee year" of circuit chautauqua. Author's collection.

circuit chautauqua successful, centering on Vawter's ability to standardize operations in the following ways:

    1. By grouping a number of towns in a circuit, and serving them with uniform programs.

    2. By using all talent full time and thus eliminating the useless expense of open dates.

    3. By further reducing talent costs through the use of long time contracts for their whole time.

    4. By reducing railroad transportation charges to a minimum, thus not only saving the money otherwise wasted, but also conserving the energy and morale of the talent folks.

    5. By building a balanced program of charm, variety, and timely interest.

6. By wholesale advertising in quantity, making possible a better as well as greater amount of publicity at no increase in cost.

7. By the concentration of expert attention upon every detail of general management throughout the whole year, to take the place of incidental management by local committees....

Redpath promotional brochures of 1924 contained an open letter from Keith Vawter to readers. In the letter Vawter explained why he thought the movement had been successful. His explanation was directed toward the original adult chautauqua attendees, many of whom by then were in retirement:

A Farmer's life is such that during his more active years it is almost impossible for him to travel and, as a rule, when he has retired from active farming the hardships of traveling do not appeal to him.

Chautauqua spreads a magic carpet on which you can sail the seven seas and get first hand knowledge of the world and its people without leaving home....

Many people have the idea that the farmer is like the man who was facing the wrong way and expressed his regret that he was missing the parade — but never thought of turning around.

We, however, know better, for we have served the farmer for years. We know that he does appreciate the opportunity to learn.... And having listened to learned men and hearing of what is going on, he gets more from it than does the ordinary listener....

The Chautauqua programme this year presents a variety of talent that is as good as a college course, administered with a sugar coating of cheery music and a dash of drama that makes it appeal to all.

The circuit chautauqua movement received "twenty year reviews" in popular magazines like the *American Mercury, Commonweal, Current Opinion, New Republic, Outlook,* and *Scribners,* in almost every local midwestern newspaper, and in major papers such as the *New York Times, Chicago Tribune,* and *Kansas City Star.* Press assessments of the circuit chautauqua movement were positive in nature. In a 1924 June edition, the *New York Times* observed that "Chautauqua must be judged not only by the good it does but by the evil it prevents." Whatever the press reported about chautauqua that year was welcomed by the owners and operators of the circuits. The sheer volume of press coverage was a major factor in drawing so many Americans to the tent that year.

DESPITE THE IMAGE OF SUCCESS

Despite the apparent success of circuit chautauqua in drawing literally millions of Americans to its programs in 1924, the movement was coming to an end. The owners and operators of the larger circuits knew, even before the year ended, that the entire operation was in financial trouble. The amusement tax, postwar inflation and rising costs, little carnival-type "chautauquas," and the impossibility of increasing contractual amounts all had long-range, negative consequences for circuit chautauqua operations. In spite of the burgeoning attendance to circuit programs in 1924, many of the largest circuit bureaus found that they were not making any profit and in some cases large deficits were incurred. To make matters worse, more than 2,000 of the 10,000 or so towns that had booked a program in 1924 simply refused to rebook circuit chautauqua for 1925. This marked the beginning of the end.

All 15 of the major circuit chautauqua bureaus operated at a financial loss in 1925. By the following year, more than half either had gone out of business, were drastically reduced in size, or had been sold. The two largest operating bureaus, the Ellison-White Chautauqua System and the Redpath-Vawter Chautauqua Bureau, were both sold late in 1926. The "Redpath-Vawter" trademark was sold along with the individual circuits that had constituted the bureau. The name Redpath-Vawter or variations thereof continued to be used by those bureaus that had pooled resources and together had purchased the Redpath Bureau. The programs promoted, for example, by the Peffer-Redpath Chautauqua or Rupe-Redpath Chautauqua or Vawter-Redpath Chautauqua in the late 1920s had no real association with the original bureau. The Redpath name as a recognizable entity, however, assisted these bureaus in attracting audiences to their tents.

In a letter to Ralph Parlette dated December 27, 1927, Keith Vawter provided the following assessment about the attitudes which apparently prevailed about circuit chautauqua at that time:

> I now seem to find there are about three types of attitudes toward Chautauqua. One is the fellow that is still in the business who seems to me to be kidding himself ... into the idea that the day of Chautauqua's greatest usefulness and perchance prosperity, is just dawning. The second group is the fellows that are ... more inclined to look on the present and future a bit pessimistically, and the third group that I come in contact with is the public, the old local boosters who again divide themselves into two groups — the old faithful

that are still struggling to keep their Chautauqua going and the younger crowd in town that feel they have made an honest effort, haven't succeeded as well as the effort justifies and are through.

The "old faithful" that attempted to keep circuit chautauqua coming to their community were usually older adults who lived in rural midwestern communities. Some had grown up with chautauqua, others had been chautauqua "boosters" and sponsors, and still others saw the large brown tent as part of a yearly ritual that needed to continue. But the ability of rural areas to sponsor chautauqua diminished each year after 1924 due to the steady decline in farm land and crop prices. As the bottom fell out of agriculture, rural banks began to fold. Banks generally held the deposits that had been set aside throughout the year to use in bringing chautauqua to the community.

As banks closed, the circuit bureaus began receiving letters like the one written by F. A. Fitterers, a member of the Gallatin [Missouri] Chautauqua Association, to the Redpath Bureau in Chicago on March 17, 1926: "The purpose of addressing you is to acquaint you of the condition of our little city, community, and county, in the past few days we have had five banks close their doors in our county ... The board of directors, after careful canvas of the situation have advised me it will be financial ruin to carry on the chautauqua." The Redpath Bureau released the Gallatin Chautauqua Association from its contract for that summer's chautauqua. Following this action, Fitterers wrote the following letter, dated March 31, 1926, to the bureau: "We appreciate your kind letter of 19th. inst. in permitting us to cancel the Chautauqua contract.... All of which was caused by our bank failures in the County, which at present times amount to eleven failures in the past twelve months."

The Great Depression was first directly felt by those individuals living in rural America. In rural communities where the banks remained solvent, dwindling crop and land prices translated into little, if any, available money for locally sponsored chautauquas. The McNary-Haugen Farm Relief Bill was first introduced to Congress and passed by the Senate in 1927. The bill was designed to assist those impacted by the waning agricultural economy. President Coolidge vetoed the bill that year and again when it was presented to him in 1928.

The situation faced by the few remaining circuit chautauqua operators in the latter half of the 1920s was twofold: first, a dwindling demand for programs, especially in urban areas and second, economic instability in rural areas where interest in chautauqua seemingly persisted. The combination of these two factors, in conjunction with the Great Crash of 1929, ended for all practical purposes the circuit chautauqua movement in the United States.

Chautauqua and Modern America

The circuit chautauqua movement in a sense enjoyed its own nostalgic climax in the Jubilee Year of 1924. Despite the intermittent praise that chautauqua received in the popular press, especially in "20-year reviews" of 1924, not all of what was written about chautauqua after the war was encouraging. Disparaging remarks began to appear that questioned the substance of the chautauqua message. In October of 1920, Sinclair Lewis' *Main Street* was published and quickly ascended to the top of the best-seller list. He wrote of circuit chautauqua that despite promises of education and uplift, "It did not seem to be a tabloid university; it did not seem to be any kind of university; it seemed to be a combination of vaudeville performances, Y.M.C.A lectures, and graduation exercises of an elocution class."

In January of 1924, the beginning of the circuit jubilee year, Bruce Bliven wrote in an article published in the *New Republic* that chautauqua demonstrated the "mental poverty of Main Street.... From its scope and direction you may learn of the national hunger for self-improvement, information, advancement.... The pabulum provided ... may not be much; but it is all there is, at least until radio becomes a serious educational force."

William L. Shirer, author of *The Rise and Fall of the Third Reich*, not only attended chautauqua as a boy growing up in Iowa, but also was a member of the Redpath tent crew for several seasons during the early 1920s. In his *20th Century Journal*, a memoir about growing up in America between 1904 and 1930, Shirer recalled that even chautauqua's most notable star, William Jennings Bryan, had little of significance to say by this time:

> But even as he continued to sway the masses with his repetitious oratory, he retreated more and more from reality, perhaps unaware of the banality, the triviality, of the haven he had found under the chautauqua tents.
>
> He no doubt was unaware, too, that his last appearance on chautauqua in 1924 marked the approach of his own end and that of chautauqua.

TENT CHAUTAUQUA IN A MEDIA AND MOBILE AGE

The 1920s saw vast strides in the improvement and availability of transportation and communication. The first federal interstate highway across the United States was completed in 1922. During the remainder of the 1920s, roads connecting to the interstate tied smaller towns to urban centers. With automobile sales rapidly increasing after World War I, Americans could now travel beyond their immediate neighborhoods and communities to pursue amusement and entertainment elsewhere.

The 1920s were also marked by the gradual popular acceptance and accessibility of the radio. At first, there was the crystal set of the early 1920s that mysteriously pulled faint signals in from somewhere, then the cumbersome battery-operated set with the big goose-necked speaker horn, and, finally, the parlor cabinet radio, which was available in 1927 through a catalog company called Sears Roebuck. Radio sales between 1925 and 1930 increased almost sevenfold. Through the medium of the radio, major events could be transmitted throughout the country almost as fast as they occurred. Americans were also interested in radio as a means of bringing entertainment into their homes.

In the final years of the 1920s, many popular radio shows emerged that provided Americans with hours of enjoyment. People listened to such radio shows as "Amos and Andy" (played by Freeman Gosden and Charles Correll), the "Fleischmann Hour" and the "Robert Burns Panatella Program" (hosted by George Burns and Gracie Allen), the "Dodge Victory Hour" (which featured Will Rogers), the "Ziegfeld Follies" (which also featured Will Rogers, as well as "Ed-Win"), the "Chase and Sanborn Radio Hour" (hosted by Maurice Chevalier and also featuring "Ed-Win"), and many others. A novel and inexpensive way to amuse friends and family, radio hurt chautauqua attendance.

Although the competition that motion pictures posed to circuit chautauqua had always been worrisome to managers, movie features began to significantly affect attendance after the war. Not only were movie houses springing up in almost every town of any size (some were converted lyceum theaters), but there was a tremendous increase in the number and types of films being made. The once clumsy and costly method of copying film had been improved, which meant that movies or serials could be released in multiples. Moreover, the coordination of sound with moving pictures lent additional excitement to the advancements being made in the movie industry.

Despite the postwar images of gaiety, fun, and relaxation associated with circuit chautauqua, it was fading from the American scene. Author's collection.

In 1926, Warner Brothers Films began experimenting with a wax cylinder recording device that synchronized a musical score with the silent film *Don Juan*, starring John Barrymore. In 1927, Al Jolson sang songs in Warner's production of *The Jazz Singer*. A mouse by the name of Mickey did speaking parts in the 1928 animated production of *Steamboat Willie*. By the end of 1929, the production of sound on film was becoming the norm rather than the exception.

The vast technological advances made in day-to-day communications and transportation, coupled with increasing availability, quickly antiquated what chautauqua had to offer. Yet the few remaining circuit managers tried to compete with "modern America" by presenting their programs as being an integral part of the new age. A mid-1920s "Redpath" brochure stated, for example, that chautauqua was the best sort of leisure time activity:

> "All work and no play makes Jack a dull boy." It also makes Jack's dad and mother a dull pair. Everywhere people are now determined as never before not to be dull — to enjoy life as they go along. They have found that they can make as much money and achieve as great professional success if they stop now and then to play. Golf and good roads, radio and the picture show, the women's clubs and the men's conventions are adding years to the lives and decades to the enjoyment of the American people.
>
> Yet none of these or any other institutions under the sun takes the place of Chautauqua. For fine fun, rubbing elbows with one's neighbors away from business cares, the delight of untangling mental snarls, listening to great religious and political and educational prophets, hearing unusual music and attending worthwhile drama, Chautauqua is matched by nothing else in America.

Even in the wake of the Great Crash of 1929, one of the last remaining circuit bureaus tried to persuade patrons that its program was better than any other form of available amusement:

> How do you get your fun out of life? Seeing the movies, going fishing, playing golf, ... reading novels, listening to the radio, going to church? ... Whatever it is, it is safe to wager that it is something that leaves you permanently better in mind or body.... That is why Chautauqua ranks so high in the pleasure of so many millions of the best type of Americans.... More than that, it leaves a pleasant taste afterward.... We are trying hard to keep pace with American tastes — the most exacting in the world.

The Program: From Applesauce to "Leisure Time"

DRAMA, SLAPSTICK, AND CORN

Drama, as had been the trend before 1924, became even more popular with chautauqua audiences and was the most frequently featured type of entertainment on the program throughout the last half of the 1920s. Most of the chautauqua play productions were performed by off-Broadway touring groups. And the majority of these companies were compensated on a per performance basis paid in advance. The vast majority of the plays were "farcelets" centering on underlying domestic and social issues facing "modern" America.

Barry Connor's *The Patsy* had opened on Broadway in 1925 and by 1927 was very much in demand by circuit audiences. A 1927 chautauqua flier characterized the heroine, through the eyes of those who had already seen the play, in the following manner: "Audiences everywhere fall in love with Patsy, the adorable flapper-Cinderella heroine of the play, and follow her fortunes with sympathy and keen amusement." Featured on the same chautauqua program as *The Patsy* was *The Show-Off*, which was advertised as a play that presented "a slice of American life so vividly and divertingly done that the play ran well into its second season in New York and enjoyed a phenomenal run in Chicago."

There were many purely "slapstick" plays — or "pure corn," as they were also called — presented from the chautauqua stage that had originated from Broadway. Winchell Smith and Frank Bacon's play *Lightnin'*, which had closed in New York in 1921, was presented on various circuit programs after 1925. The play was promoted by one chautauqua bureau as telling "Bill's story of bees and the humor of Bill's domestic difficulties." The play production of *So This Is London*, introduced to the Broadway stage in 1922, was featured on 1927 and 1928 "Redpath-Vawter" programs as follows:

> The theme of the play is that "one-half of the world doesn't know how the other half lives," and for the purposes of this play one-half of the world is labeled "American" the other half "British," and sets forth the snobbishness of London as contrasted with the "blase" roughness of the newly rich in America.
>
> The play deals with a young American in love with a sweet English girl, a millionaire father who wants to buy an English factory, and a titled English family — with much bitterness between the parents — who make the ways of the lovers proverbally rough.

At the end of 1924, the Redpath-Vawter Chautauqua Bureau hired Barry Connor to write a play expressly for use on its circuits. Connor wrote a play called *Applesauce* for the Redpath Bureau, and Keighley, still under contract with the bureau, produced it. The play was first featured on the 1925 Redpath Chautauqua program and starred Eugene

Lockhart in the leading role. An actress by the name of Martha Scott played a supporting role in the play. Scott would go on to win an Oscar for her performance in the 1938 production of Thorton Wilder's *Our Town*.

Redpath brochures pointed out to readers that *Applesauce* had been expressly written for circuit audiences and explained that the title of the play was "obtained from the modern name for 'blarney,' 'the glad hand,' etc." The plot of the play was described in Redpath advertising in the following manner: "The hero serves it [applesauce] without limit to win the hand of the girl he loves, get himself established in business and becomes one of the best liked fellows in town." In the aftermath of the breakup of the Redpath-Vawter Chautauqua Bureau, the play toured New York City and several other major cities; it was later made into a movie called *Brides Are Like That*.

A "Broadway hit of the 1928-29 season" that was frequently featured on the 1929 Redpath Chautauqua circuit was the play *Skidding*. The play, as advertised, raised questions (and purported to have some answers) about the role of women in modern America: "A rollicking comedy drama of love and politics that will make you think. Should the Judge yield to the inevitable? Should a woman run for Congress? 'Old Maids' and discontented wives. Is this generation Skidding?" This play became the basis of the popular late 1930s Andy Hardy feature film series.

A play entitled the *Detour* was usually promoted on the same 1929 program as *Skidding*. The *Detour*, which had opened on Broadway in 1921, was said to present the "story of a small American home, of a family operating a small truck farm, beset with debts and taxes and an absorbing ambition to secure enough money to buy additional land. There is a generous sprinkling of comedy and comic situations."

A variety of other play comedies were featured on late 1920s circuit programs. These plays included, among others, *A Bill of Divorcement*, *Adam and Eva*, *In Walked Jimmy*, *Seventeen*, *Six Cylinder Love*, and *Take My Advice*. All of the aforementioned plays came to chautauqua after they had run their course on Broadway. As with the general trend in Broadway productions, the drama presented from the chautauqua stage throughout the 1920s was dominated by comedy and these comedies often had trite plots. Although Broadway had experienced a brief revival of interest in Shakespearean drama during the mid-1920s, this trend was not reflected to any great degree in circuit chautauqua programs. In fact, the Ben Greet Players, known by

Broadway and chautauqua audiences for their fine performances of Shakespeare, had permanently moved to Hollywood, California in 1926.

Music: Sidesplitting "Climaxes and Anti-Climaxes"

The musical numbers featured on late 1920s circuit chautauqua programs were dominantly of a slapstick variety. The "Oh Percy" Musical Revue Company was, for example, described in a 1927 "Redpath" brochure as "a musical comedy revue presented by an aggregation of ten men, featuring the insatiable Jay Tobias. Sidesplitting minstrel show scenes are presented — a clown Saxophone band." The musical variety and novelty of the Orpheum Entertainers was described in a 1927 brochure as follows:

> The Orpheum Entertainers, belonging to the well known type of "Master Attracts," presents a program of novelty and entertainment, so attractive that it is well calculated to meet with an enthusiastic reception from the great mass of Chautauqua people. They use a combination of instruments so novel that it is bound to stimulate interest and enthusiasm.... Here is a full concert company and a prelude, this company will be just one more big musical treat.

In another 1927 program, the members of the Premier Male Quartet were characterized as being "singers and comedians of the first rank and [they] keep their audience in a continuous uproar." Dunbar's Singing Bell Ringers, once known for their more classical renditions, were promoted as a 1928 headline feature in a "Redpath" brochure as follows: "comedy skits and excerpts from their own experience in vaudeville." A musical group known as the Alamos apparently furnished 1928 audiences with a series of humorous "climaxes and anti-climaxes." The "noble" Russian Cossack Chorus, "composed largely of Russian Noblemen driven out by the scourge of the Red Revolution," performed humorous musical routines before 1928 and 1929 circuit audiences. And Native American performer Princess Blue Feather had perfected her musical routine to such a point that by 1928 she was promoted as being a "feminine competitor of Will Rogers."

Vierra's Hawaiians, who appeared on 1927 and 1928 "Redpath-Horner" programs, were also promoted on the basis of their use of special effects:

> With special scenic and lighting effects, which includes the representation of a volcano in eruption, George Vierra and his native

company of Hawaiian singers offer an exquisite dramatic and musical sensation....

The stage is realistically decorated in Hawaiian effects. A South Sea moon bathes palm trees, thatched roof houses, volcanoes and tropical seas with its romantic light.

The South Seas act called a "Night in Hawaii" was the central theme of a three-day 1929 chautauqua program. College boys dressed in Hawaiian shirts strummed ukeleles, sang "songs of the island," and constituted, according to the program, the "gay musicians from the enchanted isles of the Pacific." These young men also appeared in grease paint on the same program in a feature called "Jubilee Frolics."

The Plantation Singers, who had worked for the Redpath bureau for more than 15 years, appeared on one of the reorganized "Redpath" circuits in 1927 and 1928. This group represented one of the few remaining all-black jubilee companies on the circuit. Performing, as they had done for so many years, the songs associated with Southern plantation days of the past, the Plantation Singers were additionally recognized for their use of humor and stage props. A "Redpath" brochure described the scope of their performance as follows:

Opening with a plantation scene, this splendid negro company offers a musical production that is decidedly out of the ordinary. Stage settings and appropriate costuming are used to advantage in the first part of the program, while the latter half is devoted to negro spirituals, Southern ballads and plantation melodies. Many humorous diversions are introduced.

The renditions of classical pieces presented by Kryl's Band or Thavius' Orchestra, the New York opera productions, and the other fine musical performances by those associated with the New York Metropolitan Opera, once characteristic of traveling chautauqua, were almost entirely pushed aside by drama after 1924. Bell ringers dressed in clown suits, more and more "college boys" playing ukeleles and doubling as jubilee singers and light musical comedies were all symptomatic of the end of the circuit chautauqua movement.

The Lecturer as Media Figure

Desperately trying to compete with movies and radio, the circuit chautauqua movement in the late 1920s had even turned to Hollywood as a source for its lecturers. A promotional statement for Chief Red

Fox, contained in a 1929 brochure, for example, capitalized on the association between this Native American and the Hollywood-based Paramount production company:

> Chief William Red Fox is a full-blooded Sioux Indian of the Rosebud Indian Reservation of South Dakota. He graduated from the Carlise Indian School in 1889. His father was Chief Black Eagle, who was one of the principals in the famous Custer fight. Chief Red Fox has served seven years in the United States Navy, and was overseas twenty-two months during the World War. He co-starred with Richard Dix in "The Vanishing American," and has played several leading parts in feature pictures for Paramount.
>
> Chief Red Fox will appear at the Chautauqua in full Indian regalia. His discussion of the American Indian, past and present, will be most interesting and instructive.

Overall, the number of lectures, especially serious lectures, were few and far between on the circuit chautauqua after 1924. Whereas the lecture features had made up the bulk of most programs prior to 1920, during the 1920s the lecture was pushed aside owing to the demands made on chautauqua for drama and, to a lesser extent, funny music. The lectures typically constituted less than 20 percent of the entire program in 1925, 1926, 1927, and 1928. And the lecturers who appeared before circuit audiences during the latter half of the 1920s were usually those who had an established name among chautauqua audiences. In the last two years of the circuit chautauqua movement, however, more than one circuit did not feature any type of oratory on its program.

The well-known Billy Sunday carried on with his crusade against the "demon liquor" throughout the 1920s from what he termed the "chautauqua pulpit." (Sunday was also heard "preaching" his message over the radio by the end of the 1920s.) Although the passage of the Volstead Act in 1919 prohibited the use of alcohol, enforcing the law was another matter. Throughout the decade that followed the passage of prohibition, the proliferation of "speakeasies," bathtub gin and home brew, and racketeering all attested to the fact that the law could not be effectively enforced. Much of Sunday's rhetoric about prohibition while speaking before late 1920s chautauqua audiences centered on the dangers that surround a "lawless nation, run by the saloon."

Despite the uphill battle that Sunday waged against liquor, people flocked to see him. As late as 1929, one chautauqua brochure had this to say about Billy Sunday:

The Jubilee Year and the Vestiges of Hope   193

>Few men are more widely known than "Billy" Sunday. He is the most spectacular and most dynamic evangelist of our age. Those who know Mr. Sunday best love him most. He is as virile and dynamic today as at any time in his long and colorful career. His messages are born of conviction, and dealing with live, up-to-date issues. Those who come to scoff usually remain to pray.
>
>It has been said of "Billy" Sunday that "He draws larger crowds, gets more converts, collects more money, and is more bitterly hated and more devotedly loved than any other living evangelist." It is estimated that he has spoken to more than 100 million people. "Billy" Sunday will be one of the greatest [things] that has ever occurred in the long history of ... Chautauqua.

The celebrity status of Sunday was, at least by this time, more important than the issue for which he spoke. The other temperance speakers who appeared on chautauqua programs during the 1920s did not last for more than one summer because of lack of interest on the part of audiences about the topic. Other celebrity lecturers who could still attract a crowd to the tent late into the 1920s included Frank Dixon, Ruth Bryan Owen, Montaville Flowers, Private Peat, Ralph Parlette, and Count Ilya Tolstoy. On the other hand, the earlier "star" lecturers, who had at one time attracted literally thousands of people to chautauqua, were absent from the program.

Bryan delivered his last speech before circuit chautauqua audiences in the Jubilee Year of 1924. In the aftermath of his involvement in the 1925 Tennessee Scopes trial, in which Bryan and fundamentalism had taken on Clarence Darrow and the theory of evolution, Bryan died. Russell Conwell had left the circuit by the end of World War I to became president of Temple University, and he also passed away in 1925. Most of the other notable star chautauqua attractions, such as Champ Clark, "Gattling Gun" Fogleman, Frank Wakely Gunsaulus, Warren G. Harding, Hilton Jones, Lincoln McConnell, Carry Nation, Edward Amherst Ott, Frederic Poole, and James K. Vardaman, had either died or retired from the circuit by 1925.

The circuit chautauqua star lecturers, when engaged by a bureau, had entered into some sort of season-long contract. But beginning in 1920, and especially after the bottom fell out of chautauqua in 1925, most lecturers and entertainers who appeared on the circuit did so on a per engagement basis. Because of the diminishing popular interest in chautauqua, circuit managers tried to avoid entering into any long-term contractual agreements with performers.

Despite the decreasing emphasis placed on oratory, there were some important issues discussed by well-known public figures on the circuit. Known as "Brother Charlie" on the circuits because he was William Jennings Bryan's brother, the governor of Nebraska ran on the 1924 Democratic ticket for vice president under John W. Davis. Charles W. Bryan delivered several speeches that year on the chautauqua circuit about "good government" and the "necessity of democratic leadership." Running for national office in 1924 on the Progressive ticket were two additional chautauqua lecturers, presidential candidate "Fighting Bob" La Follette with Burton K. Wheeler as his vice-presidential running mate. After years of absence from the chautauqua platform, La Follette returned that year, resurrecting in his speeches many of the same themes he had talked about on chautauqua more than a decade ago: governmental ownership of railroads, farm relief, and laws limiting monopolies. Both "chautauqua candidates" lost to Calvin Coolidge, who had shunned requests to appear on chautauqua.

In 1925, shortly after the election, "Fighting Bob" La Follette died. The La Follette name, however, did not fade immediately from circuit chautauqua. In 1927, Congressman Phil La Follette appeared on the Independent Chautauqua Bureau's program and was described in the following manner: "Son of the late Senator Bob La Follette of Wisconsin, presenting his stirring lecture 'A Challenge.' A notable discussion of national affairs." Other "politicians" who appeared before circuit audiences after 1925 included two women who had received national newspaper and radio recognition.

Mable Walker Willebrandt had been an assistant attorney general under Attorney General Harry M. Daugherty at the time when he and several other members of President Harding's staff were implicated in an extortion plan. One circuit of the reorganized "Redpath Bureau" hired Willebrant in 1927 and again in 1928 to lecture about the "Hows and Whys of the Ohio Gang." In 1929, the first woman governor of any American state, Governor Sarah Tyson Rorer of Wyoming, presented "The Governor Speaks" on several circuit programs. The lecture centered on why women needed to become involved in community affairs and local government. In 1933, President Franklin Roosevelt, prompted by Mrs. Roosevelt, appointed Rorer to be the director of the United States Mint.

Several of the lecture topics that materialized on the late 1920s chautauqua programs dealt with subjects that were by their very nature rather daring and exciting. E. R. Root, the president of the A. I. Root

Company, which sold beekeeping supplies, spoke before 1924, 1925, and 1926 Redpath audiences about the practices and economic advantages of beekeeping. In Redpath advertising, Root was promoted on the basis of his "sensationalistic handling of bees." Root's handling of the bees was so sensational that the Redpath Bureau had received some letters of inquiry regarding the safety of audiences during his demonstrations. On March 6, 1926, E. R. Root wrote to John F. Chambers of the Redpath Chautauquas, Chicago, Illinois, to respond to this concern:

> The enclosed copy of my proposed article will explain my "tricks of the trade," for my Chautauqua audiences were always glad to have the truth explained, after I fooled them thru the use of the magic wand and my little fairy.
>
> I think you will be pleased to know that not one of my children were stung in all of my two years' experience, and I am safe in saying that not one of them will be stung during the coming season. The parents of the children are always mightily pleased, and every time a child takes a hold of a handful of bees there is a round of handclap. You can see that it is a matter of local pride that local people can handle bees, after I show the way.

Count Felix von Luckner, known as the "Sea Devil" submarine commander because of his daring wartime exploits that sank countless Allied ships, lectured several times on late 1920s circuit programs. He also promoted his book titled after his nickname. Mary Heath, who piloted her own aircraft from circuit engagement to circuit engagement, presented a lecture entitled the "Conquest of the Air." Sociologist Geoffrey Morgan spoke about the "Problems of Leisure Time" before late 1920s circuit audiences. His presentation was said to deal with how "modern inventions and shortened working hours have made a problem of how we best spend our leisure time." Among the solutions for dealing with this problem that Morgan suggested was "attending Chautauqua." For any one associated with a chautauqua circuit in the late 1920s, however, it was obvious that Americans had found other ways of occupying their leisure time.

Chautauqua as a Stepping Stone: From Late Nineteenth- to Twentieth-Century Entertainment

Throughout the history of circuit chautauqua, many of its performers were associated in one way or another with other forms of popular entertainment such as vaudeville, lyceum, Broadway, and film (and, perhaps in a broader sense, politics). As the circuit chautauqua movement became more entertainment-oriented, it attracted an increasing number of "big city" Broadway performers, directors, stagehands, vaudeville artists, bands, and other acts. Many of the performers who became associated with circuit chautauqua in fact worked back and forth between engagements in larger cities and summer chautauqua programs. Circuit chautauqua in essence functioned as a stepping stone between late nineteenth-century forms of stage entertainment and twentieth-century forms of electronic mass media — the silent film, the "talkie," full-length motion pictures, radio, and, eventually, television.

Many of the monologues that Opie Read presented to circuit chautauqua audiences beginning in 1904 were taken from his best-selling books, *The Jucklins* and *Starbucks*, printed in 1895 and 1902, respectively. In 1921, Read took a brief interlude from chautauqua and went to Hollywood, California, to act in a silent movie production based upon *Starbucks*. The movie was not successful, but Read, upon returning to chautauqua, was just as popular as he had ever been. The late nineteenth-century vaudevillian John Bunny had become by 1913 a noted Broadway actor, Vitagraph "film star," and chautauqua humorist. He began his association with chautauqua in 1908 and appeared on the program each season until his death in 1915.

Conrad Nagel of Keokuk, Iowa, began his association with the circuits as an understudy of chautauqua reader Edna Means. The year after he left chautauqua in 1915, Nagel joined the Keith Vaudeville Circuit of New York City. While on assignment as a Keith player in California, Nagel also appeared in his first silent film, a *Shorty Hamilton* feature, in the role of a cowboy. Between his return to New York City in 1916 and joining the U.S. Navy in 1918, Nagel appeared in several Broadway plays. After the armistice was signed in 1918, he returned to the Broadway stage, and in 1927, the same year that Al Jolson uttered the first words ever heard "on" film, he signed a contract with Warner Brothers. Throughout the remainder of the 1920s and into the end of the 1930s, Nagel, appearing in dozens of films, was considered a "Warner Brothers star." In 1939, he performed in his last Warner Brothers film, *The Mad Empress*.

There were a number of other individuals who became well-known "film" personalities or were associated with film production who can be identified with the World War I era of circuit chautauqua. Louella Parsons, the acid star and film critic for the Hearst papers, appeared as a reader on a 1916 Redpath circuit chautauqua which operated out of Chicago. Leo S. Rosecrans, who eventually accepted an executive-producer position at Jerry Fairbanks Productions, worked for more than a decade as a circuit chautauqua manager. Actress Dore Davidson, who had appeared with William Keighley in the 1916 Redpath production of *The Melting Pot*, had started working for Warner Brothers in the early 1920s. Count Ilya Tolstoy worked back and forth between summer chautauqua engagements and guest appearances in silent films throughout much of the 1920s.

Noted film writer and actress Ruth Gordon worked back and forth between vaudeville and chautauqua before the war as part of a musical company known as the Red Headed Quartet. After appearing in various Broadway productions throughout the 1930s, Gordon materialized as an actress in a series of Warner Brothers films. In 1940 she played with Edward G. Robinson in the production of *Dr. Ehrlich's Magic Bullet*. In the 1960s and 1970s, Gordon appeared, often as a character actress, in such films as *Inside Daisy Clover*, *Rosemary's Baby*, and *Every Which Way but Loose* with Clint Eastwood.

Originally from England, the Ben Greet Players had been engaged in 1904 to perform Shakespearean drama before New York audiences. Within several years, the Greet Players began a tour of the country, fulfilling engagements at lyceum theatres. The popularity of the company caught the attention of the Redpath Chautauqua Bureau, which subsequently made arrangements to have the Greet Players tour with its circuits, beginning in 1913. The Greet Players traveled each season on one or more Redpath circuits for more than two decades. At first the company presented light Shakespearean comedies before chautauqua audiences and then, after 1915, full-staged Broadway productions. No single dramatic company on the chautauqua circuit did more to change the disapproving attitudes that rural audiences frequently had toward drama into an appreciation for this performance art form.

Many of the actors, actresses, and directors associated with the Greet Players eventually ended up pursuing careers in film. Early 1900s Broadway actress Sybil Thorndike joined the Greet Players in 1905. She toured intermittently with the company on the Redpath circuits until 1919, at which point she returned almost exclusively to Broadway theatre. In the 1940s, Thorndike began to accept some parts in film, working back and forth between Broadway and Hollywood. In the 1950s, she appeared in two films, Alfred Hitchcock's *Stage Fright* and *The Prince and the Show Girl*, with Marilyn Monroe and Laurence Olivier.

The early silent film star, Edith Wynne Matthison, who appeared in the 1915 Lasky production of *Carmen* with Geraldine Farrar, toured with the Greet Players on the Redpath circuit. The fine Shakespearean actor Frederick Warde, who appeared as Richard III in the 1913 Stirling film version and as King Lear in the 1916 Thanhouser film rendition, acted in these roles before chautauqua audiences as a member of the Greet Players. Actress Blanche Frederici worked with several play production companies, including the Greet Players, which toured with circuit chautauqua. In 1916 and 1917, she headed her own Redpath chautauqua play company. During the early 1930s, Frederici appeared as a character actress in six Warner Brothers films. Upon the selling of the Redpath Chautauqua Bureau in 1926, the Ben Greet Players moved as a company to Hollywood, California, where members intermittently worked in film.

Most of the Greet play productions presented before Redpath circuit audiences were directed by William Keighley. Keighley worked each season for the Redpath Bureau from 1913 until 1926, the year the bureau was sold. In 1927, Keighley returned to work exclusively on Broadway productions, but only for a short period of time. After a short stint as a radio-play director in 1929 and 1930, he went to work for Warner Brothers in the early 1930s. From his first major directing project for Warner Brothers in 1934, a movie entitled *Easy to Love*, until his last, a 1957 release called *The Master of Ballantrae*, Keighley was involved in the directing and production of more than 100 Warner Brothers films. There were other actors and directors who were associated with Keighley while working for the Redpath Bureau who eventually ended up in film.

Marc Connelly assisted Keighley in the directing and editing of various circuit plays, especially those he himself had written. Connelly was awarded a Pulitzer Prize in 1930 for his play *Green Pastures*, which was made into a Warner Brothers movie under the direction of Keighley and Connelly in 1936. Connelly was involved in the production side of various films into the 1950s. Late in his career, he acted in the 1957 film *The Spirit of St. Louis* with James Stewart and in the 1960 movie *Tall Story*, featuring Anthony Perkins with Jane Fonda making her screen debut. J. Hartley Manners, the well-known early 1900s playwright and actor, also assisted Keighley with Redpath play productions. Although he did not make the transition into sound film, Manners was involved in the production of several silent films.

Two other chautauqua directors who at times collaborated with

Keighley were De Wolf Hopper and William K. Howard. Hopper began his career in acting in the 1880s and by 1910 had become a noted actor and director of both plays and musicals. In recognition of his talents, Hopper was offered a contract by the Triangle Film Corporation in 1915, and he accepted. Although interested and active in film, Hopper also directed musical productions for Broadway and, by 1916, for the Redpath Chautauqua Bureau. In the late 1930s, Hopper acted in the Warner Brothers release of *The Cowboy Quarter Back*, and during the 1940s, he appeared in a number of movies, including *Bullets for O'Hara*. The latter movie was directed by William K. Howard, who had been a set designer and director for both the Redpath and Lincoln chautauqua bureaus. Howard directed more than a dozen silent films during the 1920s and was involved in the making of more than 12 films in the 1930s.

Eugene Lockhart, the Canadian-born actor, worked under the direction of Keighley in over a dozen play productions for the Redpath Chautauqua Bureau. After permanently leaving circuit chautauqua work in 1927 and working in various New York play productions, Lockhart and his wife Kathleen Lockhart were asked by Keighley to appear in a 1936 film called *Brides Are Like That*. The film was based on Barry Connor's 1925 play *Applesauce*, the play exclusively written for the Redpath Chautauqua Bureau and in which Lockhart had had a part. The Lockharts are the parents of actress June Lockhart.

Eugene Lockhart, who was better known in Warner Brothers publicity as "Gene" Lockhart, stayed with Warner Brothers until 1949, when he appeared in his last film, *The Inspector General*. The film starred, among others, Danny Kay, Elsa Lanchester, and Rhys Williams. Rhys Williams had worked with Lockhart in a number of Keighley productions for the Redpath Chautauqua Bureau. Williams, in fact, had actually begun his acting career working for Keighley-produced Redpath productions. Williams left chautauqua after World War I to pursue an acting career on Broadway. Later he appeared in several movies, including the 1945 production of *The Corn Is Green*, starring Bette Davis, *The Inspector General*, and the 1951 production of *Lightning Strikes Twice*.

Oscar-winning Martha Scott, who on occasions acted with Eugene Lockhart in Keighley-produced circuit plays, worked with him again in the 1941 film *One Foot in Heaven*. In 1957, she appeared in the award-winning film production of *Sayonara*. During the early 1920s, Phil Tongue worked as an actor and reader/humorist for the Peffer Chautauqua Bureau, which operated primarily in New England. In 1936, he was recognized for the supporting role he played in the Broadway production of *Fresh Fields*. In 1954 he appeared with Tab Hunter and Robert Mitchum in the Warner Brothers movie version of Eugene O'Neill's *Track of the Cat*. Jay Tobias, who emerged as a musical comedy chautauqua director in 1926, went to Hollywood when the circuit movement ended and appeared in several films.

The Oscar-winning Dean Jagger worked on the Ellison-White western circuit in the early 1920s. As they were traveling to a chautauqua engagement in Arizona, the bus in which Jagger and the other circuit members were riding went off the road. One person was killed, and the others, with the exception of Jagger and a baritone, were seriously injured. The bus had contained the production company which was to perform the play *Cappy Ricks*. Jagger and the baritone had been sent with the production company to assist with stage props and lighting and to provide entertainment between scene changes. With the production company and the bus disabled, Jagger and the baritone hitchhiked a ride to the chautauqua grounds, where they found the audience assembled and waiting to be entertained.

After explaining to the audience what had happened to the dramatic company, Jagger and the baritone did an impromptu performance before the audience. The audience, according to Harry P. Harrison, "stood and cheered, and the next night and the next night, in two other small Arizona towns." Jagger stayed with the Ellison-White Bureau for several seasons before going to Broadway. In 1933, he was featured in the first Broadway production of *Tobacco Road*. By the end of the 1930s, Jagger had entered into the film industry, and in 1938 he starred with Dorothy Gish in D. W. Griffith's film *Missouri Legend*. Between 1940 and 1950, Jagger appeared in various Westerns and World War II adventure films. More recently, Jagger performed in the movie *Twelve O'clock High* and played the role of the principal in the 1960s television series, *Mr. Novak*.

Additional motion picture personalities were associated with circuit chautauqua. The list includes dancers Adele and Fred Astaire; character actress Beulah Bondi; Keystone Cop Chester Conklin; actress Ruth Donnelly, who danced a jig as Sister Michael in *The Bells of St. Mary's*; Broadway and television producer Max Gordon; actress Marjorie Main, best known for her role as Ma opposite Percy Kilbride in the Ma and Pa Kettle series; comedian Jack Oakie, who portrayed Mussolini in Charlie Chaplin's *The Great Dictator*; dialect comedian Jack Pearl, the "Baron von Munchausen"; Roger Pryor, son of chautauqua band leader Arthur Pryor; actress Esther Ralston, known in the movie trade as "The American Venus"; and actress Blanche Yurka, the "Bohemian Girl."

Circuit chautauqua performers like Edgar Bergen, Everett Edward Kemp, and Clarence Nash established a name for themselves, first on chautauqua, then in radio, and finally in film and television work. It was only after the chautauqua and vaudeville circuits began to ebb that Bergen became involved in film features, radio, and finally movies. What chautauqua and lyceum had taught Bergen (and Charlie McCarthy) in the eight years of their association with the circuit, according to his daughter Candice Bergen, was "how to dress, move on stage, write and deliver material, shape an act, sense an audience. Become performers. Vaudeville artists. This they did, and they did it quickly, having only seconds to win over what Oscar Hammerstein II called 'the Big, Black Giant'—the audience that waited impatiently under the tent." In 1934, Bergen began appearing in short film features produced by Warner Brothers and also performed on the "Rudy Vallee Fleischmann Radio Show" with Charlie McCarthy, Mortimer Snerd, and Effie Klinker. Within a few years, Bergen began his film career by acting with Charlie in a production called the *Goldwyn Follies*.

From the early 1930s into the 1950s, Everett Kemp, a former chautauqua reader and humorist, portrayed the character of "Uncle Ezra" on Kansas City's KMBC "Happy Hollow Radio Show." During the mid-1950s, he appeared in a television comedy produced by KCMO Television, also based in Kansas City, Missouri. Clarence Nash, who imitated the raspy voice of a temperamental duck before 1920s chautauqua audiences, was well known by the mid–1930s as the "Voice of Donald Duck." He, like Bergen and Kemp, had also made the transition from the circuit to radio work before being "discovered" by Walt Disney.

Moreover, many of the opera performers who had appeared before circuit chautauqua audiences—Julia Claussen, Alice Nielsen, Carmen Pascova, Leonora Sparks, among others—had at one time or another been recorded under the Victor Record label. Many of these recordings were played over the radio in the 1930s, 1940s, and into the 1950s. Other circuit chautauqua performers like Ralph Bingham, Elias Day, Fisk Jubilee Singers, Kryl's Orchestra, Arthur Pryor, Jessie Pugh, Opie Read, and Carl Sandburg were also heard over the radio at one time or another.

The "Spirit" of Chautauqua

In 1929, the United Circuit Chautauqua Bureau had printed across the front of its brochure the words "The Spirit of Chautauqua."

Whatever the motive for placing this phrase on the face of the brochure, the statement was ironically true. All that remained of circuit chautauqua by 1929 was essentially spirit. Despite the fear of movie competition, the remaining few circuits used the appeal of Hollywood to sell adults on letting their children come to the program. A 1929 "Redpath" brochure, for example, promised: "The Picture Man will take movies of the kids in the Junior Chautauqua Parade and show them the last night of chautauqua. 'Gee, I wonder if I can see myself as a Movie Star — sounds like being in Hollywood doesn't it?'"

The last few circuit bureaus that operated into 1929 and 1930 provided "movie features" which in some instances made up the bulk of the program. Transporting a projector projectionist, and a series of films was far less costly by that time than hiring and transporting performers and equipment. One chautauqua company noted that the following films were being offered on its 1929 program:

      Flying Romeos— Charlie Murray and George Sidney
      Little Shepherd of Kingdom Come— Richard Barthelmess
      The Wagon Show— Ken Maynard
      The Covered Wagon— J. Warren Kerrigan
      Legion of the Condemned— Gary Cooper and Fay Wray
      Speedy— Harold Lloyd
      Valley of the Giants— Milton Sills and Doris Kenyon
      Old Ironsides— Charles Farrell

But as this list of silent films demonstrates, the circuit bureaus integrated only silent films into their programs. By this time, the enormous cost and difficulty of moving sound-projection equipment was beyond what the bureaus could handle. As a result, however, the films that chautauquas offered on their programs were disappointing to the audiences. They expected and wanted to hear the new and fashionable "talkie." By using what was by then becoming antiquated film equipment in order to compete with the frequently featured "talkie" at the local movie house, chautauqua lost even more ground as a modern form of public entertainment.

Although it had incorporated smaller animals into magic or illusionary acts, chautauqua had traditionally discouraged large animal acts. Circuit chautauqua managers had not wanted to take any chance of being associated with the circus. Yet in the last years of the 1920s, large animal acts were integrated into some circuit programs and promoted as "Hollywood"-type entertainment. Animals were popular in

The Wonder Dog was chautauqua's version of Warner Brothers Studio's Rin-Tin-Tin. Wonder performed feats of mathematical genius from the chautauqua platform, ca. 1927. Redpath Collection, University of Iowa.

film throughout most of the 1920s. As film directors Richard Griffith and Arthur Mayer noted, "everything that ran, hopped, crept, or crawled had found a place in films."

In 1923, Warner Brothers introduced dog star Rin-Tin-Tin to the viewing world in a film called *Where the North Begins*. During the remainder of the 1920s, the studio made an additional 18 Rin-Tin-Tin features. One of the last remaining circuit chautauquas in the late 1920s, began featuring "Wonder Dog." The dog was promoted on the basis of being "better than Rin-Tin-Tin." Appearing on stage with a large blackboard, Wonder could presumably add, subtract, multiply, or divide the numbers written on the board by his "assistant." Another animal noted, in circuit promotion for its ability to calculate numbers was Mascot, "The $50,000 Horse."

By the end of the 1920s, the sophistication of motion pictures and serials, in conjunction with the "talkie," the availability of radios and radio programming, improved roads and automobiles, and, finally, the 1929 crash doomed any hope of the continuance of circuit chautauqua or, for that matter, vaudeville. When the Great Crash of 1929 occurred, the only two remaining circuits that had been created out of the Redpath Chautauqua Bureau when it was sold in 1926, the Peffer-Redpath and the Rupe-Redpath, folded. The last American-owned chautauqua company, the Associated Chautauquas, continued to operate one circuit until it was closed for good in a rural Illinois town in August of 1932. This was the same year that New York City's vaudeville Palace, at 47th and Broadway, closed its doors. Coincidentally, the circus, which did not have the same ties with modern media as did chautauqua and vaudeville, has survived into present day, although it was daunted by the depression.

Life After Death

Several American communities tried in the aftermath of circuit chautauqua to keep the concept alive through the organization or reorganization of locally operated and sponsored chautauquas. Many former circuit entertainers were hired by community-based chautauquas to appear on their programs. Places where local chautauquas continued to operate after 1930 included Fountain Park, Indiana; Wathena, Kansas; King City, Missouri; Storm Lake, Iowa; Winona Lake, Indiana; and Boulder, Colorado. Each of these communities had had a leading local chautauqua before the circuit chautauqua movement had even begun. The Chautauqua Institute, or what was once known as "Mother Chautauqua," is still in operation at Lake Chautauqua. By and large, the Institute evolved into a leading educational center for the arts.

VIII

Circuit Chautauqua as an Agent of Social Change

Without a doubt, many Americans viewed circuit chautauqua during its heyday as the "biggest event" of the year for their community. Boosters worked together to make their chautauqua the best ever. Main Street was cleaned, weeds in vacant lots mowed, and the events for Chautauqua Week planned. From the chautauqua platform, countless Americans learned about issues, concepts, and events not within their immediate grasp. They heard about tax plans and trusts, women's suffrage and the demon rum, community pride and business success, the war and foreign threats, electricity and farming, and Africa, China, South America, and the North Pole.

Long after the big tent was taken down, chautauqua patrons discussed with one another the things they had learned. Chautauqua also provided "the best" in drama, music, literature, and entertainment to patrons who otherwise would not have been exposed to such refinements. Drama evolved from readings to Shakespeare to Broadway plays. Music encompassed classical works, marches, jubilee singers, Metropolitan Opera performers, South Pacific vocal groups, harmony maids, and more. Magicians, illusionists, impersonators, storytellers, ventriloquists, and animals with "mathematical skills" all graced the chautauqua platform. Chautauqua youth programs provided children with opportunities to learn about nature and conservation, drama and music, foreign lands, and different customs. Chautauqua Town also taught boys and girls about civic leadership and community pride. Moreover, families, friends, and neighbors visited with one another at chautauqua, "a week long vacation."

Circuit chautauqua developed in a generation that truly experienced massive economic, political, social, and technological changes. Circuit programs helped Americans to deal with these transformations.

Praising rural life-styles and customs during the early years, circuit programs assured midwesterners of their importance in a country that was rapidly becoming industrialized and urban. Before World War I, the circuit programs began bridging the gap between rural and urban areas by focusing on matters of community and improvement and this effort was of importance to both segments of the population.

Once President Wilson declared war against Germany in 1917, the circuit programs extolled Americans for their patriotism and commitment to "making the world safe for democracy." Immediate postwar programs expressed the fears and doubts that many Americans had about anybody or anything considered foreign and presented economic directions for farming and business. During the last half of the 1920s, circuit chautauqua was the place that modern Americans went to see New York plays, to enjoy comedy, and to have fun.

Within approximately a quarter of a century, the circuit chautauqua movement had changed locally managed lyceum and chautauqua programs of adult education into a commercial program of mass entertainment. The strict control the individual communities had over their nineteenth-century lyceum and permanent chautauqua program was replaced by a twentieth-century movement that operated from central offices, provided a standardized program package, and delivered features that eventually all Americans could enjoy. In doing so, circuit chautauqua fostered a "melting pot" ideology that broke down the boundaries between what was considered to be rural and what was regarded as urban. Vaudeville and Broadway were always dominantly urban, while lyceum and permanent chautauquas were rural. Circuit chautauqua, as it evolved, satisfied the needs and values of both marketplaces.

In the end, circuit chautauqua was so successful in meeting the marketplace demands of Americans for entertainment that its own identity was lost. By the 1920s, circuit chautauqua no longer had its own unique message or cause or separate identity from other forms of popular entertainment. Once circuit chautauqua lost its own uniqueness, the movement began to decline. Although factors such as the "talkie," the radio, and improvements in transportation, coupled with the Great Crash of 1929, hurt circuit chautauqua, the movement was already faltering before these innovations and this economic nightmare had a major impact on the average American.

Circuit chautauqua was also an important link between nineteeth-century and twentieth-century American forms of entertainment. It encouraged and fostered the acceptance of modern forms of mass media such as film, radio, and, even to a degree, television. Many of those associated with circuit chautauqua platform arts learned how to adapt production techniques and scripts and musical scores to mass audiences comprised of both rural and urban peoples. Circuit chautauqua productions encouraged what are now referred to as networking systems. It was no accident that so many of the same people who first worked together in circuit chautauqua productions later would work together in film and television. Circuit chautauqua was also responsible in part for nurturing an acceptance of modern electronic media. As radio, film, and even television utilized the voices and images of recognizable former chautauqua entertainers, the "new" media forms were not as forbidding as they might have been.

Circuit chautauqua grew up in a cornfield, went to war, tried to be modern, and in the end returned to the farm. The chautauqua journey left unforgettable trails and images. It bridged the gap between nineteenth- and twentieth-century attitudes about education and entertainment, nourished a national ideology, and readied the nation for electronic mass media entertainment. Whether an entertainer, superintendent, tent boy, or audience member, those who were part of the journey fondly remember their community's chautauqua park, the glamour of the Chautauqua Girl, William Jennings Bryan, Kryl's Band, Reno the Great, the Fox Quartet, the Jackson Jubilee Singers, and more, much more. As one person interviewed summed it up, "Circuit chautauqua was wonderful. Oh, it was simply wonderful. I wish I could go again."

Appendix

Summary of twenty years of Redpath Chautauqua programs provided in *Twenty Years of Chautauqua Success*, Redpath Collection

1904
FIFTEEN TOWNS
NINE DAYS PROGRAM

Talent includes following:
Chicago Ladies Quartette
D. W. Robertson (Moving Pictures)
Giant Quartette (Colored)
Ash Davis (Cartoonist)
Temple Quartette with Katherine Cole
Edwin Brush (Magician)
Garretson (Juggler) (each for three days)
George L. McNutt
Maud Ballington Booth
Gen. Z. T. Sweeney
Col. Bain
Frank G. Smith
Adrian M. Newens
Dr. E. A. Ross
T. Baird Collins (Flying Machine)
Dr. Thomas E. Green, et al.

1907

Hesperian Quartette
Carl D. Thompson
W. Robbert Goss (Illus.)
Hesperian Quartette
Rt. Rev. J. Henry Tihen
Geo. E. Garretson (Juggler)
Hungarian Orchestra
Judge Ben B. Lindsey
Geo. E. Garretson
Hungarian Orchestra
Gov. E. W. Hoch
Peter McQueen (Illus.)
Sterling Jubilee Singers
Monroe E. Markley
Peter McQueen (Illus.)
Sterling Jubilee Singers
J. Adam Bede
Oberamergau by Goss

1908

The Stelzle Quartette
H. P. Miller
Ten Pueblo Indians
Ohio Male Quartette
Warren G. Harding
Opie Read
Hungarian Orchestra
Dr. Thos. E. Green
Dr. Thos. Will (Illus.)
The Bernards
Thos. Brooks Fletcher
Alton Packard
Sterling Jubilee Singers
Dr. A. E. Winship
W. Robert Goss (Illus.)
H. Ruthven McDonald
Richmond P. Hobson
Ernest Harold Baynes

1909

Burton Thatcher
Duncan McKinley
Ralph Bingham
Royal English Bell Ringers
Arthur MacMurray
Royal English Bell Ringers
Concert Trio (Nell Bunnell)
Dr. Geo. R. Stuart
Albert Armstrong (Illus.)
Mrs. Brown & Boys
Sen. R. M. La Follette
Chas. A. Payne (Illus.)
Royal Hungarian Orchestra
Charles B. Landis
Hal Merton (Magician)
Commonwealth Quartette
Mrs. La Salle Corbell Picket
Dr. Frederick E. Hopkins
Cole Steele Company
Judge Alden
Cole Steele Company

1910

Kirksmith Sisters
Mattison W. Chase
Evelyn Bargelt
Royal Italian Band
Walter Eccles
Band
Ladies' Quartette (Mrs. Watkins)
Dr. A. A. Willitts
Bishop W. F. McDowell
H. Ruthven McDonald
Henry J. Rainey
Fr. P. J. McCorry
Music Makers Quartette
Lee Francis Leybarger
Strickland W. Gillilan
Fox Sisters Orchestra
Edward Russel Perry
Sen. Irvin L. Lenroot
Lee Lathrop Fullenwider
Monroe E. Markley
The Floyds (Magic)

1911

Dunbar Singing Orchestra
Dr. Mansell
Thos. M. McClary
Weatherwax Quartette
Miss Belle Kearney
Jas. Francis O'Donnell
Clark Bowers Company
Bishop Robert McIntyre
Arthur K. Peck (Illus.)
White Rose Orchestra
William Edgar Geil
Jos. W. Folk
Thaviu Band
  and
Grand Opera Quartette
Heimerdinger Trio
Garetta (Animals)
Charles R. Adair
Riner Sisters
Chas. L. Seasholes
Jess Pugh-Riners

1912

Maurer Sisters
Charles W. Fitzwilliams
W. I. Nolan
Music Makers Quartette
Mrs. A. C. Zehner
Rosani (Juggler)
The Artists Co. (Kickbush)
Bishop Anderson
Dr. Lincoln L. Wirt
Balalaika Orchestra
Col. Geo. A. Gearhart
Sen. Burkett
Thaviu Band
  and
Grand Opera Sextette
Boston Lyrics Trio
Hugh A. Orchard
Alton Packard
College Girls
Nels Darling
Walter Eccles & Girls

Appendix

1913

Spanish Ladies
Judge A. Z. Blair
Concert
Jacob Reuter Co.
Dr. F. W. Gunsaulus
Ralph Parlette
Harmony Concert Co.
A. C. Shallenberger
Ernest Wray O'Neal
Thaviu
   and
Twelve Singers
Riner Sisters
Mary Agnes Doyle
Frederick A. Poole (Illus.)
Edwin R. Weeks Co.
Victor Murdock
Shungopavi
Dunbar Quartette & Bells
Harry A. Atwater
Joy Nite by Dunbars

1914

Dunbar Girls
A. M. Reitzel
Frederick A. Poole (Illus.)
Ethyl Hinton (Mordelia)
Geo. H. Bradford
Ben Greet Players
Rogers Grilley
Sen. Frank J. Cannon
Gov. R. B. Glenn
Sam Schildkret
Sen. Jas. E. Watson
"Any Tink You Like"
Alpine Yodlers
J. C. Nayphe
Raweis
Grand Opera Quartette
Gov. H. A. Buchtel
Montraville Wood
Quintano Band
Fr. Austin Fleming
Band

1915

Old Home Singers
Judge Manford Schoonover
Old Home Singers
University Girls
Judge Kavanaugh
Lou J. Beauchamp
Orpheum Mus. Club
Arthur Kachel
Victor Murdock
Kryl Bohemian Band
Cambridge Players
Ng Poon Chew
Ross Crane
S. Platt Jones
Byron C. Piatt
Balmers Kaffirs
Sam Schildkret
Sen. J. K. Vardaman
Schildkret Orchestra

1916

Kellogg Haines Co.
E. H. Lougher
Kellogg Haines Pty.
McGrath Bros.
H. A. Adrian
Col. Geo. W. Bain
Gwent Welch Singers
Chas. F. Scott
Welch Singers
Phillipinos
Opie Read
Sen. T. P. Gore
Kryl Bohemian Band
Chautauqua Concert Pty.
Gov. M. R. Patterson
Laurant & Co.
Ada Roach Co.
Geo. L. McNutt
Ada Roach Co.

1917

Schumann Quintette
Concert

Dr. Jas. L. Gordon
Glenn Wells Co.
Sarah Tyson Rorer
Sen. Frank B. Willis
Royal Dragoons
Cong. Abercrombie
Royal Dragoons
Elsie Baker
Concert
John B. Ratto
Kryl Bohemian Band
Judge Ben B. Lindsey
Katherine Ridgeway
Hawaiians
H. S. McCowan
Mildred Leo Clemens

1918

Jess Pugh
Private Lovell
Dr. Chas. E. Barker
Knight MacGregor
B. F. McDonald
Dr. Chas. S. Medbury
Bostonians (Orch.)
Frank Cole
Bostonians (Orch.)
Williams Jubilee Singers
L. C. Jones — Dr. Montgomery
Williams Jubilee Singers
Mikado Orchestra
Fred Dale Wood
"Mikado" Light Opera
Cyclone Davis
"It Pays to Advertise"
Pagent
Reno
Royal Grenadiers

1919

The Altheas
Concert
Dr. Chas. S. Medbury
Boston Opera Company
Harry J. Loose
Boston Opera Company

Chicago Saxaphone Co.
Concert
Sir John Foster Frasier
White Hussar Girls
Gov. Geo. A. Carlson
White Hussar Girls
Frank Dixon
The Melting Pot
Aviation
Maj. R. C. Bridgman
Quaglia's Banda Roma
Pagent
Red Cross — Miss Nelson
Ralph Bingham

1920

Columbia Players
Concert
Edwin M. Whitney
Dorothy Cole Co.
W. E. Wenner
Ralph Dennis
Solo Recital
Rev. Isaac L. Wood
Criterion Quartette
John C. Weber
   and His Band
Harry A. Barnhart
"Nothing but the Truth"
Premier Artists
Phil P. Campbell
Premier Artists
Pagent
Stone Platt Co.
Ada Ward

1921

Orchestra Troubadors
Troubadors — George Tack
Dr. Robt. S. McGowan
Rich Werno Entertainers
Granville Jones
Quin O'Brien
Weatherwax Bros.
Concert
Bertha Kuntz Baker

Prelude Recital
Gov. Chas. H. Brough
Pascova-Hardeman-Wille
David D. Vaughan
"Broadway Jones"
Gondoliers
Farmer Burns
Gondoliers
Mother Goose Party
Baker-Youna-Pryor
Jess Pugh — Joy Nite

1922

Mitchell Bros.
Homer C. Boblitt
Robt. G. Cousins
DiGiorgio Orchestra
Edwin M. Whitney
DiGiorgio
Handley Trio
John E. Pounds
D. Thomas Curtin
College Glee Club

Edna Means
Black Face Minstrels
Prelude Recital
John Temple Graves
DeZanco-Smith-Oster
J. Campbell White
"Turn to the Right"
Pagent
Paul Clemons — Marionettes
Dr. R. B. Baumgardt

1923

Dr. Thomas E. Green
Honorable L. J. Dickinson
Bill Daly
DeKoven
"The Witching Hour"
"The Meanest Man in the World"
William Keighley
"Witching Hour"
"Robin Hood"
Dr. Tehyi Hseih

Selected Bibliography

Adams, James Truslow. *Frontiers of American Culture: A Study of Adult Education in a Democracy*. New York: Scribner's Sons, 1944.
Albert, Allen. "The Tents of the Conservative." *Scribner's* 72 (July 1922): 54–59.
Bartlett, John B. "Bryan, Chautauqua's Orator." Ph.D. diss., Ohio State University, 1963.
Bede, Carl. *The American Lyceum: Town Meeting of the Mind*. New York: Oxford University Press, 1956.
Bergen, Candice. *Knock Wood*. New York: Linden, 1984.
Bestor, Arthur, Jr. *Chautauqua Publications*. New York: Chautauqua Press, 1935.
Bliven, Bruce. "Mother, Home and Heaven." *New Republic* 37 (January 1924): 172–75.
Blum, Daniel. *A Pictorial History of the American Theatre: 1860–1980*. New York: Crown, 1981.
_____. *A Pictorial History of the Silent Screen*. New York: Grosset & Dunlap, 1953.
Briggs, Irene, and Raymond DaBoll. *Recollections of the Lyceum and Chautauqua Circuits*. Maine: Bond Wheelwright, 1969.
Burr, Agnes R. *Russell H. Conwell and His Work*. Philadelphia: John C. Winston, 1917.
Case, Victoria and Raymond. *We Called It Culture*. New York: Doubleday, 1948.
"Chautauqua." *Outlook* 16 (March 1927):325–26.
Chautauqua Collection. Iowa State Historical Society, Iowa City, Iowa.
"The Chautauqua Liked by Millions Is 40 Years Old." *New York Times*, 12 July 1941, sec. 4 p.3.
Coletta, Paolo E. *William Jennings Bryan: Progressive Politician and Moral Statesman, 1900–1915*. Lincoln: University of Nebraska Press, 1968.
Commanger, Henry Steele. *The American Mind: An Interpretation of American Thought and Character Since the 1880's*. New Haven: Yale University Press, 1950.
"Current Tendencies in the Development of the Chautauqua Movement." *Current Opinion* 59 (August 1915):115–16.
Day, Beth. *The Little Professor of Piney Woods: The Story of Professor Laurence Jones*. New York: Julian Messner, 1955.
Degler, Carl N. *Out of Our Past: The Forces That Shaped Modern America*. New York: Harper and Row, 1959.

DeMille, Cecil B. *The Autobiography of Cecil B. DeMille.* Edited by Donald Hayne. N.J.: Prentice-Hall, 1959.
Earley, Mary Dawn. *Stars of the Twenties.* New York: Viking, 1975.
Gance, Abel. *The Parade's Gone By.* New York: Alfred A. Knopf, 1968.
Gilbert, Douglas. *American Vaudeville: Its Life and Times.* New York: Dover, 1963.
Gish, Lillian. *The Movies Mr. Griffith and Me.* N.J.:Prentice-Hall, 1969.
Gould, Joseph. *The Chautauqua Movement.* Albany: State University of New York Press, 1961.
Graham, Donald L. "Circuit Chautauqua, a Middle Western Institution." Ph.D. diss., State University of Iowa, 1953.
Green, Abel, and Joe Laurie, Jr. *Show Biz: From Vaude to Video.* New York: Henry Holt, 1951.
Hance, Kenneth G., Homer O. Hendrickson, and Edwin W. Schoerberger. "The Late National Period: 1850–1930." In *History and Criticism of American Public Address*, vol. 1, edited by William N. Brigance, pp. 111–52. New York: McGraw-Hill,1943.
Harrison, Harry P., as told to Karl Detzer. *Culture Under Canvas.* New York: Hastings House, 1958.
Hays, Samuel P. *The Response to Industrialism: 1885–1914.* Chicago: University of Chicago Press, 1957.
Higham, Charles. *The Art of the American Film: 1900–1971.* New York: Doubleday, 1973.
Hirschhorn, Clive. *The Warner Bros. Story.* 1979. Reprint. New York, Crown, 1982.
Hofstadter, Richard. *The Age of Reform: From Bryan to F.D.R.* New York: Alfred A. Knopf, 1955.
_____. *The Paranoid Style in American Politics and Other Essays.* New York: Random House, 1952; Vintage, 1967.
Horner, Charles. *Strike the Tents: The Story of Chautauqua.* Philadelphia: Dorrance, 1954.
Horner Chautauqua Collection. Special Collections, University of Iowa, Iowa City, Iowa.
Hurlbut, Jesse L. *The Story of Chautauqua.* New York: G. P. Putnam's Sons, 1921.
Kniher, Charles R. "The Chautauqua Literary and Scientific Circle, 1879–1914: An Historical Interpretation of an Educational Piety in Industrial America." Ph.D. diss., Columbia University, 1948.
Lake Contrary Brochures. St. Joseph Public Library, St. Joseph, Mo.
Laurie, Joe, Jr. *Vaudeville: From the Honky-Tonks to the Palace.* 1953. Reprint. New York: Kennikat, 1972.
Leuchtenburg, William E. *The Perils of Prosperity: 1914–1932.* New York: Rand McNally, 1958.
Lewis, Sinclair. *Main Street.* New York: Harcourt, Brace, and World, 1920.
Limmp, Isabel B. *King City, 1856–1940.* Kansas: Mennonite, 1983.
Loring Campbell Collection of 319 Chautauqua and Lyceum Brochures: Special Collections, University of Arizona, Tucson, Arizona.
McConnell, Grant. *The Decline of Agrarian Democracy.* Los Angeles: University of California, 1953.
McCown, Robert A. "Records of the Redpath Collection." *Books at Iowa* 19 (1973): 8–23.

MacLaren, Gay. *Morally We Roll Along*. Boston: Little, Brown, 1938.
Manderson, Mary Sandra. "The Redpath Lyceum Bureau, an American Critic: Decision-Making and Programming Methods for Circuit Chautauqua, 1912–1930." Ph.D. diss., University of Iowa, 1981.
Mason, Gregory. "Chautauqua: Its Techniq." *American Mercury* 1 (March 1924): 274–80.
Morrison, Theodore. *Chautauqua: A Center for Education, Religion, and the Arts in America*. Chicago: University of Chicago Press, 1971.
Murray, Robert K. *Red Scare: A Study in National Hysteria, 1919–1920*. Minneapolis: University of Minnesota, 1955.
Noffsinger, John F. *Correspondence Schools, Lyceums, Chautauquas*. New York: Macmillan, 1926.
Nye, Russell B. *Midwestern Progressive Politics: A Historical Study of Its Origins and Development, 1870–1950*. East Lansing: Michigan State College, 1951.
Orchard, Hugh. *Fifty Years of Chautauqua*. Cedar Rapids: Torch, 1923.
Parrington, Vernon J. *The Beginnings of Critical Realism in America: 1860–1920*. New York: Harcourt, Brace, and World, 1930.
Redpath Chautauqua Collection. Special Collections, University of Iowa, Iowa City, Iowa.
Richmond, Rebecca. *Chautauqua: An American Place*. New York: Duell, Sloane, and Pearce, 1943.
Sandburg, Carl. *Ever the Winds of Chance*. Urbana: University of Illinois, 1983.
Scott, Marian. *Chautauqua Caravan*. New York: Appleton-Century, 1939.
Shirer, William L. *20th Century Journey: The Start 1904–1930*. New York: Simon and Schuster, 1976.
Slout, William Lawrence. *Theatre in a Tent: The Development of a Provincial Entertainment*. Ohio: Bowling Green University Popular Press, 1972.
Smith, Bill. *The Vaudevillians*. New York: Macmillan, 1976.
Smith, Henry Nash. *Virgin Land: The American West as Symbols and Myth*. Cambridge: Harvard University Press, 1970.
Staples, Shirley. *Male-Female Comedy Teams in American Vaudeville: 1865–1932*. Michigan: University of Michigan Institute, 1984.
Tapia, John. "Circuit Chautauqua's Program Brochures: A Study in Social and Intellectual History." *Quarterly Journal of Speech* 67 (May 1981):167–77.
Tekkel, John. "Chautauqua: A Nostalgic Salute." *Saturday Review* 11 January 1969, 122–23.
Tozier, Roy B. "The American Chautauqua: A Study of a Social Institution." Ph.D. diss., State University of Iowa, 1932.
_____. "A Short Life — History of the Chautauqua." *American Journal of Sociology* 10 (July 1934):71.
Vawter Chautauqua Collection. Special Collections, University of Iowa, Iowa City, Iowa.
Vincent, John Heyl. *The Chautauqua Movement*. New York: Books for Libraries Press, 1885.
Wagner, Carl Vern. "The American Lyceum: A Survey from 1826 to 1947." Thesis, University of Washington, 1948.

Wiebe, Robert H. *The Search for Order: 1877–1920*. New York: Hill and Wang, 1967.
Wilson, Edna E. "Canvas and Culture: When Chautauqua Comes to Town." *Outlook* 131 (August 1922):598–600.
Wiggam, Albert. "Is the Chautauqua Worthwhile?" *Bookman* 65 (May 1927): 399–406.

Index

A. I. Root Company 195
Abraham Lincoln: The Prairie Years 167
"Acres of Diamonds" 58, 124
Adam and Eva 189
Adams, James Trusdale 11
Adams, Maude 127
Adananc Quartette 170
Addams, Jane 20, 55, 144
Adrian, Henry A. 87
Affiliated Circuit Chautauqua 69
"Aggie" and "Sci" 141
Al Baker and "Dummy Dennis" 175
Alamos 190
Albert, Allen 85
Aldrich, Arthur 133
Alice Schroeder Company 139, 143
Alkahest Chautauqua 82, 88
All American Niles Hussar Band 126
All College Glee Club and Black Face Minstrels 173
Allen, Gracie 185
Allied soldiers 117, 118
Allied powers 113, 140
Allpress All Star Company 171
Althea Players 127
America Yesterday and Today 141
American Communist Party 150
American Federation of Labor 150
"American Folktale" 167
American Girls Americanism 141
American Ladies Orchestra 99
American Legion 148
American Literary Bureau of New York 14
American Mercury 181
The American Songbag 167
"An American Vagabond" 66
"American Wonder Series" 72
"Americanism" 156

"America's Tomorrow" 151
"America's World Leadership" 157
"Amos and Andy" 185
Amsbary, Wallace 67, 94
amusement tax 157
"An Analysis of Success and Failure" 83
Andrews, Edward 133
Andy Hardy features 189
animal acts 202
"Annie Laurie" 170
Anthony, Susan B. 15, 144
Anvil Chorus 62
"Apostle of Sunshine" 60, 120
Applesauce 162, 188–189, 199
Arden Drama Company 92
Aristotle 12
Armistice 117, 149, 164
Armitage, Frank Guy 176
Armour Institute of Technology 61
Arms and Man 134
Armstrong, Albert 71
"The Art of Making Money" 15
Arthur Pryor Chautauqua Band 62
Associated Chautauqua 203
Associated Western Literary Society 14
Astaire, Adele 200
Astaire, Fred 200
At Home Plantation Singers 130
Atlanta, Georgia 179
Atlantic Monthly 30
Aubrey, John E. 85, 120
Audubon Republican 29

Bachman, Carl 167
"Back to the Constitution" 155
Bacon, Frank 188
Bain, George W. 23
Baker, Al 175–176
Baker, Bertha (Kuntz) 167

219

Baker, Charles 86
Baker, Elsie 20, 99, 177
Baled Hay 69
Balmer, H. L. 101
Bambi 137
bank closings 183
Bargelt, Evelyn 88
Barnum, Phineas T. 15
Barnum and Bailey Circus 18, 177
Barrymore, Ethel 134
Barrymore, John 186
Barthelmess, Richard 202
Battis, William Sterling 137
"Battle Ground of the Nation" 123
Battle of Chateau-Thierry 119
Battle of the Somme 118
Battlefield 92
Beach Trio 99
Beauchamp, "Take the Sunny Side" Lou 61
Bede, J. Adam 23, 54, 124, 156
Beecher, Henry Ward 13, 15
Bells of St. Mary's 200
Ben Davies Welsh Quartet 172
Ben Greet (and His Shakespearian) Players 44, 90, 91–92, 189–190, 198
Ben Hur 67
Bergen, Candice 176, 201
Bergen, Edgar 44, 174–176, 201
Bernhardt, Sarah 98
Beulah Buck Quartette 99
Bevans, Irene 91
Beveridge, Albert 44, 147
"Bibbity Bob" 65–66
Bible 67
Bill Johnson and His One Tune 70
Bill Nye and the Boomerang 69
Bill of Divorcement 189
Bingham, Ralph 70, 109, 201
Biographical History of Atchison County, Missouri 22
Birth of a Nation 123
Black Eagle, Chief 192
Blackmore, R. D. 71
Blanchard Costume Singers 172
Bliven, Bruce 184
Boblitt, Homer G. 152, 154
Bode, Carl 13
Bohemian Girl 97, 134
Bohumir Kryl (and His Great) (Orchestra and) Band 62–63, 191
Bolieau Concertiers 99
Bolshevik Revolution 150

Bolshevism 149–150, 153
"Bolshevism in Russia and America" 152
Bondi, Beulah 200
Booker T. Washington (Tuskegee) Singers 59, 101, 130, 173
booking agent, chautauqua 32–34
Booth, Edwin 109
Booth, Maud Ballington 57
Borah, William E. 147, 148
Boston, Massachusetts 12
Boston Lyceum Bureau 13
Bought and Paid For 137
Boulder, Colorado 204
Boxer Rebellion 89
Bradford, George 61
Brides Are Like That 189, 199
Brinton, E. A. 90
Bristow, Joseph L. 55
Britt Chautauqua 97, 134
Broadway 69, 70, 93, 94, 95, 133, 134, 135, 136, 179, 189, 197, 198, 199, 205; performers 196
Broadway Jones 136, 162
Broadway Players 162
Bromwell, James 155, 157
Brooks, Fred Emerson 67
"Brother Charlie" 194
Brother Jones' Sermon 70
Brough, Charles 157
Brush, Edwin 19, 75–76, 108, 142, 169
Bryan, Charles W. 194
Bryan, William J. 15, 20, 23, 33, 43, 44, 45, 56, 57, 58, 59, 60, 61, 85, 111, 112, 120, 124 147, 153, 154, 184, 193, 194, 207
Bubble 163
Buckingham Palace 109
Buehler, Ezra Christian 41
Bullets for O'Hara 199
Bunny, John 19, 44, 69–70, 94, 196
Burbank Man 87
Burkarian, Nikolai 150
Burke, Billie 134
Burns, George 185
Burns, Harry Foster 155
Byrd, Richard E. 20

Cadman, Samuel Parks 61, 124
Cadmean Chautauqua 48, 79
Calgary 79
Cambridge Players 135, 138
Cambridge Singers 171
Cameron, Missouri 131

Index

Campbell, Loring 109
Campbells 169
Cannon, Frank J. 83–84
Cannon, "Uncle" Joe 84
Cappy Ricks 163, 200
Carlson, George A. 156
Carmen 198
carnivals 158–159, 169
Caruso, Enrico 98
"Case Against Cigarette Smoking" 56–57
Cashford, Fern 167
Caupolican, Chief 131, 143
Caveny Company 88
Cedar Rapids, Iowa 48
Central Community Chautauqua 79
Century 30
"Challange" 194
Chambers, John F. 195
Chanticleer 86
Chaplin, Charlie 200
Charles City, Missouri 186
"Charlie McCarthy" 174, 201
"Chase and Sanborn Radio Hour" 185
chautauqua, circuit: boosters 35, 36, 37, 183; "chautauqua girl" 73, 207; children's program 105; commercial aspects 30–32, 79; contract, chautauqua 33; decline of 182; introduction of circuits 25; junior chautauqua 105, 174; meanings of 19–20; media industry as competition 160; "Methodist circus" 39; not-for-profit 160; overseas 32; permanent 19–25, 206; platform 40; season 45, 179–181; small 158–159; states, popular 48; success 179, 180, 181; tent 40; town 174, 205; week 45, 205
chautauqua, community assemblies: auditorium 24; community based 22–25; independents 76, 194
Chautauqua Girls at Home 19
"A Chautauqua Lady in 1921" 44
Chautauqua Movement 21
Chautauqua, New York Institute: *Chautauquan* 20; College of Liberal Arts 22; The Institute ("Mother") 19–22, 55, 64, 178, 204; Literary and Scientific Circle 20, 21, 22, 49, 95; Normal School 22; Press 20, 21; School of Theology 22; Teacher's Retreat 22; University 22
Chautauqua Six 99
Chautauqua Union 25

Chevalier, Maurice 185
Chicago 48, 68, 52, 61, 78, 179, 188
Chicago Art Institute 88
Chicago Lyceum Bureau 101
Chicago Tribune 181
child labor laws 55
Chocolate Soldier 134
Christmas Carol 67
Christmas Morning at Home 137
cigarette smoking 56
circus 176–177, 203; "Golden age" 18
Civil War 160
Clansman 123
Clare, Joseph 151
Clarinda, Iowa 24
Clark, Champ 53, 54, 111, 154, 193
Clark, Estelle 70
Class Royal Grenadiers 125
Claussen, Julia 98, 165, 201
Clements (Gates), Roena 44–45, 73, 98, 107
Clemons, Paul 176
Cleveland, Ohio 79
Cobb, Irvin S. 119
Cohan, George 162
Cohen on the Telephone 138
Coit-Alber Chautauqua 79
"Colonel Fayerweather" 138
Colonial Players and Singers 170
Colored Lochimnvar 137
Columbia's Awakening 141
Columbus, Ohio 48
Columbus Memorial Fountain 87
Comedy of Errors 91
"Comin' Thro' the Rye" 170
Committeeman's Manual 35
Commonweal 181
communism 149, 154
Communist Labor Party 150
Community Chautauqua 98
Conklin, Chester 200
Connelly, Marc 64, 198
Conner, John F. 155
Connor, Barry 188, 199
"Conquest of the Air" 195
conscription 115, 148
Conwell, Russell H. 58, 85, 87, 120, 124, 193
Cook, Frederick 72
Cooke, Edmund Vance 44, 61, 67, 72
Coolidge, Calvin 44, 179, 183, 194
Cooper, Gary 202
Cope, Leon 109

Corn Is Green 199
Correll, Charles 185
Covered Wagon 202
Cowboy Quarter Back 199
Craig, Missouri 38
Crane Ross (Rosey) 87–88
Crawford-Peffer Chautauqua 61
Croatian Tamburica Orchestra 128, 172
"Cross of Gold" 59
Crowin, Tom 139
Crumm, Edna 88
"Culture of Your Personality" 86
Cummings, Albert B. 55
Current Opinion 181
Custer, George 192

Daly, W. E. 154
Darling, Nels 84, 120
Darrow, Clarence 193
Daugherty, Harry M. 194
David Garrick 67
Davidson, Dore 92, 197
Davies, Ben 172
Davis, Bette 24, 199
Davis, J. H. "Cyclone" 83, 120
Davis, Jefferson 14
Davis, John W. 194
Day, Beth 103
Day, Elias 94, 138, 163, 201
Deane, Arthur 134
Debs, Eugene 44, 84, 149
Delsarte art of expression 24
Democratic Platform, 1916 146
Dennis, Ralph 152
Des Moines, Iowa 48, 96, 102
Detour 189
"Dickens Man" 137
Dietrick, "Sunshine" Paul 61, 169
Disney, Walt 168, 201
Dix, Richard 192
Dixie Jubilee Company 130
Dixon, Frank 23, 123, 193
Dixon, Thomas 123
Dr. Ehrlich's Magic Bullet 197
"Dr. Frederick Cook's Discovery of the North Pole" 72
Dodge automobile 122
"Dodge Victory Hour" 185
Dolliver, Jonathan P. 55
Don Juan 186
Donald Duck 168, 201
Donnelly, Ruth 200
Dopf 22

Dowling, Sylvester J. 123
Dramatic Mirror 137
Dresser, Louise 134
Drew, Sidney 134
Drinkwater, John 162, 164
DuBois, Howard W. 72
Dunbar, Ralph 44, 133
Dunbar Ladies Orchestra 125
Dunbar's Singing Bell Ringers 190
Dunbar's White Hussar Band 125
Durieux, William 177

Ealy, William S. 36
"East and West and the Borderland" 89
Eastwood, Clint 197
Easy Dawson 69
Easy to Love 198
"Eccentricities of Genius" 16
Eclair Production Company 166
"Ed-Win" (Wynn) 185
Edison, Thomas A. 20, 71
"Effective Government in the Post World War" 84
Efficiency 137
"Effie Klinker" 175, 201
Eggleston, Edward 70
Eisenhower, Dwight D. 55
electricity 122
Elixir of Youth 163
Elk City, Oklahoma 42
Ellison, Roy J. 27, 28, 29, 31, 79, 163
Ellison-White Chautauqua 31, 32, 45, 61, 79, 134, 156, 159–160, 162, 163, 168, 182, 200
Elmore, Lucy 176
Emerson, Ralph Waldo 13
Erie Canal 12
Ethiopian Serenaders 99, 100, 101
ethnic images 100
European Red Cross 119
Evening Star Chautauqua 129, 135, 155, 173
"Every Time I Feel the Spirit" 130
Every Which Way But Loose 197

Fads and Fancy 43
Fairbanks, Douglas 134, 166
Fairbanks Productions 197
"Famous Dove Trick" 108, 169
"Far East Question" 153
Farm Bloc 154
farm movements, 19th century 49
farm prices, decline in 183

Index 223

Farmers' Alliance 49, 76
"farcelets" 188
Farrar, Geraldine 198
Farrell, Charles 202
Ferrantes Hungarian Orchestra 99
festival activity 106
Fibber McGee and Molly 69
"Fight for a State" 54
Filipino Jackies 172
Finch, Flora 69
Finkbine, W.O. 102
Fink's Hussar Militaire 172
Fisk Jubliee Singers (Players) 64, 99, 101, 173, 201
Fisk University 64
Fitters, F. A. 183
"Fleischmann Hour" 185
Fletcher, Thomas Brooks 147–148
Floradora 166
Flowers, Montaville 67, 94, 117, 193
Floyds 108, 142, 169
Fluffy Ruffles 69
Flying Romeos 202
Fogelman, Harry L. 83, 120, 193
Folk, Joseph 54
Fonda, Jane 198
"Forces That Make Cities" 85
Ford, Henry 185
Fortune Hunter 137
Forty Liars and Other Lies 69
Fountain Park, Indiana 204
Fox Quartet 207
Fox Sisters Orchestra 64
Frank Lea Short Players 92
Frederici, Blanche 198
Free Baptist Chautauqua Assembly 24
Fresh Fields 200
Frohman, Charles 91
From Cannibalism to Culture 104
"Fun Maker" 109

Gale, Albert and Martha 109, 132, 143
Gallatin, Missouri 183
Gallatin Chautauqua Association 183
Garfield, James A. 64
Garretta 109
"Gates of the Soul" 61
Gattling Gun Fogelman 83
Gearhart, G. A. 23
George Tack Orchestral Troubadours 170
Gilbert, Bertha James 133

Gilbert and Sullivan 133, 134
Gillilan, Strickland 68–69, 94, 120, 167
"Girl with the Camera Eye" 95, 96
Gish, Dorothy 134, 200
Gish, Lillian 134, 149
Glenn, Robert G. 83
Glenn Wells Players 135
Golden Jubilee 178
Goldwyn Follies 201
Gondoliers Musical Program 172
Gordon, Elsie Mae 139
Gordon, Max 200
Gordon, Ruth 19, 44, 127, 197
Gore, Thomas 54
Gosden, Freeman 185
Gould, Joseph 20
"Governor Speaks" 194
Graham, Donald 31, 32
Grange 76
Grange Revolt 49
Grant, Ulysses S. 20
Gray, Estelle 165
Great Crash of 1929 169, 184, 187, 204, 206
Great Depression 183
Great Dictator 200
Greeley, Horace 13
Green, Able 18
Green Pastures 65, 198
Greet, Ben 90, 91, 92
Griffith, D.W. 104, 134, 123, 149, 161, 200,
Griffith, Richard 203
Gunsaulus, Frank Wakely 61, 87, 193
gyroscope 121

Hackett, Walter 135
Hadley, Herbert S. 54
Hale, Edward Everett 15
"Hand at the Nation's Throat" 151
Handley (Handley Trio) 43
Hanly, J. Frank 56
"Happy Hollow Radio Show" 201
Harding, Warren G. 44, 84, 145, 147, 156–8, 193–194
"Harp of the Sense, a Study in Vibrations" 120
Harrison, Harry P. 48, 49, 75, 83, 121, 177, 200
Harrison, Richard B. 64
Hart, William S. 134
Hathaway, George 15
Havensville, Kansas 45

Hawaiian Quintette 128
Hawaiian Singers and Players 99, 104
Hawn, Henry G. 138
Hay, John 89
Hayes, Rutherford B. 20
Hazard, John 162
hearing torpedo 121
Hearts of the World 149
Heath, Mary 195
Hedley, James 23
Henders, Harriette 98
Henderson, Harriette 98
Highland Lassies 172
Hilder Orchestra 97
Hillis, Newell Dwight 61
Hindus, Morris Gershon 125
Hinshaw Singing Band Opera Company 97
Hinton, Clara 63, 60, 65, 76, 86
Hinton, Ethel 109
History of the Southern Confederacy 14
History of the Standard Oil Company 55
Hitchcock, Alfred 197
Hitchcock, Raymond 69
HMS Pinafore 134
Hobart, Oklahoma 35
Hobart Republican 35
Hobson, R. P. 23
Hoch, Edward W. 54
Holbrook, Josiah 12, 13
Hollywood, California 190, 196, 197, 198, 200, 203,
Hollywood appeal 202
Holmes, Oliver Wendell 13
"Home Coming of Elmer Warts" 70
"Home Town" 84
Hoosier Schoolmaster 70
Hoover, Herbert 44, 157
Hoover, J. Edgar 150
Hopper, De Wolf 134, 199
Horner, Charles 34, 52
Horner-Redpath Chautauqua 34, 43
Hotchkiss, C. L. 42, 49
"Hour of Democracy" 124, 151
"How Should You Use Your Vote, Now That You Have It?" 145
"How to Live One Hundred Years" 86
How to Run a Lyceum Course 35
Howard, William K. 199
Howard, South Dakota 94
Howard Russell Song Review 170
Howard Tooley Opera Company 133
"Hows and Whys of the Ohio Gang" 194

Hugh McNutt's All-American Band 95
Hulbert, Homer A. 125, 153
Humoresque 167
Humphrey, Sue 45
Hunter, Tab 200
Hunt's Three Ring Circus 18

ideological linkages, 19th to 20th 206
Illustrated Doniphan County 24
"Impending Crisis" 83
In Walked Jimmy 189
Ince, Thomas H. 134
Independent Voter's Association 154
"Individual and Society" 157
"Inexcusable Lie" 148
Inside Daisy Clover 197
Inspector General 199
Instructions to Superintendents 44
international alliances 145
International Chautauqua Alliance 25
International Conference on Communism 149
International Lyceum and Chautauqua (Manager's) Association 31, 66, 117, 158, 176, 177, 178
interstate highways 185
Iowa City, Iowa 60
"Iowa Idea" 55
"Is Farming a Business" 154
It Pays to Advertise 135, 136, 162
"It's Bonnied Scotland in Sweetest Earnest Song" 129
"It's Me" 130

Jack and the Bean Stalk 176
Jackson Jubilee Singers 173, 207
Jacksonville, Florida 92
Jagger, Dean 44, 163, 200
"Japanese Silver Tongue" 89
"jar of life" 85–86
Jazz Singer 186
Jefferson, Thomas 49
Jo King and Her Harmony Maids 170
Joe Du Mond's Male Quartette 170
John Bunny Comedy 69
John Philip Sousa Marching Band 62
Johnson, Hiram 147
Joliet, Illinois 66
Jolson, Al 186, 196
Jones, Grandville 155
Jones, Hilton I. 120, 193
Jones, Laurence C. 102–103, 118
Jones, Sam 24

Jordan, David 148
"Jubilee Frolics" 191
jubilee performers 59, 64, 132, 164, 173
jubilee year 173, 178–179, 184, 193
Jucklins 67, 196
Kaffair Boys 43, 101
Kansas City, Kansas 78, 179
Kansas City, Missouri 43, 48, 163, 201
Kansas City Star 181
Kay, Danny 199
KCMO Television 201
Kealakai's Hawaiians 128
Keighley, William 91, 92, 135, 162, 164, 166, 169, 188, 197, 198, 199
Keighley-Redpath productions 162
Keith-Albee Vaudeville circuit 18
Keith-Orpheum Vaudeville circuit 18
Keith Vaudeville circuit 96, 196
Keller, Helen 144
Kelly, Gregory 127
Kemp, Everett Edward 44, 138, 167, 201
Kennedy, Charles Rann 92
Kenyon, Doris 202
Keokuk, Iowa 96, 196
Kerrigan, J. Warren 202
Kilbride, Percy 200
King City, Missouri 26, 56, 60, 204
Kinney, Hallie 39
Kirksmith Orchestra 63–64
Kling, Jeannette 137
Kohl-Castle Vaudeville circuit 18
Kryl's (Orchestra and) Band 96, 191, 201, 207
Ku Klux Klan 100

Ladies Home Journal 30
La Follette, Phil 194
La Follette, Robert 23, 44, 53, 82, 111, 154, 147, 194
Lake, Leonora 56–57
Lake Chautauqua, New York 94
Lake Contrary Chautauqua Grounds 23
Lake Madison, South Dakota 94
Lanchester, Elsa 199
"Land of the Dragon" 89
"Land of War and Women" 90
Landon, "Alf" 20
Lasky Productions 198
Laurant, Eugene 142, 143, 169
Laurie, Joe, Jr. 19, 108
"Lawlessness" 151
League of Nations 146–149, 151, 157

League of Women Voters 145
Lee, Josh 107
Legion of the Condemned 202
Leland Powers School of Expression 66
Lenin 150, 154
"Let's All Pull Together" 115
Lewis, John L. 150
Lewis, Sinclair 184
Lhevinne, Mischa 165
liberty bonds 115, 116, 118
Liberty Maids Quartet 64, 125, 126
Liberty Torch 141
Lightnin' 188
Lightning Strikes Twice 199
Limpp, Rufus 60
Lincoln, Abraham 13, 109, 140, 162, 164
Lincoln Chautauqua 48, 80, 114–115, 134, 199
Lincoln, Nebraska 48
Lindquist, William 92
Lindsey, Ben 54, 124
Link, Arthur S. 89, 111
"Little Humorist" 109
Little Minister 71
Little Professor of Piney Woods 103
Little Shepherd of Kingdom Come 202
"Little Wise Hen" 168
Lloyd, Harold 202
local chautauquas 203
Lockhart, Eugene (Gene) 162, 188–189, 199
Lockhart, June 199
Lockhart, Kathleen 199
Lodge, Henry Cabot 146–147
Lorna Doone 52, 71
Loseff's Russian (Orchestral) Quartet(te) 129, 172
Lovely Galatiea 97
Lowell, James Russell 13
Lucey, Thomas Elmore 109
Luckner, Felix von 195
Lusitania 111, 172
lyceum 69, 160, 206; pre–Civil War 12–13; post–Civil War 13–19
Lyceumite 43

Ma and Pa Kettle series 200
McClary, Thomas 23, 86, 109
McConnell, J.W. 92
McConnell, Lincoln 120, 193
McDonald, Edwin 43
McDonald, Ruthven 65
MacGown, Robert S. 157

MacGregor, Knight 129
MacLaren, Gay Zenola 47, 66, 85, 88, 94–95, 167
McNary-Haugen Farm Relief Bill 183
Mad Empress 196
Madame Butterfly 133
magic lantern 71
Maguire, Gabriel 153
mail-order catalogue 30
Main, Marjorie 200
Main Street 184
"Man Against the Masses" 123
"Man of Many Faces" 109
Man with the Bone-Colored Whiskers 138
"Man with the Joy Face" 109
"Man with the Million Dollar Laugh" 138
manifest destiny 88
Manlove, Howard 94, 109, 140, 162
Manners, J. Hartley 163, 198
Manning, H. 118
Manning College of Music, Oratory, and Dramatic Arts 94
"March of the White Rats" 63
"Mark Twain of Kentucky" 138
marketing strategies 82
Martha 166
"Martyrdom of Fools" 148
"Mary Had a Little Lamb" 168
Mascot 166
"Mascot, the Fifty Thousand Dollar Horse" 204
mass culture 206
Master of Ballantrae 198
Matthison, Edith Wynne 198
May, Earl Chapin 18
Mayer, Arthur 203
Mayflower 98
Maynard, Ken 202
Maytime 166
Meanest Man in the World 162, 169
Means, Edna 95–96, 167, 196
medicine shows 158–59
Mellinger, W. L. 153
Melting Pot 42, 92, 93, 134–135, 112, 179, 197
"melting pot" ideology 206
Merchant of Venice 91
Mergrue, Cooper 135
Message from Kansas 54
Metropolitan Grand Quartet 99
Mickey Mouse 168, 186
Midland Chautauqua 48, 118, 128, 129, 135, 139

Midland Lyceum Bureau 15
The Mikado 133, 166
Milbury, Massachusetts 12
Mildred Morrison Concert Party 127
Miller, DeWitt 23
Miller, Lewis 19
Miller, Milo 122
Mills, Grace Halsey 91
Mills, Richmond 123
Minakuchi, Yutaka 89
Mine Workers 150
Minneapolis, Minnesota 94
"Mission of Mirth" 86
missionary diplomacy 89, 90
Missouri Legends 200
Missouri Ozarks 39
"Mister Duck" 108, 142, 169
Mr. Novak 200
Mitchell Brothers 170
Mitchum, Robert 200
Model T Ford 185
"Modern Arabian Knights" 153
"Modern Mormon Kingdom" 83
Mohammed Ali 125
Monroe, Marilyn 197
Monroe Doctrine 88
Montague Light Opera Company 133
Montgomery Ward 30
Morgan, Geoffrey 195
Mormon missionaries 84
Morris, William 86
"Mortimer Snerd" 201
Mossman, W. H. 20
"Mother" Chautauqua *see* Chautauqua, New York Institute
Mound City, Missouri 41, 57, 62
movie houses 185, 186
movie industry 165
movies 185–186; sound 186
Mrs. Rastus Johnson's Joy Ride 70
Mrs. Wiggs of the Cabbage Patch 70
Much Ado About Nothing 91
mud modeling 87
Murray, Charlie 202
Musical Merry Makers 171
"My Old Kentucky Home" 130

Nagel, Conrad 44, 95, 196
Nash, Clarence 168, 201
Nashville, Tennessee 98
Nation, Carrie 24, 44, 56, 193
National Lyceum League 13
National Male Quartet 171

Native American performers 73, 130
Nayphe, Julius Caesar 90
Neapolitan Grand Opera Company 166
"Necessary Political Reform" 55
"Nelle Gray" 130
Nelson, Mary K. 119
networking in theatre and media 207
neutrality 111–112
New England town hall 11
New Republic 181, 184
New York City 12, 52, 78, 94, 96, 149, 161, 179, 188, 189, 196, 204
New York City Marine Band 99
New York Institute *see* Chautauqua, New York Institute
New York Metropolitan Opera 98, 99, 134, 191
New York Redpath Lyceum Bureau 79
New York Times 165, 181
New York Tribune 14
Nichols, James T. 90
Nielsen, Alice 44, 97–98, 201
"Night in Hawaii" 191
Nightingale, George E. 118
Niles Hussar Band 126
Noe, Cotton 138
Noffsinger, John 15
Nonpartisan League 154
normalcy 145, 147
North American Review 15, 30
North End Club chautauqua boosters 38
Norwich, New York 177
Not Understood 137
Nothing But the Truth 162
Nye, Bill (Edgar Wilson) 19, 69, 94, 109, 167

Oakie, Jack 200
Ocean Park, Maine 24
O'Connor, Alfred H. 118
"Off ag'in, on ag'in, gone ag'in, Finnigan" 69
Off Broadway companies 188
"Oh Percy" Musical Revue 190
Ohio Valley 13
Olathe Register 34
Old Fashioned Girls 127
Old Home Singers 170
Old Ironsides 202
"Old Kentucky Home" 170
Old Order Changeth 55
Olivier, Laurence 197
One Foot in Heaven 199

"The One-Mile Town" 85
O'Neill, Eugene 200
opera 161
"Opie Read of politics" 120
Orchard, Hugh 28, 34
Orphan's Benefit 168
The Orpheans 99
Orpheum Entertainers 190
Ott, Edward Amherst 23, 61, 120, 193
Our Town 189
Out to Old Aunt Mary's 70
Outlook 181
Owen, Ruth Bryan 153, 193
Owen, William 92

Packard, Alton 44, 75–76, 169
"Pagoda Land" 89
Pair of Sixes 136, 162, 163
Palace Theatre 174, 204
Palmer, A. Mitchell 150–151
Palmer, Mrs. Potter 43
Palubicki, John 156
Pamahasika and His Pets 109
Panama Canal 89, 90
Panama-Pacific International Exposition, 1916 128
Pankhurst, Emmeline 55
Paramount Production Company 192
Paris Peace Conference 146
Parker, Theodore 13
Parlette, Ralph 85–86, 182, 193
Parsons, Louella 196
Pascova, Carmen 165, 201
Patience 134
Patsy 188
Payne, Charles 72
Pearl, Jack 200
Pearson, Paul N. 158
Peary, Robert E. 72
Peat, Harold 118–119, 148–149, 193
Peffer, Crawford A. 79, 91
Peffer Chautauqua 134, 199
Peffer-Redpath Chautauqua 182, 204
Peg o' My Heart 136, 162, 163
"Pending Perils and Problems" 151
Pennybacker, Mrs. Percy 145
Perkins, Anthony 198
Perplexed Husband 136
"A Personal Note to Our Thousands of Patrons" 51
Peter Pan 127
"Phantom Bride" 142
Philippine Quartet 172

Phillippes, Dora De 171
Phillips, Wendell 13, 15
Pied Piper 133
Pilgrim Girls (Orchestra) 64, 125, 126
Piney Woods Country Life School 102
Plancon, C. Pol 165
Plantation Singers 191
plays, negative connotation of 94
The Pleasure Seekers 136
Plymouth Male Quartet 171
Poe, Edgar Allan 109, 138
Polly of the Circus 164, 177
Poluhni 139
Pond, J. B. 15, 16
Poole, Frederick 89, 193
populist movement 49
Populist party 76
Portland, Oregon 79
Powell, Ernest 118
Power, Tyrone 134
Powers, Leland T. 66, 67
Premier Male Quartet 190
presidential campaigns: 1916 111; 1924 194
Price, Lucy 144
Prima Donna Soprano 98
Prince and the Show Girl 197
"Prince of Peace" 60, 124
Princess Blue Feather 190
Princess Bright Star 132
Princess Pat 166
Princess Stock Company 96
Princess Te Ata 132, 143
Princess Watahwaso 132, 143
print media 34
prison reform 57
Private Peat 148–149
"Problems of Leisure Time" 195
"Problems of Peace" 151
program brochures 34
Progressive ticket, 1924 194
Prohibition ticket, 1920, 56
Pryor, Arthur 62, 63, 166, 201
Pryor, Roger 200
public land disposal acts 12
Pugh, Jessie 70, 201
"pure corn" 188

Quayle, William A. 61
"Queen of the Chautauqua Platform" 137

Radanovits, Sandor 133
Radcliffe, W. L. 79
Radcliffe Chautauqua System 79
Rader, William 90
radio 185
railroad expansion 13, 29, 80
Ralph Dunbar Maryland (Jubilee) Singers 44, 101
Ralston, Esther 200
Rankin, Jeannette 55, 144
"Rare Fun Well Done" 75–76
"Razzazza Mazzazza" 63
Ratto, John B. 94, 140
The Raven 138
Raweis 104, 105
Read, Opie 23, 44, 67–68, 94, 120, 167, 196, 201
readings vs. drama 93
"Real Discovery of the North Pole" 72
"Re-created World" 124
Red Cross 115, 116, 117, 118, 119
Red Flame 154
Red Fox, Chief 191
Red-Headed Quartette 127, 197
Red Mill 133
Redpath, James 14, 15, 68
Redpath Chautauqua 29, 43, 48, 55, 56, 69–70, 79, 80, 93, 98, 108, 113, 118, 119, 120, 121, 123, 133, 135, 134, 137, 138, 142, 144, 145, 151, 152, 153, 155, 156, 157, 159, 162, 164, 166, 167, 168, 169, 170, 172, 174, 175, 179, 180, 189, 195, 197, 198, 199,
"Redpath Chautauqua" 168, 187, 190, 191, 194, 202
Redpath comedy hits 162
"Redpath-Horner" Chautauqua 92, 121, 137, 163, 166, 190
Redpath Lyceum (and Chautauqua) Bureau 14, 15, 23, 25, 27, 29, 32, 43, 45, 48, 61, 66, 79, 94, 102, 169, 183
Redpath Special 80
"Redpath-Vawter" Chautauqua 52, 129, 130, 152, 160, 162, 163, 167, 170, 172, 174, 182, 188, 189
Redpath-Vawter Junior Chautauqua 141
Redpath-Vawter trademark 182
Redpath's Oratorio Artists 99
Reed, John 150
reform themes 53
Regeneration 137
Regnier, Joseph 168
Regniers 99

"Renewed America" 156
Reno, Edward (the Great) 108, 142, 169, 207
Reno, Madame 108, 142
"Representative Government" 53
Rice, Alice Hegan 70
Rice, Phidelphia 67, 94
"Riddle of the Russian Revolution" 151
Ridgeway, Katherine 44, 67, 137, 167
Riley, James Whitcomb 69, 70, 109
Rin-Tin-Tin 203
Ringling Brothers Circus 18
Rip Van Winkle 137
Rise and Fall of the Third Reich 184
Rivals 135, 136
"Robert Burns Panatella Program" 185
Robin Hood 133, 143, 166
Robinson, Edward G. 197
Rockport, Missouri 22, 23
Roebuck, Alvah C. 30
Rogers, Will 185, 190
Romancers 92, 136
Romeo and Juliet 162
Roosevelt, Alice 63
Roosevelt, Eleanor 194
Roosevelt, Franklin 194
Roosevelt, Theodore 44, 84, 89, 93, 98, 147
Root, E. R. 194–195
Root, Elihu 147
Rorer, Sarah Tyson 194
Rosani, Carl 108, 109, 142
Rose, Laura 119
Rosebud Indian Reservation 192
Rosecrans, Charles E. 87
Rosecrans, Leo S. 197
Rosemary's Baby 197
Rositzky, Simon (Si) 38
Royal Dragoons 170
Royal English Hand Bell Orchestra 62
Royal Hawaiians 128
Royal Opera Company 98
Rudolph's Swiss Singers and Players 129
"Rudy Vallee Fleischmann Radio Show" 201
Rupe-Redpath Chautauqua 182, 204
rural character 50–53, 76
Russell, Lillian 98
Russell, Sol Smith 109
Russell H. Conwell and His Work 58
"Russia or America; Which?" 152
Russian Cossack Chorus 190
Russian Revolution 152

Russian Socialistic Federation 150
Russo-Japanese War 89

S. de Zanco-Smith-Oster Trio 170, 171
Sacco, Nicola 151
St. Joseph, Missouri 23, 62, 102
Sam Schildkret's Hungarian Orchestra 63, 96
Sandburg, Carl 43, 44, 94, 66–67, 167, 201
Sarett, Lew 67
Saturday Evening Post 119
Savannah, Missouri 26, 60
Sayonara 199
School of Speech Arts 138
Schroeder, Alice 139, 143
Schwartz, Alexander 152
"Science Made Plain" 121
Scopes (Monkey) Trial 59, 193
Scott, Martha 44, 189, 199
Scribners 181
"Sea Devil" 195
Search for Order 50
Sears, H. W. 30
Sears, Roebuck and Company 185
Sears, Roebuck Catalogue 30
Second Congress of the Third International Conference 152
Sells-Foto 177
Sennett Mack, 134, 161
Serl, Elmer Willis 179
Servant in the House 92, 97
Seventeen 127, 189
Shakespeare, William 66, 90, 93, 135, 197, 189, 189, 190, 197, 205
Shame of the Cities 55
Shaw, Anna Howard 144
Shaw, George Bernard 134
She Stoops to Conquer 91
Shepherd of the Hills 164
Shirer, William L. 184
Shorty Hamilton features 196
Show-Off 188
Shungopavi, the Medicine Man 107
Sidney, George 202
"Significance of the Frontier in American History" 11
silent film 19, 161, 166
Sills, Milton 202
Sinclair, Upton 20
Six Cylinder Love 163, 189
Skidding 189
Sky Pilot 71

"slapstick" 188
Smilin' Through 162
Smith, Winchell 162, 188
So This Is London 162, 188
socialism 149, 154
Songs and Stories of the Redman 132, 143
"Soul of Things" 138
"Sour Grapes" 61
Sousa, John Philip 62
Sparks, Leonora 98, 201
"Special Privilege" 53
Speedy 202
Sperry, Nan 123
Spirit of St. Louis 198
Spirit of 1776 141
sponsors 183
Spratt, Leah 131
Stage Fright 197
stage lighting 42
Stalin, Joseph 109
Standard Chautauqua 54, 75, 127, 139, 164, 166
Standard Oil Company 54
Standard Redpath Chautauqua 27–28, 48
standardization 49–50
Stanley, Henry M. 15
Star lecture courses 15
Star Lyceum Bureau 94
Starbucks 68, 196
State University of Iowa 102
Steamboat Willie 186
Steffens, Lincoln 44, 55
Stelzls 99
Sterling Jubilee Singers 64
Stevens, Robert 92
Stewart, James 198
Stirling Films 198
Stoddard, Mary 99
"Stories About Lincoln" 167
Storm Lake, Iowa 204
Story of Tahan 104
Stowe, Harriet Beecher 70, 164
strikes, 1919 150
SueInui, Kiyo 89
suffrage, women's 55, 113, 144
Sullivan, John L. 56
Sumner, Charles 15
Sunday, Billy 20, 56, 123, 192–193
Sunday program 46
superintendent, circuit 38–40
superintendent, report book 47

"Survivor of the Somme" 118
Sussex 111
"Swanee River" 130
Swarthmore Chautauqua 48, 155, 179
Swarthmore, Pennsylvania 48
Sweden's Royal Opera 165

Taft, Lorado 88
Taft, William Howard 44, 86, 89, 98
Taggart, Charles Rose 67, 94, 109
Tahan, Chief 143
Take My Advice 189
"talkie" films 202, 203, 204
talking machines 128
Tall Story 198
Taming of the Shrew 92
Tammany 54
Tanhouser Films 198
Tapia (Saunders), Merlyn J. 40
Tarbell, Ida 55
Taylor, Jessie Rae 140, 168
technological advances, impact 187
Temple of Apollo Lyceus 12
Temple University 58
Temporary Husband 163
tent boys/crews 36, 39–42, 96
textile workers 12
That Printer of Udells 138
Thaviu's Great Orchestra (and Grand Band) 63, 96, 97, 126, 191
Thaviu's Orchestra 191
Thomas, Edna Francis 139
Thoreau, Henry David 13
Thorndike, Sybil 197
ticket agents 37
ticket prices 36
"Tickles and Trickles" 69
Tillman, "Pitchfork" Ben 84
"To Hell and Back with a Smile" 148
Tobacco Road 200
Tobias, Jay 190, 200
Todd, Helen 144
Tolbert, Frank 151
Tolbert, Raymond B. 124
Tolstoy, Ilya 20, 152, 193, 197, 199
Tongue, Phil 199
Tooley, Howard 133
Topeka, Kansas 48
town hall 11
Track of the Cat 200
"Tragedies of the Unprepared" 148
"Tragedy in Popular Government" 152
transformation, culture 205–6

traveling shows 158
Treaty of Versailles 146–148, 151
Tredwell, Louise 165
Trefz, Edward 157
Triangle Film Corporation 134, 199
Trotsky, Leon 150
Troy, New York 15
Turn to the Right 139, 162
Turner, Frederick Jackson 11
Tuskegee Black Performers 101
Tuskegee Jubilees 173
Tuskegee Normal and Industrial Institute 102
Twain, Mark 15, 94, 109, 138
Twelfth Night 91
Twelve O'Clock High 200
20th Century Journal 184
Twenty Years of Chautauqua Progress, 1904 to 1923 179–181
"Two Years in Hell and Back with a Smile" 118
"Two Years in the Devil's Playground" 118
Tyrolean Alpine Singers (and Yodelers) 43, 99

Ulrich, Margaret 92
ultraviolet ray 121
"Uncle Ezra" 201
Uncle Tom's Cabin 64, 70–71, 134, 163, 164
Underwood, Oscar 148
Underwood Tariff Bill 148
Union of Russian Workers 150
United Artists 166
United States Mint 194
United States Navy 121
"University of Hard Knocks" 85–86
University of Kentucky 138

Valley of the Giants 202
"Vanishing American" 192
Vanzetti, Bartolomeo 151
Vardaman, James K. 83, 193
vaudeville 18, 19, 69
Vaughan, David 151
Vawter, Keith 27, 28, 29, 46, 51, 55, 56, 70, 79, 82, 159, 180, 181, 182
Venetian Trio 129
Venetian Troubadours 129
Victor Records 63, 70, 99, 201
Vierra, George 190

Vierra's Hawaiians 190
"Village Storekeeper" 84
Vincent, John Heyl 19, 20, 21, 64, 94
Vinton, Sumner 89
Vitagraph Production Company 69, 196
Vivian, Percival 91
"Voice from the Black Belt" 102
Volstead Act 192

Wachtel, Ina 59, 62, 63
Wade, Frederick 67
Wagon Show 202
Waikiki Hawaiian Singers and Players 128
war: casualties 145; debt 145; declaration of 113–114; tax 116, 117, 157
War Camp Community Service 115
"War from an Officer's Viewpoint" 118
War Savings Stamps 115
Ward, Ada 39
Warde, Frederick 198
Warner Brothers 93, 186, 196, 197, 198, 199, 200, 201, 203,
Warren, Harriet Bird 119
Washington, Booker T. 20, 102, 103
Washington, D.C. 78
Washington, George 140
Washington, Howard C. 99, 100
Wathena, Kansas 56, *204
Wathena Chautauqua 56
Watkins, V.S. 137
Webster, Daniel 54
Wesleyan University 120
Western Federation of Chautauquas 25
Western Redpath Chautauqua 31, 133
Westinghouse, George 20
"What's in the Farmer's Mind" 154
Wheeler, Burton K. 194
Wheeler, Frederick 99
"When You and I Were Young, Maggie" 170
Where the North Begins 203
White, Clarence H. 79
White, Shannon 179
White, William Allen 55
White and Black Minstrels 173
White-Myers Chautauqua 138, 153, 163, 164, 166, 170, 171, 172, 177, 179
"White Savage" 104, 143
Whitman, Walt 66–67, 69
Whitney, Edwin 138, 162
Wickersham, L. B. 23
Wiebe, Robert 29, 50, 104

Wild West shows 130
Wilder, Thorton 189
Willebrandt, Mable Walker 194
Willey, Sarah 92
Williams, Hattie 69
Williams, Rhys 44, 199
Williams Jubilee Singers 130
Williams Lecture and Musical Bureau 15
Willis, Maude 67, 94
Willitts, A. A. 23, 60
Wilson, Alonzo 114
Wilson, Woodrow 43, 44, 59, 83, 84, 111, 112, 113, 117, 140, 146, 147, 150, 157, 192, 206
Winona, Indiana 56
Winona Lake, Indiana 204
Winona Lake Chautauqua 56
Witching Hour 163
"With an Irishman Through an African Jungle" 153
Women's Christian Temperance Union 107
Women's Days 144
"Wonder Dog" 302
Wonder Worker 142
"Wonder Worker and Novelty Entertainer" 108

Wood, Montraville 121
World Congress of Historians 11
World Disarmament Conference, 1899 88
World War I 30, 32, 60, 93, 96, 102, 104, 110, 121, 130, 137, 142, 145–147, 157, 158, 160, 164, 169, 172, 193, 196, 206
World War II 121
World's Fair: 1893 11, 43, 46, 101; 1904 46; 1916 128
Wray, Fay 202
Wright, Harold Bell 138, 164

Yale University 125
Yarrow, George 86
Yeuell 72
Your Best Friend 93
youth program 105
Yurka, Blanche 200

Zabelle, Flora 69
Zangwill, Israel 92, 135, 179
Zedler Symphonic Quintette 171
"Ziegfeld Follies" 185
Zimmermann note 113

www.ingramcontent.com/pod-product-compliance
Ingram Content Group UK Ltd.
Pitfield, Milton Keynes, MK11 3LW, UK
UKHW041943140426
5217IPUK00014B/638